WALES AND THE FRENCH REVOLUTION

General Editors: Mary-Ann Constantine and Dafydd Johnston

For Matthew, Rufus and Jemima

English-Language Poetry from Wales
1789–1806

ELIZABETH EDWARDS

UNIVERSITY OF WALES PRESS
CARDIFF
2013

www.uwp.co.uk

British Library Cataloguing-in-Publication Data
A catalogue record for this book is available from the British Library.

ISBN   978-0-7083-2568-1
e-ISBN   978-0-7083-2569-8

Typeset in Wales by Eira Fenn Gaunt
Printed CPI Antony Rowe, Chippenham, Wiltshire

'one of these excursions, travelling . . . [t]hrough Wales'

William Wordsworth, *The Prelude*, Book XIII.

WALES AND THE FRENCH REVOLUTION

The French Revolution of 1789 was perhaps the defining event of the Romantic period in Europe. It unsettled not only the ordering of society but language and thought itself: its effects were profoundly cultural, and they were long-lasting. The last twenty years have radically altered our understanding of the impact of the Revolution and its aftermath on British culture. In literature, as critical attention has shifted from a handful of major poets to the non-canonical edges, we can now see how the works of women writers, self-educated authors, radical pamphleteers, prophets and loyalist propagandists both shaped and were shaped by the language and ideas of the period. Yet surprising gaps remain, and even recent studies of the 'British' reaction to the Revolution remain poorly informed about responses from the regions. In literary and historical discussions of the so-called 'four nations' of Britain, Wales has been virtually invisible; many researchers working in this period are unaware of the kinds of sources available for comparative study.

The Wales and the French Revolution Series is the product of a four-year project funded by the AHRC and the University of Wales at the Centre for Advanced Welsh and Celtic Studies. It makes available a wide range of Welsh material from the decades spanning the Revolution and the subsequent wars with France. Each volume, edited by an expert in the field, presents a collection of texts (including, where relevant, translations) from a particular genre with a critical essay situating the material in its historical and literary context. A great deal of material is published here for the first time, and all kinds of genres are explored. From ballads and pamphlets to personal letters and prize-winning poems, essays, journals, sermons, songs and satires, the range of texts covered by this series is a stimulating reflection of the political and cultural complexity of the time. We hope these volumes will encourage scholars and students of Welsh history and literature to rediscover this fascinating period, and will offer ample comparative scope for those working further afield.

Mary-Ann Constantine and Dafydd Johnston
General Editors

Contents

Figures

Preface

This anthology aims to introduce a wide-ranging but representative selection of Anglophone Welsh poetry from the period 1789–1806. Pulled together for the first time – in some cases published for the first time – this body of writing creates a new poetic map of Wales that unfolds over a decade and a half of revolution and war. My introduction points out contexts for the poems and connections between them, but necessarily selective due to limitations of space, it also leaves the reader to take their own route through the texts, and to make their own links with other works not discussed in this anthology but which should suggest themselves time and again. I hope that this selection of texts, which contains many overlooked or hard-to-find items, may encourage excursions into less familiar writings about Wales, a nation that emerges here as a Romantic-era melting pot: heroic but subdued, defiant but suffering, beautiful, hostile, mysterious and inspiring, constantly reimagined and endlessly marginalized.

   Viewed collectively the texts present several difficulties of interpretation. There is little uniformity of style or cultural locality or positioning here: the poems include works by native writers and those who spent time in Wales during an extraordinary period of European history and who read contemporary situations through Welsh people, landscape and history (and vice versa). Seeing a path, then, through poems written from divergent or even conflicting perspectives has sometimes seemed an almost impossible task. Some of the texts reveal uncomfortably colonial undercurrents, while even writers who are apparently sympathetic tourists exploit Wales in their poetry, consuming it or recreating it to fit their own purposes. However, the construction of Wales in works by non-native poets offers new illustrations of how this small nation was viewed in wider political contexts. Poetry and prose by Welsh writers often accentuates the loyalty of the Welsh people to a larger British state, but texts by visitors show the extent of the disparity between this standpoint and the perceptions of tourists. (George Davies Harley, for example, draws forbidding Welsh landscapes into the broader theatre of the war with France in his *Holyhead Sonnets*, nos. 42 and 43.) Although Wales may sometimes seem 'at risk' in poems by tourists, the contrasts between these views and the self-images of the Welsh are revealing. Finally, some of these poems may seem neither exclusively Welsh nor English but to share cultural memories, or histories, that take shape at the meeting points between two perspectives.

The 'Wales and the French Revolution' project would not have been possible without generous funding from the Arts and Humanities Research Council and the University of Wales. For help while researching this anthology I am grateful to staff at the National Library of Wales, John Rylands University of Manchester Library, Cardiff University Salisbury Library, Cheshire Record Office and Denbighshire Record Office. I am grateful to the University Librarian and Director of John Rylands Library for permission to quote from the Thrale-Piozzi papers. I count myself lucky to have worked with an inspirational team of researchers at the Centre for Advanced Welsh and Celtic Studies: I am grateful to the Director of the Centre, Dafydd Johnston, and to Cathryn Charnell-White, Ffion Jones and Heather Williams for their encouragement and advice. Special thanks to Marion Löffler for her constant scholarly generosity and moral support, to our project leader, Mary-Ann Constantine, for constructive comments on every section of this book, and to both for sharing countless ideas and suggestions. I am grateful to our editorial officer, Gwen Gruffudd, for her careful copy-editing of the text and the production team at the University of Wales Press, especially Sarah Lewis, Siân Chapman and Dafydd Jones. Thank you to members of the project's advisory panel, especially John Barrell and Caroline Franklin, and to Mary Chadwick, Nia Davies, Nicholas Davies, Harriet Guest, Bethan Jenkins and Catriona Kennedy for help of various kinds along the way. Finally I am very grateful to Glenys and Bryan Edwards for help with child-care that enabled me to work on this project, and to Matthew for his endless patience and willingness to hold the fort. This book is for him, and for our children.

February 2013   Elizabeth Edwards

Acknowledgements

The National Library of Wales: Fig. 2

© Tate, London 2012: Fig. 3

© Trustees of the British Museum: Fig. 4

Abbreviations

BBCS	*Bulletin of the Board of Celtic Studies*
CC	John T. Koch (ed.), *Celtic Culture: A Historical Encyclopedia* (5 vols., Santa Barbara, 2006)
CIM	Geraint H. Jenkins, Ffion Mair Jones and David Ceri Jones (eds.), *The Correspondence of Iolo Morganwg* (3 vols., Cardiff, 2007)
DWB	*The Dictionary of Welsh Biography down to 1940* (London, 1959)
KJV	The King James Version of the Bible
NLW	National Library of Wales
ODNB	*Oxford Dictionary of National Biography* at *http://www.oxforddnb.com*
OED	*Oxford English Dictionary* at *http://www.oed.com*
PL	Edward A. Bloom and Lillian D. Bloom (eds.), *The Piozzi Letters* (6 vols., Newark, 1989–2002)
THSC	*Transactions of the Honourable Society of Cymmrodorion*
WHR	*Welsh History Review*
WWMH	John Keegan and Andrew Wheatcroft, *Who's Who in Military History From 1453 to the Present Day* (2nd rev. edn., London, 1996)

Introduction

A remote corner of the empire?

In 'Owen of Llangoed', a poem published in October 1804, the Anglesey poet Richard Llwyd applauded Henry Addington for his patronage of Robert Burns's eldest son. 'May Heaven his efforts bless,' Llwyd declared:

> Who guides an Empire's cares;
> For his *own heart*, a moment steals –
> A *thought* for Genius spares. (No. 51, lines 114–16)

In a gloss on this passage, Llwyd developed his tribute to Addington, who had been forced from office as prime minister earlier that year: 'that the mind that directs the concerns of his Country at a period of unexampled difficulty and danger, should recollect the orphans of genius, in a remote corner of the Empire is surely no common praise'. Llwyd's note on Addington's private concern for provincial 'orphans of genius' obviously foregrounds Burns, and Scotland. It invokes a writer who was 'the most influential and important figure in the history of labouring-class poetry',[1] and a particular touchstone for Llwyd, who was a former domestic servant. But beyond the footnote, beyond the biographical, the poem as a whole brings another outlying, colonial locality into view – Wales.[2]

'Owen of Llangoed' is a four-part, lyrical ballad-like tale of a boy from Anglesey and his ultimately ill-fated adventures as a sailor during the Revolutionary and Napoleonic wars. Richard Llwyd's reflections on patronage and poetry, the place of the arts in wartime, clearly take place in the context of an imperialist Britain weathering the storms of a drawn-out conflict and successive invasion crises. Full of local detail and a sense of place, the island setting of 'Owen of Llangoed' also brings the regions into clearer focus. As he imagines Britain's struggle for empire, for liberty vis-à-vis France, so Llwyd calls attention to its internal empire: the colonized fringes of the constituent parts of Britain pictured in the quotations above as distant, dispossessed and dependent.

Welsh poems of the late eighteenth and early nineteenth centuries, their landscapes, politics, soundscapes and narratives, have found little place in recent accounts of the writing of the 1790s and beyond.[3] Even works that explicitly focus on place or on the geopolitics of Romanticism rarely mention Wales: Scotland and Ireland currently supply the grounds for comparative approaches.[4] 'Owen of Llangoed' suggests various starting points for shifting the balance, since Llwyd's polemical poem brings the lives of the Anglesey rural poor onto the wider stage of war with France, and into the labouring-class poetic tradition.[5] The poem foregrounds the local, personal and everyday – what Llwyd terms 'a noiseless story . . . the hamlet's humbler cares, / A peasant's joys and troubles' (lines 6, 15–16) – developing a rich particularity, a distinctively Welsh identity, out of these local dynamics. At the same time, 'Owen of Llangoed' is also a poem about Wales's relation to the wider world: the narrative of the poem turns on Owen's curiosity about places *beyond* the horizons of Anglesey – busy Liverpool, the frozen north, or the sandy shores of Africa. Foregrounding the indigenous and regional and yet geographically always on the move, clearly set within a cosmopolitan context, the poem offers new perspectives on 'Romantic ethnicity'[6] and Wales's place within increasingly devolved geographies of Romanticism.

The new landscape of 'four nations' or archipelagic criticism is, however, still patchy and uneven. Scottish literature has long been overshadowed by politically and culturally ascendant English contexts and models,[7] and Ireland has perhaps fared even worse. Until recently, only writers whose work has 'been co-opted into the "British" canon'[8] have received serious scholarly attention. In some cases, conventional boundaries of period and/or nation have been problematic: Scotland and Ireland need to be seen, it has been argued, within broader political, economic and cultural frameworks in order to generate fresh views of their literature. A 'defamiliarization of some of the fundamental categories that structure literary history, including the temporal borders of periodization and the topographical borders of nationality', may transform matters.[9]

This revisionary perspective is equally helpful in approaching Wales, a subject at least as incomplete and indistinct as Scotland or Ireland, though for reasons that may appear contradictory. Wales has 'suffered from a chronic in-betweenness',[10] earlier incorporated by England than the other 'Celtic' nations, and much more stable in political terms than either by the period around the French Revolution. Largely as a result of the predominance of the Welsh language, however, Wales can also seem more foreign and 'other' than Scotland or Ireland: at once safe and familiar *and* potentially alien and incoherent. Visitors to Wales clearly illustrate these views: they show signs of unease on their travels, uncertain in their interactions with places or landscapes and especially with the local people, most of whom spoke Welsh only.[11] This duality, which is highly visible in the texts of the period, has not been explored by critics of the poetry, and Richard Llwyd is a case in point. An antiquary and provincial writer widely known in his own time as the 'Bard of Snowdon', little trace can be found of him today, despite the continuing importance of labouring-class poets and regional voices.[12] Given the general neglect of eighteenth-century and Romantic Wales, it seems likely that the relentlessly Welsh fabric of Llwyd's Anglophone poetry, which details his knowledge of history and early manuscripts in a mass of footnotes, has contributed to this forgetting.

Wales may also seem incomplete or shadowy, then, as a result of a 'missing' literature. Who wrote poetry about, or from, Wales in the years after 1789? What did they say about Wales and the Welsh? How did they represent England, or Britain, or Continental Europe and matters of revolution and war? For non-Welsh speaking literary scholars in particular, much of this material has simply been inaccessible, and for that reason ignored or over-looked, as Mary-Ann Constantine has pointed out.[13] There is also, however, a significant body of forgotten Anglophone Welsh verse from the period.[14] Recovering texts in Welsh and in English will contribute towards a more accurate and detailed understanding of Revolution-era poetry in Britain. And rediscovering a lost literature also matters from Welsh national and cultural perspectives. In post-colonial terms Wales has long been a 'stateless nation' whose national identity has substantially been kept alive in the work of its writers.[15] This anthology speaks to that tradition, working into a Romantic-era gap in Welsh literary history.

Several very well-known accounts of Wales exist from the years around the French Revolution, of which Wordsworth's ascent of Snowdon in *The Prelude* or 'Lines written a few miles above Tintern Abbey' will be among the most familiar to readers today.[16] But beyond a few canonical pieces, Wales largely awaits discovery in the Anglophone poetry of this period. Drawn from a variety of sources, the poems in this anthology range from topical newspaper poems to manuscript fragments, to more final versions of texts taken from published volumes. Some use conventional, even predict-able verse forms, others are more experimental. The selection includes public poems concerning current events at home and abroad, poems on particular individuals (some well known, others obscure or unnamed), or on regional crises. Other verses are much more private in orientation, giving poignant accounts of personal hardship or windows onto introspective, solitary mo-ments. Poems taken from manuscript sources suggest a different sort of privacy, since they may have seemed unpublishable in the difficult political climate of the 1790s: provocative poems critical of the king, the government, religious leaders or the ongoing war. Many of the poems are fugitive pieces, drafted quickly in response to events as they happen (and whose outcome could not possibly have been known at the time), with a hurried or uneven quality that suggests the turmoil of the times through which they were written.

Major themes recur throughout the poems. Politics, history, landscape, war and life at home, singly or in any combination, are constant preoccupations for writers in Wales in the period 1789–1806. Poets sometimes directly discuss events in France and the war that followed; at other times they focus on the situation in Wales in these years, especially after the hardships of wartime (intensified by harsh winters and failed harvests) brought poverty and suffering to many people. Loyalism and 'defensive patriotism'[17] are strong themes here, but more ambiguous reactions to the war with France and at times a spirit of popular protest focusing on social distress are also expressed. Many works explore landscape and history, central themes particularly in poems by tourists. Wales was variously a landscape of reaction[18] and a land-scape of opposition in the wake of the French Revolution: violently sublime, inhospitably historical, an asylum, a living grave, or a blood-soaked scene of past battles that conjure up modern war contexts.

The period around 1789 saw a Welsh literary-cultural revolution take place alongside the political, constitutional one in France, a parallel that may not be entirely coincidental.[19] Literary history was in the process of being trans-formed in Wales in the late eighteenth century by a series of republications of early poetry, from the ninth-century saga poems republished as *The Heroic Elegies and Other Pieces of Llywarç Hen* (1792) to the fourteenth-century lyric poetry of Dafydd ap Gwilym (1789). The process was largely controlled by the expatriate London Welsh, especially the wealthy furrier Owen Jones (Owain Myfyr), who funded the work, the lexicographer and antiquary William Owen Pughe, and the visionary but deeply unreliable Edward Williams (Iolo Morganwg), who brilliantly forged a series of Welsh medieval poems and then attributed them to Dafydd ap Gwilym.[20] They were building on, adapting and reinventing works salvaged by Welsh antiquaries and scholar poets earlier in the century – figures such as Evan Evans who discovered the manuscript of the early Welsh poem *Y Gododdin*, a work that directly inspired Iolo Morganwg's 'Ode; Imitated from the Gododin of Aneurin' (no. 12).[21]

These reissued editions of Welsh poetry moved the recovery effort into a new phase, and fresh perspectives on the past and contemporary relations with it followed these rediscovered texts. This refocused consciousness of history in textual form inspired English as well as Welsh writers, as, for instance, the relationships between Iolo Morganwg and William Blake or Robert Southey show.[22] Crucially, the period covered by this anthology was characterized by a rapid succession of dramatic events, and, amid confusion and uncertainty, a sense that the final outcome of these events could not be safely predicted. For several writers in this selection the often equally tumultuous chronology of Welsh history, especially the medieval period, existed in a dynamic imaginary relation with the present.[23] An impression of history-in-motion repeatedly echoes through the pages of poems that are only indirectly 'about' subjects from the past.

Responding to revolution also had distinctive aesthetic dimensions linked with the discourse that was being used at the time. Eighteenth-century travellers to Wales often viewed its landscapes through the medium of Thomas Gray's 'The Bard' (1757), a poem that became a problematic text in the later eighteenth century because its wide influence meant that it 'seriously threatened to stand in for genuine Welsh examples'.[24] But in an interesting contrast, the pale spectre of Gray's bard rarely features in poems by Welsh-language writers.[25] This split along linguistic lines reflects the distinctive situation of poetry in Wales, and the historical archive on which this anthology draws is fragmented in a number of ways as a result. Most important is the language divide, a feature that sets Wales apart from the other 'British' nations in the period.

Around 1800 nine out of ten people in Wales spoke Welsh; seven out of ten spoke no English at all.[26] As a result, Anglophone Welsh writing in the period was a minority concern that has been largely ignored by later literary historians. For bilingual writers such as Iolo Morganwg and Richard Llwyd, writing in English was a deliberate choice. The reasons behind this decision are complex, but both writers were selecting an audience through their use of language: Iolo aspired to success outside Wales, while Llwyd may have written in English in order to appeal to and inform the Anglicized gentry within Wales. From contemporary, twenty-first century perspectives, however, the choice may still seem surprising, especially given the language situation in Wales in the eighteenth century.

What used to be called Anglo-Welsh writing – a term that has fallen out of favour because it suggests 'a partial, incomplete and inferior "Welshness"'[27] – is a notoriously fraught field. In the twentieth century, Anglo-Welsh literature became linked with a sense of shame or trauma, and haunted by a 'cultural cringe' that inscribes literary works with insecurity, awkwardness, or even satire at the expense of Wales.[28] This perspective rarely appears in late eighteenth-century Anglophone writing: the letters of the London Welsh in the 1790s, for example, illustrate the confident sociability that connected figures like Iolo Morganwg, David Samwell (Dafydd Ddu Feddyg),

Owain Myfyr and others.[29] Iolo Morganwg usually wrote his letters in English, though his ability to switch to Welsh and back again at any given point produces the 'lively demotic' that characterizes his correspondence.[30] When these writers do question the use of English, as Owain Myfyr did in a letter written to Iolo in 1783, the tone is sharp and direct, with no hint of self-doubt:

> Ti a eist yn ynfyd Iorwerth! Llythyr Seisnig at Owain Myfyr? Onid oes digonaidd o Saesoneg yn Llundain? Oes, oes! Bwrw heli yn y mor yn buost. Dod y tro nesaf ini amheuthun, sef llafn o lythyr Cymraeg lan loyw.

> (You have gone mad, Iorwerth! An English letter to Owain Myfyr? Is there not enough English in London? Yes, indeed! You have been throwing salt water into the sea. Next time give us a rarity: a mighty letter in pure, shining Welsh.)[31]

Yet, virtually all the poems in this anthology hinge on some aspect of the meeting-points between England and Wales, between two languages and two cultures. Many of them keep Welsh-language literary history in view, especially its bardic tradition, although it is difficult to gauge exactly what writers in this period would have known as 'literary history'.[32] What is clear is that the work of poets with a Welsh-language frame of reference has been shaped by a dual inheritance, by a different poetic tradition reaching back over centuries with its own very specific themes, forms and rhythms.[33] In this way, Wales offers unique temporal and national contexts for Anglophone poetry – settings coloured by histories of conflict and underpinned by earlier verses.

Two languages in dialogue: it is worth noting that the action of Llwyd's 'Owen of Llangoed' takes place, in theory, entirely in Welsh up to the point at which Owen leaves Anglesey for Liverpool.[34] Llwyd portrays Liverpool as hectic and overwhelming, and Owen's sense of isolation among its busy crowds brings out his ethnic difference:

> There – though in a constant crowd,
> He found his footsteps lonely;
> For Owen's tongue, as yet, was tun'd,
> To antient British *only*. (Lines 149–52, my emphasis)

Until this point, readers cannot know that an act of linguistic elision or exclusion is taking place in the poem: that the English-language poem they are reading is a mediated version of events, spoken and understood only in Welsh. A poem unfolding in Welsh but recited in English is an unusual, and in some ways unsettling, prospect. Arguably the most Welsh space of 'Owen of Llangoed' – the Welsh-language space – remains inaccessible in this poem spanning two languages. In one sense, Llwyd is suggesting that Welsh life and language is 'culturally unassimilable'[35] in an English-language Romantic-era poem. In another sense, his poem plays out the mixed and contingent allegiances that lie behind depictions of Wales in this period.

Some of the conflicts within eighteenth-century Welsh writing in English have recently been sketched out by Sarah Prescott in her discussion of what she terms 'Cambria poetry'. Prescott argues that verses from Wales, among them those by Evan Evans and John Walters, present an emergent 'discernable English-language poetic tradition . . . which takes Welsh history and literature as its theme'.[36] This tradition is often oppositional in character, presenting scenarios that reveal the unevenness within notions of Britishness in the eighteenth century. By the period of the French Revolution, then, there was a body of work already in place that may have established conventions for later poems. Some of the clearest differences between eighteenth-century Welsh and English approaches crystallize, Prescott explains, around the concept of patriotism, where the Welsh works emphasize 'the glory of Wales's bardic past and the resilience of the Welsh language'[37] as opposed to military or naval victories. This is particularly visible in poems written in the Napoleonic era, under fears of invasion and defeat, though these later works also spotlight native Welsh military heroism, new and old. Other themes shift in their meanings across the period. The changing significance of 'ancient Britishness', for instance, in poems appearing against the crisis years of 1803–5 compared with those published immediately after the Revolution is striking. Throughout the anthology the poems present contested and malleable accounts of their subjects, offering a range of cultural and political perspectives. No single, authoritative gaze on a landscape or account of historical events emerges here, but instead multiple and not always harmonious, or, taken collectively, even coherent viewpoints.

These differences in perspective need to be added to the biculturalism that already characterizes texts such as 'Owen of Llangoed'.[38] The split between poems by native writers and by visitors to Wales, between travellers 'looking in' and native Welsh 'writing out', in this anthology creates a series of visions of Welshness. As a result, these works lay claim to being read as 'Welsh' in various ways, playing out several kinds of local and national identities; responses to Wales that are differently imagined according to the particular contexts that produced them. Why, for instance, did some writers in Wales feel that it was a place where things could be forged anew while others show nothing of the sort in their writings, depicting Wales as strikingly, almost deliberately unpoliticized, a refuge from politics rather than a space in which to exercise it? Does this suggest a failure to understand their Welsh surroundings on the part of some writers, or perhaps a refusal to do so? The picture is darker and more complex in poems by Welsh writers such as Iolo Morganwg and Richard Llwyd, in whose work the image of an oppressed and dispossessed Wales looms large, casting shadows onto the wider scene of British poetry in this period and even the concept of a united, coherent nation state under the name 'Britain'.[39]

In the late eighteenth century Wales became the site of the British 'petty tour', a domestic replacement for the Continental grand tour during the wars with France.[40] As a result the 1790s was a decade of new encounters within Britain, in which tourists saw Wales against different contexts.[41] These tours also brought a sense of introspection, a new pressure to look within. Travelling through Wales threw some of the internal differences within Britain into relief; tourists often noted the strangeness of Wales and its people, a view that when taken to its logical extreme points towards the strangeness of Britain and the almost arbitrary nature of its union of disparate peoples and cultures.[42] William Sotheby's account of his travels through Pembrokeshire shortly before the Revolution, published in 1790 as 'A Tour Through Parts of South and North Wales' (no. 2), includes an account of meeting a young, unnamed shepherd girl. In the poem she is picturesquely located on the battered periphery of the coastline (lines 49–59), a wild, lonely, primitive figure whose inability to give Sotheby directions on his travels – she is a monoglot Welsh speaker – appears, to him, proof of her provincial barbarity. In the poem Sotheby stresses the narrowness of the shepherd girl's world-view ('the narrow bound / Of her rude range') but the dismissive, and deeply colonial, nature of his portrayal of this native Welsh figure, his sense of alienation from her, suggests that there is little or no broader unity under-writing his perception of Wales. A number of pieces in the following selection clearly display their allegiance to a unified British nation (often, but not always, in the context of war and invasion), but scratch a little deeper into the poetry of the period and there is often scant sense of a common British-ness in their authors' perception and experience of Wales. By contrast with Sotheby's shepherd girl, Owen of Llangoed, another poor shepherd figure on the edge of the nation, sees nothing but possibilities beyond the shores of his small island, his inability to speak English no barrier to his ambition. The spaces between these two views, Sotheby's and Llwyd's, and the meeting-points between them, are central themes throughout this anthology.

Dawn of liberty 1790–3

'For poets, as for others living at the time, there was no doubt that the French Revolution was the era's crucial event and key literary subject.'[43] Revolution is the master-narrative of all the texts included in the following selection, but what was Wales like as the Revolution travelled through polemical writings, correspondence, news or hearsay into the poetry of this period? By the time revolution rocked France, Wales had experienced its own provincial Enlightenment, led by antiquarians and artisans who recognized the importance of preserving the nation's language and literature against Anglicization and industrialization.[44] Beyond Wales, a displaced public sphere had developed in London in the eighteenth century, largely through the patriotic societies founded there by expatriate Welshmen.[45] And yet, despite these pockets of intense activity, the Welsh of this period have also been described as a 'non-historic' people:

> small, of no account, the debris of a past – a people whose history and traditions had been disrupted, whose language had lost status and threatened to dissolve into a mess of patois . . . a people which lacked even the vestiges of a state and was doomed to disappear.[46]

The French Revolution acted almost irresistibly upon this small nation, argues Gwyn A. Williams, by speeding up the tendency towards 'revival and reassertion' in the face of the 'hegemonic external culture'[47] – English culture – that weighed heavily upon it.

The egalitarian ideals of the Revolution would have been welcomed by those Welsh people who linked their own sense of nation with civil, political and religious oppression, sentiments clearly set out in Iolo Morganwg's 'Address to the Inhabitants of Wales' (no. 13). However, Wales appeared on the horizons of poems about the Revolution and its consequences with varying degrees of clarity and coherence. As Marion Löffler has shown, Wales was not perceived by the newspapers on its border – which, in the absence of a native press, served both north and south regions – as a 'political unit'.[48] Developing the rather loose and disjointed sense of Welshness suggested by the border newspapers, poems from the period may model a strongly local identity, or, at the other extreme, offer unfixed or provisional impressions of Wales. The opening group of poems in this anthology shows a variety of perspectives on Wales's relationship with the Revolution, from the broad sweep of David Samwell's celebratory ode for the year 1790 (no. 1) to the detailed view of local industry and its links with France in the anonymous 'An Ode to Commerce' (no. 3). Along with poems by Richard Llwyd and

David Thomas (Dafydd Ddu Eryri), these works begin to illustrate the way in which verse was a vital part of the print conflicts of the British Revolution controversy. William Sotheby's depiction of travels that are haunted by the past and the present in 'A Tour Through Parts of South and North Wales' (no. 2) opens up the recurring theme of the unevenness and ambiguity that runs through depictions of Wales (especially its castles, landscapes, people or history) in the period, an approach that also offers a way of articulating uncertainties about events in France.

David Samwell's ode welcoming the Revolution belongs to a collective positive response to the events of 1789 voiced by writers as different as Anna Seward, William Roscoe, and the unnamed Irish poet whose rejoicing at the 'wonderful hubbub' in France is a prelude to his pleas for Irish freedom in verses later published as the opening text in the republican songbook *Paddy's Resource* (1795).[49] Samwell optimistically looks forward to a new decade and a new age of freedom begun by the Revolution in this poem articulating hopes that the first lights of liberty in France will spread to other regions suffering tyranny and injustice.

By 1789 Samwell was an important member of the expatriate London Welsh, part of 'a bohemian intelligentsia living by their pens and wits'.[50] His letters vividly document this world: there were meetings in public and private to discuss the events of the Revolution, dinners to commemorate the fall of the Bastille, affectionate but subversive banter secreted in letters to Iolo Morganwg:

> Let me, like Belial at thy elbow, knock,
> And say I dine at two o'clock.
> Belial will have thee, soon or late –
> Iorwerth's, Tom Paine's & Dafydd Feddyg's fate.
> Perhaps it may be known some ages hence
> Iorwerth, Tom Paine, & Dafydd Ddû had scones.[51]

The Welsh language, only rarely used in letters between Iolo and Samwell, offered a space for hiding radical sentiments. In a note rearranging a meeting with Iolo – the original date clashes with an anniversary dinner celebrating the Revolution – Samwell adds a Welsh postscript that suggests some nervousness about the way in which political opposition is being policed in London: 'Gadewch im eich gweled cyn gynted a galloch, rhag ofn ir milwyr ein gyrru ni o'r Goron ag Angor i Baradwys.' (Let me see you as soon as you can, in case the soldiers should send us from the Crown and Anchor to Paradise.)[52]

Outsiders in London, a shared sense of Welsh identity bound together a disparate set of men, overriding their political differences where necessary.[53]

While these London networks were largely social and cultural in orientation, politics often outweighed all other concerns, especially in the Caradogian Society (active *c.*1790–8). London-Welsh circles were, however, overshadowed by state surveillance and repression by the mid- to late 1790s.[54] Independently minded figures such as Iolo Morganwg or the tavern keeper and translator John Jones (Jac Glan-y-gors; 1766–1821) experienced first hand the dangers of being linked with radical activity in the capital,[55] and the forces that put down the British reform movement may also have affected the political character of the Caradogian Society. Reports of the Caradogian's debates on subjects such as the 'Gagging Acts'[56] suggest a sort of Welsh extra-parliamentary court of opinion, a situation that cannot have gone down well with the authorities in the 1790s. 'We hear no more of the Caradogian Society after 1798',[57] notes E. G. Bowen, but this is not surprising given that the reform-minded Caradogian was exactly the sort of grouping under attack from the wartime British government.

By 1790 any sense of a positive consensus about events in France was already unravelling. It would continue to fragment in the following months and years, through a pamphlet war of ideas, the rising tide of loyalism of late 1792, and the beginning of the real Revolutionary war in February 1793. These shifts in events and perspectives can be traced through the poetry. Although William Sotheby's 'A Tour Through Parts of South and North Wales' recounts a journey taken in the summer of 1788, it appeared in 1790 with events in France as a backdrop to its descriptions of Welsh people, places and history. Read through the new prism of the Revolution, Sotheby's *Tour* offers more than one version of events.

Sotheby's travels through south Wales include visions of the 'ceaseless revolution' of contemporary industry and the softer imagined meanings of historicized Welsh landscapes. Published against the expanding Revolution controversy, the poem represents a threshold in Anglophone Welsh poetry: both an end and a new beginning of ways of writing about Wales. Sotheby's *Tour* comes late in the history of the genre of topographical poetry that he sometimes seems to aspire to writing in this work – the *Tour* travels right through the landscape of John Dyer's 'Grongar Hill' (1726), for example (lines 259–71). But his poem is also at the forefront of a new wave of views of Wales marked by contemporary events.

A number of poems in this collection offer a sense of the Revolution being refracted through Wales, and the Revolutionary picture is often out of focus as a result. The troubled histories of the Welsh landscapes in which these works are set, or which inspired them, distort things further. Visiting the ruined castles of south Wales leads Sotheby to a string of reflections on liberty, prison, feudalism, oppression, superstition – in short, a picture of a

Figure 1. S. Alken, after J. Smith, 'Caraig-cennin Castle' (1794)

sort of *ancien régime* Wales that brings to mind France, and particularly the Bastille, destroyed the summer before the publication of Sotheby's poem.[58] The poem is unsteadied by problems of vision: Sotheby's views of Wales are characterized by 'wavering mists', by an imagined 'thin blue veil' that 'half conceal[s]' the landscapes he is trying to portray. The occluded nature of Sotheby's descriptions perhaps suggest that he has reached no clear decision or judgement about contemporary events.

By 1790 the French Revolution was also beginning to make more specific impressions within Welsh life. In Bersham just outside Wrexham, for instance, the ironmaster John Wilkinson was known for his French sympathies. Wilkinson's foundry belongs to the 'abrupt crisis of modernisation'[59] that had struck Wales in the eighteenth century, but viewed more closely it reveals particular connections between Wales and the French Revolution since Wilkinson – who was Joseph Priestley's brother-in-law and his firm supporter – quickly became a figure of suspicion. Industry was unlocking Wales in this period, creating 'a more open and varied society' and trans-forming its political cultures.[60] When 'An Ode to Commerce' was published anonymously in the *Chester Chronicle* in December 1790,[61] supporting French affairs was not yet synonymous with the betrayal of British interests in the way that anti-revolutionary forces would make it out to be in the coming years. As an account of contemporary Britain, 'An Ode to Commerce' is more particularized, grounded in actual place and specific references, than David Samwell's vague, luminous vision of liberty. The poem surveys the almost sublime reach of Wilkinson's business empire ('parts of a whole which is almost beyond comprehension', line 81n), which extended to France, framing struggles towards liberty in terms of wealth and progress in a typical 'Modern Whig' perspective.[62]

Strongly local in its dedication to Wilkinson and in its place of publication, the ode points towards a larger patriotic unity founded in commercial exchange. And yet it also hints at the troubles that were unfolding in north-east Wales. Wilkinson had directly benefited from earlier conflicts such as the American wars, for which he produced cannon at his Bersham ironworks.[63] From the 1780s onwards, he issued trade tokens and later (some thought in imitation of Revolutionary France) assignats. The 'Ode to Commerce', a poem invoking a global theatre of war, mentions Wilkinson's trade tokens – his 'elegant and useful coinage' with 'its extensive circulation' (line 89n) – but the poet does not point out the fact that here are some of the earliest signs that upheaval in France may translate to trouble in Wales. Bersham stands out as an example because Revolutionary anxieties surrounding the figure of Wilkinson can be directly traced on the wider canvas of British affairs: in January 1793 assignats were banned, a move calculated to stop the circulation of Wilkinson's paper money.[64] It is easy to see why the authorities took fright at Wilkinson. He had arms in the form of the cannon he was manufacturing, he had his own currency, a potentially substantial body of men in his workers, he collaborated with France in business and, it was widely thought, ideology, and he supported well-known British radicals.

In the years that followed, north-east Wales would repeatedly show itself as an unsettled space, a place of disturbances and seditious proclamations. There were riots in Wrexham, Hope and Denbigh against enclosures, poverty and famine,[65] and at times unambiguously political protest.[66] These moments did not, however, often find their way into poetry. A historical lens on current events that only indirectly comments on the present is much more typical of the period. This was the strategy used by Richard Llwyd in shaping an explicitly Welsh response to Revolution in two occasional odes published in the *Chester Chronicle* in 1791 and 1792. These verses show Llwyd channelling Samwell's broad portrait of universal freedom into a narrower national context. In Llwyd's poems, scenes of Welsh history are overlaid with the language of liberty that animates Samwell's ode; like Samwell, Llwyd celebrated the 'gen'rous flame' of freedom recently lit in France and the triumph of reason that 'Spurns a tyrant's mad decrees' (no. 4, line 52). But these two poems by Llwyd are politicized in a different sense because they clearly assert a patriotic allegiance to Wales, which takes centre stage as an ancient location of liberty and peace in 'An Ode for the New Year':

> Such as o'er the trackless heath,
> Unharass'd yet in fields of death,
> Unfetter'd freedom ran;
> Ere yet the moated rampart knew
> Oppression's callous steel-clad crew,
> Her foes, and those of man! (Lines 16–21)

In this poem the Revolution fits into a wider account of Wales's lost liberty (lines 47–50): at the point in late 1790 when the poem was probably written, Llwyd was clearly seeing the history of the Welsh nation in the context of the French Revolution.

Contemporary nuances interlace Llwyd's poetry. His 1792 'Ode, for the Anniversary of St. David' (no. 5) depicts liberty as first a uniquely British force ('Nurtur'd in the British isles, / On other realms, lo, Freedom smiles', lines 25–6) and beyond that a particular characteristic of the Welsh: 'Cambria . . . bade her native offspring be, / To time's remotest period, free' (lines 22–4). This poem is a compressed meditation on history, Llwyd's self-portrait as, in traditional bardic fashion in Wales, the 'muse of retrospective lore' (line 10). Elsewhere in the poem images of slaughter and exodus under the British queen 'Boadicea' – 'While Europe from each crowded shore / Pour'd her savage outcasts o'er' (lines 13–14) – equally suggest a spectacle of exile in terms of the emigrés who had crowded out of France in their thousands after the events of 1789.[67] Finally, while Britain and France were not yet at war, internal struggles in France, and between France and its Continental neighbours (war with Austria began in April 1792), bring contemporary resonance to Llwyd's picture of 'death-fraught plains'.

Such double meanings only intensified in poems published later in the decade. Writers responded with uncertainty, rising to horror, to the beginnings of war in Europe and, by the late summer of 1792, the shift from Revolution to extreme republican violence in France. With the radiant optimism of the initial reception of the Revolution clouding over, a proclamation against seditious writings in May 1792 also brought a legal aspect into play that closed down some of the possibilities for discussing politics in literature. By the end of the year loyalist associationism was taking hold in Wales.[68] For all these reasons, writing poetry became a more complicated matter over the course of 1792.

When William Sotheby's 1790 *Tour* was republished with illustrations in 1794, its ambiguous approaches to freedom and repression could only have sounded deeper, perhaps even ironic or knowing. The *Tour* shows that the meanings of poems kept pace with changes in France and corresponding responses in Britain; perspectives mix up, lose the neatness of one-way vision as a result. In 'The Banks of the Menai' (no. 6), for example, David Thomas offers an ancient Welsh angle on contemporary affairs, through which the Jacobin Terror of 1792 seems to seep into the bloodstained landscape of his cautious counterpoint to the French Revolution. Thomas's poem, publicly recited in London in September 1792 at the new bardic gathering, the Gorsedd, sounds a new, narrower conception of liberty: 'Each bosom warm in freedom's cause, / And yet *obedient to the laws*' (lines 33–4 – my emphasis).

David Samwell's ode on the mythical giant Rhita Gawr (no. 7), performed at the same meeting of bards in 1792, offers a contrasting perspective on the use of the past as a means of commenting on present events that shows the breadth of Welsh responses to the Revolution, even within a fairly small grouping such as the Gorsedd.[69] This poem links Welsh poetry with the rights of man (lines 55–60), presenting Wales and its literature as a place of natural rights in a much more republican way than, say, Richard Llwyd does. Like Thomas, Samwell sees the Welsh in the 1790s as heirs of an earlier poetic tradition that includes writers such as Aneirin and Taliesin. But more provocatively, Samwell also depicts bardic activity as a ritualized, institutional but not obviously political way of receiving the French Revolution in Britain. In a mark of how extreme Samwell's position is in this work, the poem anticipates regicide in France, linking the execution of Charles I with the imagined or foreseen death of Louis XVI ('Saw ye on the scaffold fall, / The owner of the purple pall'), and at no point resisting the death of the French king.

By the 1790s recycled Celtic material had long featured in English eighteenth-century verse. The reworking of Welsh myths and histories in mid-century poems such as Thomas Gray's 'The Bard' (1757) and William Mason's *Caractacus* (1759) turned out influential variations on the theme of heroic resistance. In sustained periods of conflict such as the Seven Years' War, ancient British heroes (especially Caractacus and Boadicea) were 'pressed into service to support the war effort as exemplary ancestors of the contemporary British warrior'.[70] As the century progressed, however, the nature of the patriotism of texts such as Gray's or Mason's looked increasingly unclear. With an eye on the dual origins of British culture – both Celtic and Saxon or Germanic – Welsh writers replied in terms that drew the double, even 'combative' meaning of the term Briton to the fore.[71] As a result, the whole notion of a national community came into an uncertainty sustained by the debate 'between nationalism, defined in cultural and linguistic terms, and political unity in this period'.[72]

Poems by Llwyd and Thomas discussed above give a Welsh genealogy for liberty and a Welsh take on traditions of resistance, as well as a sense of a native literary history. When the Oxford poet George Richards (1767–1837) explored similar subject matter in *Songs of the Aboriginal Bards of Britain* (1792), then, he did so from a very different perspective. Remote history, the raw material for a nationalist or even Jacobin poetry in the hands of, respectively, Llwyd or Samwell, appears noticeably more introspective and defensive under the darkening shadow of ideological, and soon to be actual, conflict with France.

Richards's 'The Captivity of Caractacus' (no. 8) retells the story of the Celtic ruler taken prisoner by the Romans whose dignity in defeat saves the day. The poem plays on ideas of Wales as historical home of liberty, resistance and defiance that shapes a later common British identity: an allegory of present-day British resilience. The precise dating of Richards's *Songs*, however, suggests that this depiction of British heroism, this attempt to catch the 'spirit' and 'genius' of earlier times, is rich with polemical significance. The dedication to the collection is dated 15 November 1792, or to a point in time when Britain was slipping towards war with the new French republic. Richards resets the rising tensions of the situation in a Celtic scene of patriotic opposition and independence, in which the bards call for war against Roman invaders: their 'bold inspiring strain . . . disdain[s] a foe's controul' (lines 16–18). *Songs* was widely praised for its 'noble and elevated sentiments',[73] but by the following year Richards had turned from ancient Britons to *Modern France* (1793), a pamphlet-length anti-revolutionary poem pulsing with French violence. This poem pictures how, by 1793, 'Spirits of Death walk frighted Paris o'er',[74] but Richards's 1792 verses on Wales should also be seen as part of a spectrum of his responses to contemporary affairs in the wake of the Revolution, setting out a militant symbolic patriotism ahead of preparations for war.

'The Captivity of Caractacus', a poem whose action all takes place at a distance, in the past, brings history onto the perimeters of the present. At just the same time, William Sotheby was making the opposite move in 'Llangollen' (no. 9), a poem twice dated to autumn 1792.[75] Writing on Wales again, Sotheby reverses the temporal perspective of Richards's poem, sinking the present into history via a first-person real-time narrator, which provides a compass point for the context, when the course events would take was still unclear. The poem is another tourist piece, explicitly figured as a return to Wales ('Genius of wild Llangollen! once again / I turn to thy rude haunts, and savage reign', lines 3–4), and a revision of Sotheby's earlier account that measures Wales against the 1790 *Tour* and against changes in the landscape of contemporary affairs.

Closing the poetry collection Sotheby published in 1794, 'Llangollen' is an introspective, down-beat piece. Sotheby's sense of Llangollen as a 'dark retreat' is based on the region's history, detailed in brutal stories of murder, deception and betrayal (lines 55–78). The poem's autumnal mood obviously has to do with the passing season, and the sometimes gloomy subject matter, but the shadow of a very specific autumn – 1792 – hangs over the poem as a whole. Looking at the River Dee swirling below him, Sotheby is drawn into reflections on the 'fate of nations, fall of kings' (line 120), and here the poem's elegiac feel and atmosphere of decline suddenly broadens out. At this moment in the text Llangollen becomes a hazy historicized parallel for contemporary France, just as Sotheby would later allegorize the Peninsular war in *Constance de Castile* (1810), a poem about dynastic politics in fourteenth-century Spain.[76] Invoking nations and kings in the plural in this way, Sotheby's poem stretches beyond the obvious, uppermost context of the vale of Llangollen and its history to the suppressed and yet perhaps equally obvious context of France.

The horrors of war 1794

Whether their authors acknowledged it or not, all of the poems discussed so far appeared against the context of the Revolution controversy; the pamphlet war involving Richard Price, Burke, Wollstonecraft, Paine, and others.[77] However, 1793 brought a crucial new context. With Britain at war with France it became increasingly difficult to represent the French Revolution as in any way analogous to the Glorious Revolution, as Price had done in *A Discourse on the Love of Our Country* (1789). 'Jacobinism' became a sensationalized term in Britain, identified with those who were in favour of reform as well as supporters of Revolution, despite the significant distance between these two positions.[78] As Britain was 'taken to the edge of panic'[79] in 1792 over the publication of the second part of Paine's *Rights of Man*, so the space for anti-establishment views closed in – a point especially relevant to Wales where Dissenters were keenly aware of their inequality in religious matters.[80]

A year of war transformed the prevailing mood of the poetry published in 1794. The tentative or hopeful qualities of the verse published in the first years after the Revolution now fell away, replaced by devastating accounts of the conflict. Loyalist writers predicted certain victory over the French and their uprising; their opponents reacted with moral horror at the glorification of war that this perspective on events usually required. But beyond the poles of these responses, which Iolo Morganwg satirically dramatizes in 'The Horrors of War' (no. 14), how did those in Britain depict and respond to the war as it unfolded overseas and then shaped life at home?[81]

Jane Cave's fast-day poem, 'Thoughts on the Present Times' (no. 16), vividly portrays events in 1793–4. Balanced between mock incredulity and a real sense of dismay about developments between France and Britain, the opening of the poem deftly sketches a world at war:

> A FAST proclaim'd! another Fast!
> Nature recedes with dire alarms;
> We dread the future, – mourn the past; –
> And all the world repairs to arms! (Lines 1–4)

Cave's poem is direct and engaging, deceptively conversational in its depiction of the shocks of 1794. It belongs to a body of work that illustrates the ways in which the French Revolution made its mark on Britain, not literally as a revolution but as a series of political, social and legal events that transformed British life in the mid-1790s.[82] Brought up in Talgarth, near Brecon, in a Methodist family, Jane Cave had moved to Bristol by the 1790s. Sarah Prescott has recently explored the importance of Cave's Welshness for her authority as a religious writer, an important feature of her work in general and of 'Thoughts' in particular.[83] Cave may seem to appear almost out of nowhere as a writer in the 1780s and 1790s, but Welsh Dissent offers one way of understanding her emergence as a confident commentator on contemporary political as well as religious matters.

Cave's work was the product of different, overlapping contexts, among them her background in the borderlands of mid Wales, framed by the Usk and Wye valleys, and her father's, and later her husband's, occupations as excisemen working for the Crown. But perhaps the Methodist connection is the most important factor in terms of her writerly identity: as Jane Aaron has explained, there are important continuities between Cave's upbringing within the 'democratic influences of . . . Welsh Nonconformist culture' with its 'intellectual and emotional intensity' and her critical and artistic engagement with events in the 1790s.[84] While the Methodists did not officially leave the Established Church until 1811, they were a clearly distinct grouping by the late eighteenth century, a suspicious minority even in Nonconformist Wales as a result of what Damian Walford Davies describes as the 'madly kinetic'[85] nature of their religious gatherings.

The 'simultaneous modernity and mysticism'[86] represented by Methodism in the period suggests the potential for a crisis of identity which materialized in the mixed sense of fear, self-justification, even paranoia, that can be seen within Welsh Methodism in the 1790s.[87] From the opposite perspective, then, Methodism may also suggest the need for the sort of robust individual identity that also enabled Cave to picture herself as a political writer. Although 'Thoughts' is a bold poem it is not uncharacteristically so for Cave, who also wrote other poems on significant contemporary events, including those local to her in Bristol.[88] It is worth emphasizing that Cave's poems were published just over the Welsh border: Bristol was not part of Wales but nor, like its northern counterpart Liverpool, was it easily separated from Wales in this period.[89] Although the extent to which Cave saw herself as Welsh is not particularly clear from her poetry,[90] she could easily have maintained a strong sense of Welshness in Bristol.

Jane Cave's better-known contemporary Hester Piozzi presents different difficulties of identity and allegiance. Piozzi clearly, and frequently, identified herself as a Welsh woman, in manuscript and in print, but her Welshness is complex.[91] Born on the Llŷn Peninsula to an impoverished Welsh gentry family, she spent much of her adult life as the wife of the wealthy brewer Henry Thrale. Following her remarriage in 1784 – for love, and somewhat sensationally – to an Italian musician, she relocated from London to north Wales in 1794.[92] Along with the French Revolution, the move to Wales transformed her writing career in the 1790s.[93]

Wales undoubtedly represented a place of refuge for Piozzi. The source of her noble lineage, it offered an escape from fashionable sociability (now tarnished by negative reactions to her second marriage) and, more importantly, a stronghold against what Piozzi saw as the shortcomings of the British nation at large as it reacted to the French Revolution.[94] Her pride in Wales was twofold, based on ideas of its people as exemplars of bravery and resistance, and on an impression of its lands as static and peaceful, symbolizing virtue. These views were of course deeply polemical, but this is the context against which the pro-war, anti-Gallican and counter-revolutionary poems and prose pieces Piozzi wrote in the 1790s, for the most part while she was living in Wales, should be read.

Piozzi characteristically responds to important developments in this period with a mixture of fear and defiance, in a patriotic bravado that always points back to the need to contain and maintain social order. The first poem by her in this anthology (no. 17) comes from the philological work she published in April 1794, *British Synonymy*, under the entry for 'VICTIM AND SACRIFICE'. This passage reflects on what Piozzi now saw as the bloody savagery of France, a place of show trials and mass murder – 'the human VICTIM destined to glut the rage of their new idol, falsely called Liberty'.[95] But she also turned out cannier poems exploiting the violence in France, as in 'The Chapter of King Killers', a political ballad composed in Denbigh in the summer of

1794.[96] In a further step, 'See, see the mad marauders come' (no. 23) shows Piozzi attempting to take on the radical movement. Written around the time of the treason trials in October/November 1794, 'See, see' was a reply to the republican song 'Plant, Plant the Tree', in whose lyrics the Attorney-General Sir John Scott saw 'every species of treason known to the law of England'.[97]

William McCarthy has summarized Piozzi's 1790s works as 'a war effort',[98] and she may well have seen it as her duty to write on behalf of the anti-revolutionary cause – in her 1798 pamphlet *Three Warnings to John Bull*, she puts it this way: 'Those who cannot fight must write for their country: *all must join, all must agree*.'[99] Loyalist counter-voices such as 'See, see' cultivate a liveliness and briskness that may reflect the speed with which they were composed but which also suggest a deliberate attempt to connect with an imagined audience in the tavern or the street. Piozzi may also have seen opportunities to get her work noticed in the political slant of her texts. In her letters she openly expresses hopes that her poems will reach a wide popular audience,[100] and she is gleefully confident that work is just as good as other poems making shockwaves in 1794. 'See, see the mad Marauders come' is, Piozzi confides to her journal, just as good as 'Plant, Plant the Tree': 'I should really be glad that these Verses found Admirers too; they are certainly as witty as the wicked ones'.[101] However, Piozzi misjudged the way in which her writings would be received and overestimated the impact they would make. Her sense that *British Synonymy* would make her a major anti-revolutionary writer came to nothing,[102] and as the voice of loyalism from north-east Wales, she was probably less successful than she had expected.

1794 became a key date for Welsh poetry in English on the publication of the two-volume collection *Poems, Lyric and Pastoral* by the Glamorganshire writer Edward Williams (Iolo Morganwg) in January of this year, which launched one of the most important and distinctive voices from 1790s Wales. Iolo was a stonemason by trade and *Poems* was his attempt to corner the market in Welsh labouring-class writing. He aspired to the success of Robert Burns or Ann Yearsley, presenting his collection as 'the real unsophisticated productions of the *self-tutored Journeyman Mason*'.[103] Yet the positions Iolo sets out in the poems were, not surprisingly, much more complex than he suggests here, often uneasily balancing Jacobin sympathies with the traditional role of the Welsh bard as the mouthpiece of society, or of history.[104] The image of the artless stonecutter quickly fades in *Poems, Lyric and Pastoral*, replaced with increasingly discordant, politically oppositional visions of conflict and brutality, and sublime, if at times schematic, accounts of Ancient British 'Bardism', Iolo's highly theatrical invented political system.[105]

Unlike Hester Piozzi's hurried pieces, this collection developed over a long period of time, and it ultimately appeared against contexts Iolo could not possibly have foreseen; it was overtaken by events despite his efforts to include poems drafted or altered at the last possible opportunity.[106] And yet the French Revolution was not the making of Iolo as a poet. Like the radical printer Thomas Spence, who included Iolo's 'Trial by Jury' (no. 25) in *Pig's Meat: or Lessons for the People* (1795), Iolo was a product of the 'intellectual and political awakening offered by the popular enlightenment in the provinces'.[107] Geraint H. Jenkins's recent intellectual biography of Iolo outlines the evolution of his democratic principles well before the 1790s: Jenkins traces, for instance, the regicidal radicalism Iolo derived from reading Milton, the role of Rational Dissent in his anti-clericalism, or the anti-Methodism which was based on the Methodists' adherence to Church and King and failure to 'reach out to the politically disenfranchised or [to] encourage them to voice their grievances'.[108] By 1789, Jenkins concludes, Iolo 'was more than ready to enter the public sphere of politics',[109] but his abstract, almost hallucinatory accounts of evil on a grand scale in *Poems* – warfare, corruption in Church and government, and the repression of civil and religious rights – also took on new life in the crucible of war and alarmism in which they were published in 1794.

Poems, Lyric and Pastoral offers one of the period's strongest examples of metropolitan radicalism remade from the periphery. However Iolo was not passively aware of his peripheral status: burningly aware of issues both sides of the border, caught up in cross-currents of class as well as nationality, language and politics, he also resisted it. In 'Winter Incidents' (no. 10), he adopts a Cowper-like position of rural retirement,[110] very likely set in Wales though the setting is not explicitly stated, a place of independence from which to speak out as a critical voice. In this poem Iolo creates a 'politically interventionist provincial poetry'[111] that provides the rationale for other poems such as 'The Horrors of War' (no. 14), in which rural retirement – anti-monarchical, anti-militaristic, resisting all forms of civic pro-war patriotism – becomes the moral high ground. However, the problems involved in fashioning a Welsh pacifist, pro-reform poetry quickly became apparent. In manuscripts probably dating from 1793–4 'Ode on Converting a Sword into a Pruning Hook' (no. 15) became a test case, and in another sense, a manifesto, for the sort of verse Iolo now wanted to write. In a succession of possible prefaces to the poem (none of which was ever printed), he rejected the notion of a just war, in direct opposition to Paine's claims for the necessity of self-defence during the American Revolution.[112] Throughout these prefaces war appears as a sort of national organizing principle, steering his argument that the nation needs to be reformed along pacifist lines:

> We want Government, not to embroil us in Wars with our neighbours on every frivolous occasion, but to guard us from its evils, to restrain us from committing depredations, not only on each other internally, but also in our collective capacity as community, on our external neighbours, on other nations and governments.[113]

Perhaps few of Iolo's contemporaries would have agreed that the execution of Louis XVI counted as a 'frivolous occasion', but there is no missing the strength both of his pacifism and his support for the French in this passage playing down the seriousness of the grounds for going to war in 1793.

Iolo's correspondence shows that the 'Pruning Hook' ode belongs to the later stages of the creation of *Poems, Lyric and Pastoral*, and to a period in which damaging rumours were circulating about his political loyalties. Among them were suggestions that he was, or had been, in Revolutionary France. He had not, Iolo stated, in an equivocal letter which leaves open, perhaps deliberately so, the question of how far he was writing 'against government':

> . . . what brightness of character can I ever expect to achieve in a country where so many endeavour to blacken it? I shall send you a printed sheet soon that contains the severest thing that ever I wrote against government and then you will be able to judge whether I attempt to raise disturbances or not. It is an 'Ode on converting a sword into a pruning hook.' . . . As for the treasonable correspondence that I have with France, let any one believe it if he pleases, that will not make it more true.[114]

However, a double bluff lies within this letter, written to his wife Peggy, who was back in Glamorgan with their children. Taken in isolation it may read as a disavowal of radical activity, perhaps intended to reassure his wife that he was not getting into trouble in London. But read in contexts to which Peggy Williams could not have had access, it is also part of Iolo's extreme opposition to the Tory government of William Pitt and the war with France.

Iolo emerges as a more dangerous figure in his manuscript writings than in published poems. The unpublished prefaces to the 'Pruning Hook' ode show in detail the oppositional stance that lay behind its composition; the idea of war as 'murder royal',[115] a crippling societal perversion, is spun through Iolo's imagination into towering visions of horror firmly based on real contemporary events.[116] Calling for peace, however, and reminding readers of the volume and violence of the losses taking place on the Continent, as he did in the unpublished song 'Bella! horrida Bella!' (no. 21), would take increasing bravery in the early years of the war, as other writers and painters found to their cost.[117] The 'Pruning Hook' ode is not a dangerous work in terms of the content of the published poem, but for readers with access to his manuscript writings it looks very threatening indeed.[118]

Perhaps because of his failure to channel the radicalism of his private papers into a final printed text, Iolo later changed his mind about the force of the poem. As soon as it was published, he saw it as part of what he now called his 'weak attempt to abet the cause of truth, justice, and humanity'.[119] He particularly regretted that the footnotes to the 'Pruning Hook' ode, along with those of the 'War-song of British savages' (a pacifist version of 'God Save the King'), were 'the most obnoxious, but unluckily, I fear, not sufficiently so'.[120] 'Too general, no particular application', Iolo concluded. His disappointment with the poem, however, is not entirely warranted. There may well have been a stern element of self-censorship involved in writing 'Ode on Converting a Sword into a Pruning Hook' since the context in which it was published – in London, in 1794, during a war that was going badly for Britain – is key to understanding how the poem may have been received. It was also publicly recited at Primrose Hill in September 1793 at the third of Iolo's Gorsedd ceremonies, which were correctly suspected of dressing up Jacobin principles in ancient Welsh bardic ritual.[121] It is very difficult to see how, either in the context of September 1793 or January 1794, this egalitarian anti-war poem could have been anything other than general and imprecise in its published form.

While the 'Pruning Hook' ode was not prison material it was written by someone who certainly had the potential to produce the sort of poetry that would have got him into serious trouble in 1790s London. Part of the problem with Iolo's verse is his tendency toward a declamatory style, an exaggerated rhetoric that tells rather than shows: he makes his point with far more force, for example, in the understated, subtle 'Winter Incidents'. However, the distinctive constellation of influences in Iolo's background as a Welsh bard may have complicated matters for him. The idiom of the 'Pruning Hook' poem – loud, theatrical, full of grand flourishes – was perhaps too closely related to the idiom of court or Establishment patriotic poetry, too close to the 'official' language of power, to be a persuasive means of articulating resistance to that power. But, historically speaking, Welsh bards were affiliated with courts and employed by powerful patrons for whom they composed praise poetry. So Iolo's sense of himself as a modern bard may have been split by conflicting commitments – for example, the bardic convention of loyalty to those in power versus political sympathies that go *against* the grain of power in 1790s Britain – that show through the fabric of his poetry.[122]

As 1794 advanced, Iolo's position became increasingly unsustainable. Gripped by a sense of the need to support the domestic reform movement,

Iolo seems to have been scared off by William Pitt's 'Reign of Terror', a period in which radicals became the target of various forms of intimidation and persecution that systematically harmed or shut down their writing careers.[123] At times the threat of intimidation may have been more imagined or feared than real, and although Iolo claims that he was interrogated by government officials and that his personal papers were searched,[124] this more nebulous threat of repercussions, usually suffered in private and most of all experienced inwardly, at the level of the imagination, had most impact on his writing life. The immediate result for Iolo's poetry in 1794–5 is a sense that he was being pulled by contradictory positions. On the one hand he fiercely wanted to join the period's dissident voices, whatever the cost, but on the other it seems that he could not overcome his fears for the consequences if he did so. In the longer term, perhaps not least as a result of this hesitancy or indecision, Iolo became part of a 'lost generation' of radicals, and more specifically part of a missing group of Welsh radicals, in the mid-1790s.[125]

Iolo's belief that he was a marked man fighting an impossible corner in the mid-1790s comes to life in 'Church and King rampant' (no. 18), an unpublished pessimistic account of the conditions for political opposition in this period. But by contrast there is also the defiant and much better-known printed broadside 'Trial by Jury' (no. 25), written in late 1794 or very early 1795, a jubilant, almost gleeful poem celebrating the acquittal of John Thelwall, Thomas Hardy and John Horne Tooke in the treason trials, and sung by Iolo at the Crown and Anchor tavern in February 1795. Perhaps this poem represents the public face of Iolo's views (his Revolutionary sympathies, his belief in the need for political and religious reform, especially for the poor, and, at times, specifically for the Welsh), while the other hints at the private underside, the hidden anxieties that lay beneath a veneer of rebellious confidence. He was clearly a divided figure, tempted towards activism and attracted to the idea of political martyrdom, but equally worried about the prospect of persecution for himself in repressive times, and especially the possible repercussions for his family.[126] And there were other limitations to Iolo's writing life in the 1790s. He never, as far as we know, became a member of radical societies such as the LCS but his chronic inability to finish anything, his addiction to laudanum as well as his often fragile state of mental health,[127] may equally have prevented him from joining the paper wars of the 1790s.

Like other writers trying to avoid accusations of wrong-doing in this period, Iolo turned to topical figurative language in order to muddy the meanings of works that could turn out to be seditious. This approach drew brilliant pieces of satire from oppositional writers in the mid-1790s, not least in the form of cryptic broadsides constructed as fake playbills designed to be

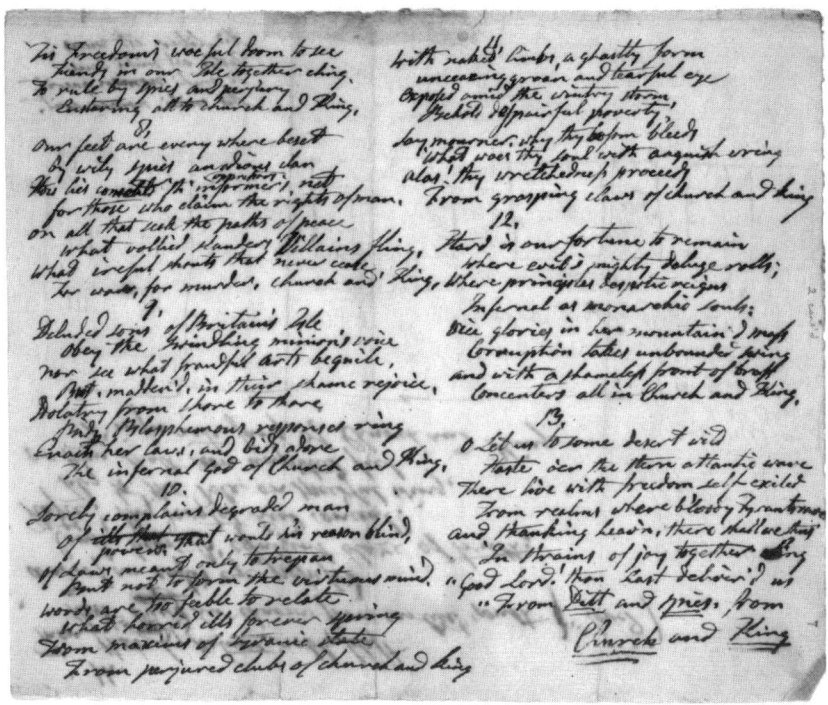

Figure 2. Extract from Edward Williams (Iolo Morganwg), 'Church and King rampant or Satan let loose for a thousand years' (NLW 21401E, f. 6)

handed out in the street or posted on walls. John Barrell has noted that 'the apparently republican content of these satires caused considerable alarm' in early 1794,[128] or at just the same time that Iolo had been writing new poems.[129] These probably included poems such as 'John Bull's Litany' (no. 19); perhaps Iolo's caricatures of figures like Edmund Burke in this poem – '. . . Edmund O Paddy, that bull-making dolt, / Who cannot ne'er could distinguish a pig from a colt' (lines 21–2) – was inspired by the fake-playbill format that was ubiquitous in this period.[130] This ludic aspect of Iolo's writing, its exuberance arguably drawn from metropolitan radicalism, also fed into Welsh-language poems such as 'Breiniau Dyn' (Rights of Man).[131] But aside from this body of work, a tide of crisis drifts within Iolo's manuscripts. The revisions, cancellations, suggestions for alternatives which fill these drafts suggest a deep new uncertainty about how to depict the events and people of this period in literature.[132]

Dangerous times 1795–9

The radical Unitarian weaver Thomas Evans (Tomos Glyn Cothi), an important figure in the Welsh-language response to the French Revolution, did not – at least as far as we know – write any original poetry in English. But he did copy English verses into his notebook, among them a strongly worded piece on the nature of life as a political dissenter in the second half of the 1790s. According to a note in the manuscript, this poem, 'Dangerous Times', was copied from the *Cambridge Intelligencer* of 11 February 1797. The poem is a satirical list of the challenges facing radicals – or even moderate reformers – in a period in which it was, the poem claims, unsafe to read, think, write, or meet (especially in public); dangerous to live, or even to be born:

> Yes, these are gloomy, dangerous times
> As all reformers know!
> When prose blank verse, & simple rhymes,
> May work tremendous woe.
>
> When force unjust man's rights assault,
> 'Tis dangerous not to wink;
> Integrity's a dangerous fault,
> 'Tis dangerous e'en to think.
>
> From dull stupidity's dark sway,
> 'Tis dangerous to be freed,
> 'Tis dangerous reason to display,
> 'Tis quite unsafe to read.
>
> . . .
>
> 'Tis dangerous good advise [*sic*] to give,
> Or infamy to scorn,
> 'Tis dangerous in <u>free states</u> to live,
> 'Tis dangerous to be born.[133]

Evans was the editor of one of three short-lived radical periodicals written in Welsh in the 1790s, *The Miscellaneous Repository neu, Y Drysorfa Gymmysg-edig*, published between the summer of 1795 and early 1796. The periodical, which strongly focused on 'the politico–religious message of Unitarianism',[134] disappeared suddenly, though not before Evans had published impassioned criticisms of the 'cruel and tyrannical government' ('lywodraeth greulon drahaus').[135] Long watched with suspicion by the authorities in south Wales for his political and religious nonconformity, Evans was convicted of sedition in 1801 and sentenced to two years in prison.[136] Perhaps the events of 1801 came as no great surprise to him. He had, after all, been confiding a private record of paranoia and persecution to his notebook in the years since the abrupt, apparently unplanned ending of his periodical.

'Dangerous Times', hidden away by Evans in his private papers, becomes a metonym of the difficulties for rebels and protesters who risked intimidation and punishment if their dissident views were discovered. It stands in for the English-language poems Evans perhaps could not allow himself to compose, even if he had wanted to. When radical poems *were* written in Wales, the delicacy of the contemporary moment cut right down to the choice of individual words. Dangerous times infected the language of Iolo Morganwg's poetry, played out textually through indecision, verses twisting with changes and hesitancy inscribed through the texts. It is worth picking out, for example, the way in which Iolo cannot decide whether to call himself a democrat or a Jacobin in one of several manuscript versions of 'Newgate Stanzas' ('A jacobin _{Democrate} bold he can scare with a frown / The scoundrel of Banditties at th' Anchor and Crown').[137] In an age in which the precise terminology of revolution was still being translated and assimilated into Welsh contexts,[138] the nuances of these labels clearly mattered a great deal, even aside from the courage of conviction required to commit them to paper in a period when no writer could be completely sure that spies were not keeping watch, or that their possessions would not be searched, even in quiet parts of Wales.

The mid- to late 1790s brought dangerous times in another sense. Corn riots were a relatively common feature of life in eighteenth-century Wales, but the outbreak of disturbances from north to south in 1795 brought 'the atmosphere of a year of revolution'.[139] By August 1795, food prices had reached an all-time high, and the resulting desperate plight of ordinary people in Wales was captured in an anonymous anti-war poem signed from Denbigh, 'For the Chester Chronicle' (no. 26). Denbigh had been the site of sustained rioting in April 1795,[140] and to some observers, further disorder in the region looked likely. By November 1795, Hester Piozzi was nervously describing the threatening behaviour of agitators towards eminent local figures such as Thomas Pennant ('They will have his Head on a *Pike* they say') and the Bishop of St Asaph.[141] Any peace made with France at this point would, she believed, only fuel these levelling, revolutionary impulses: '. . . when our fine Peace shall be signed they will have more Jacobins come over to teach them these amiable Lessons – and for one Riot *now* extant – a hundred *then*'.[142]

Serious rioting, culminating in an attack on the carriage of George III, had also broken out in London just days before Piozzi's comments. The government responded with the 'Gagging Acts', a determined effort to crush the reform movement, in part by cracking down on public political gatherings. How did such events weigh on the poetry of the later 1790s? In a period in which 'All liberal acts are indiscreet, / 'Tis scarcely safe to move', as the author of 'Dangerous Times' described it, the advocates of Welsh history and culture continued to excavate earlier works of poetry from fragile manuscripts on the cusp of being permanently lost.[143] London was still a focal point of activity; it was here that the first volume of the literary and antiquarian magazine *The Cambrian Register*, edited by the lexicographer and translator William Owen Pughe, was published in 1796. And while cultural reawakenings in Wales clearly predated the Revolution, domestic wartime disturbances brought sparks of contemporary light into the deep historical orientation of the poetry written alongside the ongoing recovery project.

Thomas Ryder's introductory ode to *The Cambrian Register* (no. 27) gives a sense of the bloody, violent qualities of the earlier Welsh poetry that the magazine reprinted. However, 1796 was in some ways a sensitive moment for the reappearance of this material, since it was almost impossible for writers to mention war at this point without drawing attention to their political sympathies.[144] In an introductory poem that offers a window onto the contents of the magazine, Ryder uses the figure of Llywarch Hen – the eponymous character of a ninth-century Welsh saga who loses twenty-four sons in battle – to evoke the loss of children through war (lines 85–106).[145] *The Heroic Elegies of Llywarç Hen* had been newly edited and translated by William Owen Pughe for a modern audience in 1792. It was published with an unsigned polemical preface by Iolo Morganwg, which reimagined Bardism along French Revolutionary lines, drawing the Llywarch Hen poems into a politicized space that 'located the ideals of liberty, equality and peace as the surviving body of a specifically Welsh (and Glamorgan-based) Bardic philosophy'.[146] In the 1790s, then, this early Welsh song of conflict, suffering and loss was first radically reimagined and then set into a modern war context.

Perhaps some of these currents in Welsh literature were too obscure for many visitors to Wales to have been drawn into. Joseph Hucks, however, saw the potential of Wales as a distilling point of concerns that were, on the surface at least, disconnected. Hucks had seen, and strongly criticized, the suffering in north Wales as a result of the war in the summer of 1794.[147] But the political picaresque of his walking tour also develops out of events taking place elsewhere, especially the war with France and the treason trials, the high point of William Pitt's pursuit of British radicals. Hucks's poem on Denbigh castle (no. 20) sets the monument of the old castle against a contemporary British political landscape, a meditation on Welsh history side-tracked into the present by the (mis)fortunes of the reform movement during that summer.[148]

The poet who published under the pseudonym 'Eliza', by contrast, did not draw parallels between ancient Wales and the revolutionary 1790s in the same way, though her poem 'Sketched on a Party down the River Wye' (no. 28), haunted by phantasmic bards singing war-songs against the invading Romans, uneasily recognizes a world of conflict on the banks of the Wye and beyond.[149] Nor did Anna Seward, whose 'Llangollen Vale' (no. 29) reimagines a brutal medieval battle scene extensively drawn from Thomas Pennant's *A Tour in Wales* (1778–84).[150] 'Llangollen Vale' was clearly an influential work in north-east Wales, as poems written in response, such as Margaret Holford's *Gresford Vale* (1798) and Robert Holland Price's *The Horrors of Invasion* (no. 46), show. But the poem does not really reveal the assured Seward of the 1780s, writing poised public addresses and verses on monumental occasions, though it takes on a much more confident character when Seward writes about her Anglo-Irish friends, Eleanor Butler and Sarah Ponsonby, 'the Ladies of Llangollen'. Before this point the voice of the poem is squeezed by a succession of traumatic spectacles – plague, wounding, death, and cosmic symbolism written against the sky – resulting in a slightly superficial or sensational account of the historical scenes around Llangollen, very different from poems by Welsh writers that also draw on history, and portray it in, and through, landscape. For Richard Llwyd, for example, mountain landscapes represent the last stronghold of Welsh liberty; like the ruins of medieval castles, physical reminders of political losses that affect Wales down to the present day, as in his long topographical poem about Anglesey and Snowdonia, *Beaumaris Bay* (no. 39).

Seward's poem speaks to a 1790s vogue for Wales sustained by the new picturesque tourism for which Llangollen was an entry point. Problematic-ally, however, some readers judged that Seward was giving the history of Wales 'to fame' again through 'Llangollen Vale'.[151] Like 'The Bard' before it, 'Llangollen Vale' became a work that threatened to displace genuine Welsh examples: one response called on the Welsh to rejoice ('Cambria, exult!') in the 'voice' that Seward had given them, their 'rock-skreen'd Valleys, mute no more'.[152] Perhaps predictably, Seward gave no sense of contemporary disturbances as she travelled across Wales in the unsettled summer of 1795.[153] Instead, she works hard to make the loyalist picturesque of 'Llangollen Vale' persuasive: her description of Butler and Ponsonby's house and garden (lines 108–19) emphasizes its tranquillity and security, 'locked against invasive threat from outside'.[154] Viewed as a sort of imperial

Figure 3. J. M. W. Turner, 'Dinas Bran, with the Dee in the Foreground' (1798)

georgic, the poem depicts an idyll of national unity – the Irish peacefully and productively settled in Wales, the whole faithful to the Crown[155] – smoothing over the historical roughness of the fight for Welsh independence with which the poem begins.

At around the same time, Robert Southey was taking the opposite approach. In contrast to Seward's feminized, domesticated depiction of Llangollen, Southey explored the ways in which Wales could be imagined as oppositional terrain. In a series of poems published in the anti-ministerial newspaper the *Morning Post* in 1798, he sketched out Welsh landscapes that reflected his own radical patriotism and rejected 'the reactionary politics of a benighted England.'[156] Southey's links with Wales were complex and lasting. Born in Bristol, he was passionately interested in Welsh history in the 1790s, the fruit of which was *Madoc* (1805), the poem he thought would be his master-work. For a time he could easily have settled permanently near Neath and become, so he joked, looking back in old age on his time in Wales, a kind of Welsh poet laureate.[157]

Southey's ode on Aberffraw (no. 36), published at the close of 1798, balances English imperial aggression with an image of Wales as 'the true home of Freedom' and peace:[158]

> From her own mountains Freedom hath not fled,
> She never shall forsake

> Her old and fav'rite seat,
> And with her, erst a stranger, sojourns Peace. (Lines 49–52)

That sense of liberty and peace had been shattered in February 1797 when the French landed at Fishguard in Pembrokeshire. Surviving accounts of the expected or reported French attack brim with either panic or defiance,[159] but the invasion was in reality a short-lived, disorganized attempt on the part of the French, who were swiftly overcome by local volunteer forces. Unlike some subsequent readings of the Fishguard landings, however, the invasion was neither a fiasco nor a farce.[160] There was good reason for the alarm that quickly spread from west Wales to London (financial panic broke out in the City when news of the invasion arrived) and equally good reason for local people to defend their interests against the French.[161]

'The False Alarm' (no. 30) brilliantly caricatures the wave of terror that radiated from events in Fishguard, though written from some considerable distance in north Wales, and crucially when the crisis was already known to have come to nothing: 'all this Bustle, Stir, and Cry / Was but a false report' (lines 43–4). If the invasion was not the national emergency that it could have been, then it was an opportunity to redefine Wales in relation to the British Isles as a whole, fighting for survival against the French. In 'The Victory of Fishguard' (no. 31), then, the events of the invasion are tied into a tradition of Cambrian heroism sharpened with anti-Gallicanism, and based on what Katie Gramich has called geographically deterministic icons of Wales as 'Freedom's sacred Land' (line 18); a place of hostile mountains, sinister storms, and a fierce warrior-like people.[162]

However, other responses in poetry to the failed invasion present a more ambiguous network of allegiances. Fishguard was clearly a rallying point for a Welsh-inflected national defence patriotism that easily travelled beyond Wales: English commentators on the invasion also 'attributed the loyalty of the local people to their native ancestral feelings'.[163] But in May 1797, the *Chester Chronicle* reprinted Thomas Gray's 'The Triumph of Owen', a translation of a poem by the twelfth-century court poet Gwalchmai ap Meilyr, dating from the early 1760s.[164] The subject of the poem is defeat of invading forces, including the English, and the editor or compositor of the newspaper comments that the Fishguard invasion – 'the repulse recently given to the invading foe, by the men of South Wales'[165] – is the ideal moment for revisiting Gray's translation. Given that resisting the French in 1797 was, to most observers, part of a wider defence of British liberty, reprinting a poem on defeat of the *English* by the Welsh traces (perhaps unwittingly) some of the conflicts within notions of Britishness in this period.

Although Denbigh was a site of significant protest in the 1790s, it also staged some intense performances of loyalism in this period. In October 1801 its inhabitants celebrated peace with France with bell-ringing, bonfires, volleys of gunshot, drinking and singing.[166] The lyrics to one of these songs were printed, untitled and unsigned, in the *Chester Chronicle*:

> I sing the Tree of Liberty,
> Believe me, 'tis no Joke, Sir;
> The best e'er found on English Ground,
> I mean the Tree called Oak, Sir.
> In Body fair I do compare
> Unto our gracious King, Sir;
> Its Limbs so great, the Lords of State,
> I loyally will sing, Sir.[167]

In late 1801 the people of Denbigh were of course taking part in the ground-swell of patriotic ritual that greeted the end of the Revolutionary war.[168] However, the strains evident within another, earlier upswing of patriotism in the same area illustrate how uneven the events of this period may have seemed to the people who lived through them. Back in October 1797 Hester Piozzi had internalized the tensions between loyalist sentiment and the constant republican threat to a point that, she suggests, affected her ability to write. Describing the celebrations near her Denbighshire house of Admiral Duncan's victory at Camperdown, she sounds distracted: 'we made a gallant Bonfire ten feet high upon the Hill in honour of Admiral Duncan – These Republican Rogues strike to the *Monarch* you see; but I cannot even make a Ballad, I am so half-Ill and fidgetty'.[169] Piozzi had written a ballad on the Spithead naval mutiny (no. 32) earlier in the year,[170] and was drafting her pro-war pamphlet, *Three Warnings to John Bull*, in Denbighshire over the winter of 1797.[171] But uneasiness about the ongoing crisis of the moment inhabited and perhaps inhibited her writing at this point.

The closing years of the 1790s were characterized by changing perceptions of the Revolutionary war, and particularly by 'a sense that the war was now "defensive"'.[172] This shift in attitudes towards the conflict may be tracked through the increased visibility of volunteer poetry in Wales, especially during fears of invasion between 1803 and 1805. Two poems from the earlier invasion crisis (1797–8) emphasize the local, regional identity cultivated by the volunteer movement alongside a sense of national unity and loyalist consensus.[173] David Thomas's 'Verses written on the late Victory gained over the French Squadron by Sir John Borlase Warren' (no. 37) and Iolo Morganwg's 'Song for the Glamorgan Volunteers' (no. 33) both foreground the ancient liberty of the Welsh as armour against modern foreign oppression.

For some readers, Iolo's poem for the Glamorgan or Cowbridge volunteers has blotted the history of his political radicalism. It seems to be a moment of apostasy, 'a blatant piece of hypocrisy' given his earlier support for the Revolution.[174] Two years earlier, Robert Burns had suffered similar accusations for his 1795 ballad, 'The Dumfries Volunteers'. This poem appears to celebrate coercive loyalism, not least in its vision of hanging those who refuse to sing 'God Save the King', but as Liam McIlvanney has argued, urging resistance to a French invasion is not necessarily inconsistent with a radical stance: 'From a civic perspective, liberation by foreign arms is a contradiction in terms. Liberty is maintained by active exertion in the cause of one's country; it cannot be secured by proxy.'[175] And although volunteering could involve loyalism of a specifically anti-radical nature, the volunteer movement in general included some strikingly democratic elements – for example, plebeian membership and egalitarian organization[176] – that may also have appealed to independent-minded writers like Iolo and Burns.

The fiercely local attachment of the poem is the key to its meaning. Iolo's defence of Glamorgan, the 'dear native place' (line 14), is not defence of a modern British province or territory but of an ancient ethnic identity and independence in spirit at least if not in legal terms: 'No nation before us this region possess'd, / To this day 'tis our own' (lines 15–16) Ironically, Iolo's attempt to hold a meeting of the Gorsedd on Garth Mountain in 1797 was suppressed by the Glamorgan Yeomanry – dramatic proof, argues Damian Walford Davies, 'that the *gorsedd* was taken seriously as a Jacobin threat and as a dangerous paradigm for reform'.[177] Iolo's 'Song for the Glamorgan Volunteers' is, after all, an intensely anti-war poem, a paradoxical perspective for a poem written in support of volunteering. The threat of invasion in 1797 may have seemed to give Iolo a change of political heart but on the contrary it gave him a sharp new hook for his pacifism:

> Return, lovely Peace, with thy banners unfurl'd,
> And, from our loved isle, give thy laws to the world,
> . . .
> May brutal resentments that hunger for blood
> Domestic and foreign be nipp'd in the bud . . . (Lines 88–93)

Peace – and war 1800–6

The Revolutionary war between Britain and France ended with the Peace of Amiens in March 1802. Relations with the French were briefly transformed; Continental travel became possible again.[178] By May 1803, however, the peace had broken down, and an era of Napoleonic warfare begun that would not conclude until 1815. A new surge in the writing of war poetry accompanied the revived conflict. These works were dominated by figures of invasion, volunteers and defence, cottage life (often involving deserted women, widows and orphans), and social and emotional distress. Like some of the Welsh ballads of this era, these poems include 'newsy' elements, keeping close to topical events.[179] At the same time different emotional arcs run though the poetry, from those involving historical Wales – a subject reinvigorated by the new war that truly finds its moment in this period – to a mood of deep suffering, often figured through the ravaging forces of winter.

In 1800 the poet laureate Henry Pye (1745–1813) published 'Carmen Seculare for the Year 1800', a retrospective view of British history written to mark the dawn of the nineteenth century. Fulfilling the official role that required him to write new year odes and birthday odes for the king, Pye's song of the age was jingoistic and anti-revolutionary, portraying America's break from Britain in the 1770s and 1780s as an act of depravity, and liberty as a 'black contagion' that had spread from American to European shores. The poem was savaged at length by one reviewer as a 'miserable ode',[180] but Pye's poem almost certainly inspired Iolo Morganwg to write his own counter-cultural synopsis of recent events.

Iolo's 'Carmen Seculare' (no. 40) weighs the events of the 1790s against the next, upcoming phase of time. Uncertainty for the future balances against expectation, and against disappointment. Would 1800 be a turning point, and a turn from what and to what if so? 'O! tell me,' the speaker of the poem pleads, 'shall Wisdom and Peace? / Shall new Golden ages return?' (lines 56–7). As this point on the 'return' of earlier ages may suggest, however, nothing is linear here. Iolo's preoccupation with time filters down into the texture of the language of the poem, which revisits the style and imagery of verses written in 1793–4 in the middle of revolutionary crises and against a backdrop of violence and war.

The career of Napoleon after he seized power in November 1799 split radicals according to the extent to which they sympathized with him. Former supporters of the French now became alienated by Napoleon's 'ambitious grasping for dynasty', which contributed towards the new 'cynicism and conservatism' of writers such as Coleridge, Wordsworth and Southey.[181] By contrast, Iolo's attempts to hold onto, or to recreate, the 1790s in 'Carmen Seculare', or in new transcriptions of earlier poems such as 'Newgate Stanzas', suggest the depth of his radicalism since, in the early 1800s, this oppositional reworking of the previous decade positioned him on the radical end of the spectrum.[182]

Iolo revised 'Carmen Seculare' in 1803, shifting its time frame to an imagined future point – '1900' – which brings an eerie, dystopian quality to the text. Like the playful but essentially private disenchantment expressed in successive manuscript versions of 'John Bull's Litany' in c.1794, his revisions to the piece illustrate his disillusionment with the current times.[183] The moral imagination behind Iolo's writing of the early to mid-1790s survives in these texts from 1800–3, but so do the limitations of his earlier work, especially his tendency towards hyperbole and a certain brashness and obviousness in his depiction of those who he saw as political opponents or targets. Although the 1803 copy of 'Carmen Seculare' may well have been written during peacetime, Iolo's poem is a reminder, or a warning, that it is too soon to celebrate the dawn of better times: '*Still* Kings are unconquer'd, the tygers of war / *Still* throng to their murderful plain' (lines 10–11, my emphasis). This point explains the circular aesthetic of a poem that now becomes a song for the interrupted, incomplete radical project of the 1790s. Where Pye severs the political business of the outgoing decade from the new century, Iolo's vision of the future still teems with Revolution-inspired fantasies, from an unyielding commitment to liberty and the rights of man (lines 20–4) to inflated, punitive visions of the individuals deemed responsible for the war (lines 32–9).[184]

Although it ends with an idealized vision of peace, 'Carmen Seculare' was not really a poem for a new peace, or even a new decade. As Iolo's uncertainty – 'shall . . . Peace . . . return?' – suggests, it was just as much a work marking the advent of a new war. Peace poems had appeared in the *Chester Chronicle* throughout 1801–2, from anonymous, probably local, verses anticipating or celebrating the peace to odes by established writers such as John Thelwall and Helen Maria Williams.[185] However, the return of war quickly made its mark in the literature of 1803 through the defensive poetry written in response to the rising invasion crisis of that summer. The intensity of the threat from France meant that there was considerable consensus among radicals and conservatives about resuming the conflict with France.[186] Consequently, a clear break appears in the nature of the poetry written after May 1803, a shift from oppositional elegies and thank-offerings for the peace to a strident invasion idiom characterized by the triumphs of English military history (among them Agincourt, or the defeat of the Armada), the figure of John Bull, roast beef and beer, as in Richard Braine's 'Serious Advice to Bonaparte', published in August 1803, or the anonymous 'Stop to a Stride', published in November 1803.[187] Self-consciousness about the method, as well as the message, emerges in some of these works, as in untitled verses ['What's to be done to save the State?'] published in August 1803, which draw attention to the importance of poetry as part of the defensive effort.

'Several long hand-bills, rousing the public spirit, have been dispersed; a few words, well adapted [as poetry], would better strike the public mind', notes the author of these verses exhorting the public to 'arise, and save the State; / Arm! fight! unite! or dread your fate.'[188]

One of the poems circulating as a handbill in the summer of 1803 was 'English, Scots, and Irishmen, A Patriotic Address to the Inhabitants of the United Kingdom', by the Scottish poet John Mayne.[189] But Wales is conspicuously absent in the unionist patriotism of this poem, as though 'English' and 'Englishmen' is shorthand for 'England and Wales'.[190] The invisibility of Wales in the popular invasion imagination would not, however, have been recognized by Welsh poets writing at this point, even during the height of the invasion scare. The period from the summer of 1803 onwards was, perhaps paradoxically, one in which ethnic Welsh difference came to the fore most intensely, and in some ways most successfully. Where English poems line up the triumphs of English history and goad the French – 'half-starv'd with meagre frog-soup' – with English 'beef and pudding',[191] the Welsh response to national defence and military matters involves a turn to national and cultural specificities, most obviously located in Wales's separate history.

A number of poems written between the start of the invasion crisis and the death of William Pitt in January 1806 reflect Welsh loyalist patriotism. The loss of Nelson at the battle of Trafalgar in October 1805, for instance, inspired a clutch of elegies (nos. 53 and 54) hardly distinguishable from poems published in London newspapers and periodicals.[192] Others shape a more distinctively Welsh form of patriotism in which the historical British heroism that featured in poems written in the early 1790s – Sotheby's *Tour* or Richards's *Captivity of Caractacus* – now found dramatic new contexts.[193] The ancient liberty and separate identity of the Welsh is a prominent feature of 'The Saxon Invasion' (no. 52), whose account of the determination of the Welsh to defend their independence against an invading tyrant, fenced round by the hills of liberty and by their enduring 'native tongue' (line 20), offers a blueprint for responses to the feared French attack. T. Ellis Owen's 'Anglesey Volunteer Song' (no. 49) outlines a catalogue of Welsh, rather than English, military successes from Roman to modern times, celebrating the defeat of the French at Fishguard (lines 33–6), and Welsh involvement in the Irish rebellion (lines 29–30) and Nelson's Egyptian campaign (lines 37–44). The heroism claimed by Owen as inherently part of the Welsh psyche is never in doubt in this poem, but the example of a beleaguered Wales repeatedly suffering occupation – the Romans, the Saxons, the Normans – also suggests sharper points of contact with the present-day crisis.

Owen's poem details a time when 'first, amazed, Britannia saw / The curse of bold Invasion' (lines 3–4) at the same time as darkly gesturing towards the 'universal ruin' (line 48) posed by the current threat. In its depiction of the Welsh toughened by centuries of conquest, the poem casts doubts on English resilience in a polemical picture of a united Britain that here appears to *need* the Welsh in the quest for its defence. This fantasy of the importance of Wales to the war effort creates a sort of inverted contributionism.[194] Would England survive the incursions of the French? Would Britain continue to exist, as Wales had not, or not as an independent nation at least. Wales is here simultaneously a source of epic, exemplary heroism and a warning, a cautionary tale of lost sovereignty.

Richard Llwyd's 'Address of the Bard of Snowdon, to his Countrymen' (no. 45) is one of the most interesting and most widely circulated explorations of some of these themes.[195] The poem was an early response to the invasion crisis, composed in June 1803 and published in the *Chester Chronicle* in August 1803. The story of successive oppressions, from Roman to Norman, is told again in this poem, a polemical back story to the subject of self-defence in modern times that locates 'genuine Freedom's holy flame' (line 57) in Wales. A decisively Welsh perspective on defence of a united British nation can also be seen in Llwyd's self-proclaimed bardic identity as the 'Bard of Snowdon', a title he acquired after the publication of *Beaumaris Bay* in 1800. Urging the 'Sons of Snowdon' to defend 'Country, Parents [and] Children' (lines 69–71), Llwyd performs the public duty of the Welsh bard, at once a remembrancer and a legislator of the world. At the same time, a sense of disruption creeps into the poem through its Welshness. Building on ideas of the Welsh as ideal soldiers and patriots, Llwyd introduces the contrasting notion of Wales as a place of 'native Peace' whose people have been 'forc'd to arms' (line 12). Then follows, in the footnotes, a portrait of historical Welsh estrangement from the rest of Britain to which it is now joined:

> The invasion of the Normans – the decisive battle of Hastings – and the immediate and disgraceful submission of the Saxon or English people, was looked upon by the Britons as a war between two *strange nations* – a quarrel with which they had nothing to do. (Line 29n, original emphasis)[196]

Although the poem as a whole propels the Welsh towards self-defence, it also hints at the alienation of Wales from events taking place beyond its borders, and at a reluctance to be drawn into 'British' conflicts even as Llwyd urges defence of the realm. Ethnic difference introduces ambivalence, and rupture, in a scenario that brings to mind Mark Philp's caution of the difficulties and inconsistencies in the poetry and prints of the early Napoleonic era that undercut any notion of 'unequivocal evidence of a deep patriotism' in Britain.[197]

At times fears of invasion overshadowed everyday life in Wales, whether in 1797 or 1803. A string of defences bound the south coast of England, but the Welsh coastline also appeared vulnerable to attack, especially after the attempt on Fishguard. In February 1804, the Swansea-based newspaper the *Cambrian* printed resolutions from a meeting held at the Town Hall in Swansea on 5 November 1803, which included the purchase of 'four brass six-pounders . . . to be placed upon the Hills commanding the Harbour of Swansea and adjacent coast'.[198] Swansea never became a particular target of the French, but such preparations and precautions brought the danger home to south Wales in a powerfully material way. At the same time, the invasion threat gathered momentum in the poetry columns of the *Cambrian*, which provided a new outlet for local verse when the newspaper appeared for the first time in January 1804.

The spiralling fears inspired by the idea of invasion filtered down into other kinds of writing in the period. Invasion emergency filled the pages of topical, ephemeral newspaper poetry and popular broadsides, but longer works also registered the effects of the panic. In 1804 Robert Holland Price, a young writer from the Llangollen area, published the second edition of his pamphlet-length poem *The Horrors of Invasion* (no. 46). No copy of the first edition is known to exist, but it was successful enough for Holland Price to issue a call for subscribers to a revised and enlarged second edition.[199] The poem is characterized throughout by a sense that Holland Price is searching for a modern form of Welsh bardism; aspiring to a role as a public voice with the ability to commemorate, exhort, record and inspire, against the impending invasion threat: 'Bonaparté threats to cross the waves, / And turn our free born Britons into slaves!' (lines 23–4).

Many invasion pieces graphically, sometimes almost gratuitously, depicted the raids that British subjects, especially women and children, would suffer in the event of a French victory.[200] These works present a constant narrative of murder, rape, looting and torching, a scene of Britain ransacked by invaders: 'Towns, hamlets burn, in one great ruin lie! / Their smoke ascends in columns to the sky' (no. 46, lines 93–4). In some poems these shock tactics predicting the consequences of invasion create stylistic tangles rooted in the confusion and terror of the prospect of French success. In another pamphlet-length work from 1804, *Invasion! A Poem* (no. 47), Joseph Reade imagines an attack by the French as brutal and grotesque as anything published in response to the crisis. But more interesting than the sentimental horror of the set-piece (lines 180–268) are Reade's stylistic idiosyncrasies. Reade prefaces his poem with an address to the public that warns of the unusual quality of the blank verse that follows:

He has attempted to vary his Stile with his Subjects; where argumentative, his Muse essays her plainest Tone, in Exhortations she assumes somewhat of a loftier Note, when locally descriptive, bold or soft as the Situation described demands, and in Parts representing a Scene of Agitation, a hurried, breathless Stile seems appropriate, consisting of short, disjointed Sentences, and a kind of explicable Confusion (if the Term may be allowed).

Invasion! is obviously an experimental work. Reade was clearly capable of turning a steady, balanced line but his poem is unpredictable throughout, full of jolting line structures and unexpected rhythms.

Reade's summary of his style as 'explicable Confusion' points up the difficulty with which the poem is channelling contemporary uncertainties. *Invasion!* may be the work of an inexperienced writer, but it does give a sense of form in conflict. The external enemy is real and vivid enough in this poem, and in *The Horrors of Invasion*, but so too is the sense of the search for an aesthetic that meets the needs of the subject matter and reflects the inward, psychic turbulence of invasion fears. The idea of the role of poetry is central to this search. Reade postscripts his poem with a defence of its peculiarities – 'stark staring Mad his Muse', he wryly imagines the critics declaring[201] – and his boldness in publishing it:

> The Fault is not my own, had our Bards been awake
> And exerted their Prowess, to strive I should quake,
> While the Times teem with Topic, barren is their Field,
> Must a rich-manur'd Soil with such Aid, nothing yield?
> Rogers, Jerningham, Hayley, Pye, Southey say where
> Fled is your faithless Genius with the fickle Air?[202]

Major writers are not, he argues, leading by example in the creation of a national poetry that deals with the invasion crisis, leaving space for – creating a need for – provincial amateurs like Reade and Holland Price.

Concepts such as 'Briton' and 'Britain' continued to be unstable in the invasion period. Always potentially signalling both an ethnic identity stretching back centuries and a modern allegiance to the nation state, the messy tensions within these terms have not yet, as Cathryn Charnell-White points out, been fully resolved.[203] The successive crises of the period 1789–1806 were not ones in which they easily could have been, but invasion brought opportunities for thinking about nation in new ways. Different identities had long been interlaced in Wales, at least since the Acts of Union in the sixteenth century. For instance, onboard a trading vessel, Richard Llwyd's Owen of Llangoed happily recognizes the Union Jack as a symbol of Britishness:

'young Owen saw with pride, / His Country's crosses' (no. 51, lines 169–70). However the war years also revealed ways in which national identity was less than fixed and could be reshaped to fit changing situations. In Mary Robinson's 1797 novel *Walsingham*, for example, the press-ganged soldier Griffith Blagdon describes himself as Welsh first and foremost, but as English when fighting the French.[204]

The contingent nature of national identity in this example from Robinson may be explained by a defensive patriotism in which association with Englishness rises in proportion to the intensity of the threat to Britain and the necessity of its defence. Some writers, however, explicitly resist the absorption of Welshness into Englishness, or Britishness, even at points of crisis. Llwyd's invasion poem 'Address of the Bard of Snowdon' is a compressed, list-like work followed by extensive explanatory footnotes. What is a brief reference in the poem to King Arthur's use of the dragon emblem as his standard (line 58) becomes, in the footnote, a provocative meditation on what Llwyd (if not his fictional character Owen) saw as the marginalization of Wales in its British context. The Act of 1800 that had, not least because of fears of invasion, uneasily bound Ireland into the Union,[205] now raised questions about the place of Wales within a larger Britain. Llwyd's complaint centres on the new Union Flag that marked the addition of Ireland.[206] As a symbol of the nation, the flag (like previous Union flags) made Wales invisible, playing up its status as peripheral, inconsequential or simply indistinguishable from England. For Llwyd, the omission of Wales from the national flag was a missed opportunity to appease the Welsh, currently in the heat of a cultural nationalist revival, and an error of judgement which impoverished Britain as a whole. The new flag, he argued, gave the 'appearance of a paucity which does not exist in an Empire composed of four Nations' (line 58n).[207]

Of all the writers in this anthology Llwyd perhaps gives the most vivid sense of Wales as a troubled nation. *Beaumaris Bay* (no. 39) traces continuities between present and historical grievances, while his adaptation of 'Ode of the Months' (no. 50), a medieval prison poem, depicts Wales as damaged, brutalized and dispossessed. The emotional colouring of the poem is fairly monochrome, from darkness and despair to a deeper version of the same, but, in an age in which the Welsh had little sense of a political nationalism,[208] this register of cultural mourning is suggestive. Edward I appears as an archetypal tyrant king in Southey's ode on Aberffraw and Llwyd's *Beaumaris Bay*, while criticizing tyrants and tyranny is a specific aspect of a more general anti-monarchical animus in Iolo Morganwg's writing. For all three of these writers, the figure of the tyrannical monarch is closely linked with the injuries sustained by the Welsh nation through history and now aspiring, perhaps struggling, towards national consciousness.[209] 'Ode of the Months' suggests parallels between Wales and a benighted, pre-Revolution France; both nations in bonds, the Welsh '[i]mmur'd within a living-grave' (line 146) as Llwyd puts it.[210] In the case of eighteenth-century Wales, however, 'tyranny' is an accumulated effect of history rather than a particular present-day target (such as the Bastille, in the French context) – a point that may account for the somewhat unfocused nature of the sense of defiance, mourning and anger in poems from the period. How might a nation's people overthrow a whole history, the events of which continue to shape the present? The result is bound to be vague and ill-defined since the enemy – is it England? – is at once everyone and nobody.

The despondent mood of 'Ode of the Months' highlights a strand of austere, ruminative poetry published during the early 1800s. Short in length and topical in feel, these poems summon up a cold, desolate atmosphere: social and emotional sufferings are often backed by winter in these works. The period after 1800 was one of continued hardship in Wales: hunger riots broke out in Caernarfonshire in November 1800, led by slate-workers, which required mounted cavalry to be stationed as a peacekeeping force in Caernarfon and Bangor in 1801.[211] The situation was barely better in north-east Wales, to judge from 'The Widow' (no. 44), understated but poignant verses exploring the distress and anxiety that characterized life among the poor at this point. In this poem, poverty brings a scene of unending labour for all that scarcely enables the widow and her charges to survive. Nothing in the poem explains the speaker's status as a widow, nor the deaths of the parents (famine? disease? events relating to the war?) whose children she now cares for. But it is worth noting how politicized a figure the widow is in this period – an emblem of suffering at home, the surviving symbol of a decimated private, domestic sphere, all of which is suggested in this poem. Read in this way, the nature of the sense of desperation that animates 'The Widow' is liminal, unspoken.

So, too, are the meanings of winter in poems published at the beginning and end of 1806. 'On Winter' (no. 56) describes the desperate situation of the poor and sick in Carmarthenshire in south Wales (lines 10–16), while 'Written late in the Evening' (no. 59), by 'Mary', links a creeping inner anxiety – 'How dismal sounds the whistling of the wind . . . The ills it whispers fill my boding mind' (lines 1–3) – with scenes of terror taking place elsewhere, at sea (lines 13–16), almost certainly within the context of the war. The poem ends with a severe portrait of Britain as a nation tainted by its involvement in slavery and war,[212] and with a challenge to mend its ways:

> Britain! knock off the chains thou hast forg'd,
> Wipe out the stain that has our isle disgrac'd,
> Give pity, mercy, freedom, to the scourg'd,
> Nor let thy character in blood be trac'd. (Lines 41–4)

'Mary's portrait of the peasant retreating from the storm – 'His is a bliss beyond what Kings enjoy' (line 12) – recalls several pieces from Iolo Morganwg's *Poems, Lyric and Pastoral*, among them 'The Happy Farmer',[213] or 'The Horrors of War' (no. 14, lines 11–20), with their insistent, defiant portraits of the virtues of a retired rural life far from the court and the corrupt ways of politics. In its depiction of home as a safe haven during dangerous times, 'Written late in the Evening' especially evokes Iolo's turbulent, snowbound 'Winter Incidents' (no. 10). As Mary Favret has explained, winter has long been understood as an allegory of war, physically traceable in the power of snow to obliterate or in the destructive energy of storms, and emotionally legible in 'the long winter of wartime and the chilling numbness that it spreads'.[214] Winter brings a chilly landscape of tyranny to Iolo's poem: the 'terror of a wintry sky' (line 56) plays bleakly against barely glimpsed episodes of mindless violence – from the deliberate killing of a thrush to the bloody horrors of war – that situate oppression, vagrancy and dispossession in the winter of wartime. What Favret terms 'a freeze or collapse of historical narrative'[215] becomes possible in poems about winter and war. Precisely dated to the evening of 15 December 1806, 'Mary' gazes into a particular winter moment through her poem, suspending time at that point. The poem contemplates wartime sufferings on a personal and local scale – and in that sense ones that are specifically Welsh, though they are also not confined to Wales – and with an international, even global reach in the case of war and slavery.

In January 1804, the *Chester Chronicle* printed a short excerpt from the Scottish poet David Carey's *The Pleasures of Nature* (1803). This passage, an address to winter ('hail! dread tyrant of the year!'), is set beside a bright fireside that contrasts the snowy storm-beaten scene outdoors.[216] Sitting directly below Carey's poem, the next item is a column on the crisis in Europe titled 'The anarchy of the Continent, in its political relations'. In the mosaic-like structure of the newspaper page these pieces on wintry tyranny and towering political emergency read as misshapen mirror images, different forms of reporting or responding to the same contemporary reality.[217] Two years later, in another winter, that sense of diplomatic chaos had collapsed into graphic combat scenes in untitled verses published by 'D.' in the *Cambrian*:

With heaps of blood the plains are strew'd,
Blood gluts th' ensanguin'd field;
And nations once with conquest proud,
To a fell despot yield. (No. 60, lines 1–4)

'All things are bound in Winter's icy chains' (no. 56, line 10), 'J. H.' had earlier written in the same column in a poem on distress in Carmarthenshire. Within these poems, or in the suggestive juxtapositions of the newspaper page, the overwhelming uncertainty of the contemporary situation finds momentary fixity and, perhaps, terrible clarity in winter. Like the frost or snow, however, that fixity is forced and violent, as well as temporary. But by the end of 1806 perhaps no more lasting close could be imagined when – although 'J. H.', 'Mary' and 'D.' could not have known this at the time – the best part of another destructive decade would still have to run its course.

Figure 4. John Hill, after Henry Wigstead, 'Penmanmawr' (1799)

Notes

[1] John Goodridge, "'That Deathless Wish of Climbing Higher'": Robert Bloomfield on the Sugar Loaf', in Damian Walford Davies and Lynda Pratt (eds.), *Wales and the Romantic Imagination* (Cardiff, 2007), pp. 161–79, here p. 173.

[2] See Kirsti Bohata, *Postcolonialism Revisted* (Cardiff, 2004), and Jane Aaron and Chris Williams (eds.), *Postcolonial Wales* (Cardiff, 2005), for detailed discussions of Wales and post-coloniality.

[3] Mary-Ann Constantine summarizes the neglect of Wales and Welsh writing from this period in 'Beauty Spot, Blind Spot: Romantic Wales', *Literature Compass*, 5, no. 3 (2008), 577–90. In her study of nineteenth-century Welsh women's writing, Jane Aaron notes that 'little is known, in Wales as in England, of the literature published during the revolutionary years which deployed Welsh contexts': *Nineteenth-Century Women's Writing in Wales* (2007; 2nd edn., Cardiff, 2010), p. 10.

[4] See David Duff and Catherine Jones (eds.), *Scotland, Ireland and the Romantic Aesthetic* (Lewisburg, 2007); Murray Pittock, *Scottish and Irish Romanticism* (Oxford, 2008); and Bob Harris, *The Scottish People and the French Revolution* (London, 2008), for recent examples of the Scotland-Ireland axis.

[5] On some of the problems concerning publishing for labouring-class writers and the difficulties surrounding the reception of their work in this period, see particularly Simon J. White, *Robert Bloomfield, Romanticism and the Poetry of Community* (Aldershot, 2007), pp. 31–57.

[6] Damian Walford Davies and Lynda Pratt, 'Introduction', in *eidem* (eds.), *Wales and the Romantic Imagination*, p. 3.

[7] Leith Davis, Ian Duncan and Janet Sorenson, 'Introduction', in *eidem* (eds.), *Scotland and the Borders of Romanticism* (Cambridge, 2004), p. 3.

[8] Julia M. Wright, *A Companion to Irish Literature* (2 vols., Oxford, 2011), I, p. 5.

[9] Davis, Duncan and Sorenson, 'Introduction', *Scotland and the Borders of Romanticism*, p. 10.

[10] Constantine, 'Beauty Spot, Blind Spot', 585.

[11] See David Chandler, 'Walter Savage Landor and Wales in the 1790s', in Davies and Pratt (eds.), *Wales and the Romantic Imagination*, pp. 141–60, for an example of tense and ultimately hostile reactions to Wales and its people.

[12] Unlike many other writers (some obscure, others well known) from England, Wales, Scotland and Ireland, Llwyd does not feature in John Goodridge's six volumes of labouring-class poetry from the eighteenth and nineteenth centuries. See *Eighteenth-Century English Labouring Class Poets* (London, 2003) and *Nineteenth-Century English Labouring-Class Poets* (London, 2005).

[13] Constantine, 'Beauty Spot, Blind Spot', 580. The other volumes in the series 'Wales and the French Revolution' provide translations of printed and manuscript Welsh poetry and prose.

[14] Sarah Prescott takes a similar approach to the earlier part of the eighteenth century in *Bards and Britons: Eighteenth-Century Writing from Wales* (Cardiff, 2008), focusing

'on lesser-known writers whose work provides new insights' (p. xxiv) to the period. Pre-twentieth-century Anglophone Welsh writing has long been a neglected field: see Jane Aaron, 'Twentieth-Century and Contemporary Welsh Gothic Fiction', *Literature Compass* 7, no. 4 (2010), 281–9; here 289.

[15] See M. Wynn Thomas, 'Introduction', in *idem* (ed.), *Welsh Writing in English* (Cardiff, 2003), p. 3, for Wales as a 'stateless nation'. See also Jane Aaron, 'Bardic Anti-colonialism', in *idem* and Williams (eds.), *Postcolonial Wales*, pp. 137–58.

[16] See J. R. Watson, 'Wordsworth, North Wales and the Celtic landscape', in Gerard Carruthers and Alan Rawes (eds.), *English Romanticism and the Celtic World* (Cambridge, 2004), pp. 85–102, for a discussion of Wordsworth's travels in north Wales in the early 1790s and their importance for *The Prelude*. Damian Walford Davies emphasizes the Welsh historical contexts behind 'Tintern Abbey' in *Presences that Disturb: Models of Romantic Identity in the Literature and Culture of the 1790s* (Cardiff, 2002), p. 9.

[17] 'Defensive patriotism was a broader, more pervasive phenomenon than loyalism; it stretched to include for example, groups of religious dissenters and the lower ranks who, by and large, had remained outside the loyalist reaction of the earlier 1790s.' Harris, *The Scottish People and the French Revolution*, p. 4.

[18] The phrase describes the tranquil, loyalist Wales of the earlier eighteenth century as depicted in the art of Richard Wilson. See David Solkin, *Richard Wilson: The Landscape of Reaction* (London, 1982). For the contrasting view of Wales as 'an oppositional terrain – an inspiring political, topographical and cultural alternative to England', see Davies and Pratt, 'Introduction', *Wales and the Romantic Imagination*, p. 4.

[19] Prys Morgan, *The Eighteenth-Century Renaissance* (Llandybïe, 1981), gives an overview of the cultural revival in Wales. For an account of possible overlaps between Revolutionary ideas and the reprinting of Dafydd ap Gwilym – poetry that celebrates liberty, especially sexual liberty – see Dafydd Johnston, '*Barddoniaeth Dafydd ab Gwilym* 1789 a'r Chwyldro Ffrengig', *Llên Cymru*, 35 (2012), 32–53. See also note 23 below.

[20] For Iolo as a forger, see Mary-Ann Constantine, *The Truth Against the World: Iolo Morganwg and Romantic Forgery* (Cardiff, 2007), especially pp. 27–41.

[21] John T. Koch, *The Gododdin of Aneirin: Texts and Context from Dark-Age North Britain* (Cardiff, 1997).

[22] For Iolo and Blake, see Marilyn Butler, 'Romanticism in England', in Roy Porter and Mikuláš Teich (eds.), *Romanticism in National Context* (Cambridge, 1988), pp. 37–67, especially 49–50; Jon Mee, '"Images of truth new born": Iolo, William Blake, and the Literary Radicalism of the 1790s', in Geraint H. Jenkins (ed.), *A Rattleskull Genius: The Many Faces of Iolo Morganwg* (Cardiff, 2005), pp. 173–93; and Caroline Franklin, 'The Welsh American Dream: Iolo Morganwg, Robert Southey and the Madoc Legend', in Gerard Carruthers and Alan Rawes (eds.), *English Romanticism and the Celtic World* (Cambridge, 2003), pp. 69–84.

[23] See Susan L. Aronstein, 'Wales: Culture and Society', in S. H. Rigby (ed.), *A Companion to Britain in the Later Middle Ages* (Oxford, 2003), pp. 541–57, for

an overview of this period in Wales, and see Dafydd Johnston, 'Radical Adaptation: Translations of Medieval Welsh Poetry in the 1790s', in Mary-Ann Constantine and *idem* (eds.), *'Footsteps of Liberty and Revolt': Essays on Wales and the French Revolution* (Cardiff, forthcoming), for responses in the poetry of the 1790s.

[24] Prescott discusses Welsh responses to Gray in *Bards and Britons*, pp. 56–83; here p. 76.

[25] Poets did, however, compete for the best Welsh translation of 'The Bard' at bardic meetings in London and Glamorgan in 1798. See Cathryn Charnell-White, *Welsh Poetry of the French Revolution 1789–1805* (Cardiff, 2012), p. 32.

[26] Geraint H. Jenkins (ed.), *Language and Community in the Nineteenth Century* (Cardiff, 1998), p. 2.

[27] See *CC*, s.v. Anglo-Welsh Literature.

[28] Diane Davies, 'Towards Devolution: Poetry and Anglo-Welsh Identity', in Keith Cameron (ed.), *National Identity* (Exeter, 1999), pp. 19–30, summarizes these elements in 'Anglo-Welsh' writing. For an overview of the distinctions between ethnic and national literatures, see C. L. Innes, *The Cambridge Introduction to Postcolonial Literatures in English* (Cambridge, 2007), pp. 97–118.

[29] Iolo's letters beautifully illustrate their world – see *CIM*.

[30] Constantine, 'Beauty Spot, Blind Spot', 586. See Iolo Morganwg to Hugh Jones, 4 June 1794, for a brilliant letter by Iolo that plays out several conflicts of identity. The letter describes Iolo's response to a Church-and-King mob: 'They press every one that passes by into this infernal service [declaring God Save the King, Church and King for ever] . . . I jabber'd Welsh, squeaked out "Church *sans* King", in as broken a manner as I could, and passed for a Dutchman with all but a Welshman or two, who laughed at me.' *CIM*, I, p. 676 – original emphasis.

[31] *CIM*, I, pp. 240–3, Owen Jones (Owain Myfyr) to Iolo Morganwg, 14 October–5 November 1783.

[32] This literary history was still in the process of being established. See Mary-Ann Constantine, 'Welsh Literary History and the Making of "The Myvyrian Archaiology of Wales"', in Dirk Van Hulle and Joep Leerssen (eds.), *Editing the Nation's Memory: Textual Scholarship and Nation-Building in Nineteenth-Century Europe* (Amsterdam, 2008), pp. 109–28; and Ffion Mair Jones, *'The Bard is a Very Singular Character': Iolo Morganwg, Marginalia and Print Culture* (Cardiff, 2010), pp. 14–48.

[33] For an overview of these forms, see Dafydd Johnston, *A Pocket Guide: The Literature of Wales* (Cardiff, 1994), pp. 34–6. These forms also play a key role in Charnell-White's delineation of the 'Welshness' of the poems written in Welsh in this period – see *Welsh Poetry of the French Revolution*, pp. 2–3.

[34] Owen's journey is typical for the period. See Gwyn A. Williams, *When Was Wales? A History of the Welsh* (Harmondsworth, 1985), p. 145, for the 'British imperial economy', which 'enmeshed' north Wales with Liverpool and south Wales with Bristol.

[35] Homi K. Bhabha, *The Location of Culture* (London, 1994), p. 128.

[36] Prescott, *Bards and Britons*, p. 115.

[37] Ibid., p. 85.

38   See M. Wynn Thomas, *Corresponding Cultures: The Two Literatures of Wales* (Cardiff, 1999), for a study of the 'subtle nexus of relationships between the Welsh- and the English-language "discourse communities" of Wales, as inscribed in their respective literary cultures' (p. 1).

39   I am following Prescott's *Bards and Britons*, which 'aims to complicate the view that the Welsh were passively assimilated into an Anglo-British consensus in the eighteenth century' (p. xiii).

40   See Hywel M. Davies, 'Wales in English Travel Writing, 1791–8: The Welsh Critique of Theophilus Jones', *WHR*, 23, no. 3 (2007), 65–93, for an overview of Welsh tourism in the 1790s.

41   Benjamin Colbert has recently described the 'dislocations' of home tourism in these terms: 'Travellers to and from the four nations . . . have long found themselves at once "at home" and on foreign ground as they move beyond borders that demarcate their senses of belonging.' See 'Introduction: Home Tourism', in *idem* (ed.), *Travel Writing and Tourism in Britain and Ireland* (London, 2012), p. 2.

42   Linda Colley has influentially (if not controversially) argued that 'Britishness was superimposed over an array of internal differences' in response to contact with the Other and especially conflict, in *Britons: Forging the Nation 1707–1837* (New Haven, 1992), p.6.

43   Simon Bainbridge, 'Politics and Poetry', in Pamela Clemit (ed.), *The Cambridge Companion to British Literature of the French Revolution in the 1790s* (Cambridge, 2011), pp. 190–205, here p. 191.

44   R. J. W. Davies, 'Was there a Welsh Enlightenment', in R. R. Davies and Geraint H. Jenkins (eds.), *From Medieval to Modern Wales: Historical Essays in Honour of Kenneth O. Morgan and Ralph A. Griffiths* (Cardiff, 2004), pp. 142–59, discusses this aspect of eighteenth-century Wales. See also, Colin Kidd, 'Wales, the Enlightenment and the New British History', *WHR*, 25, no. 2 (2012), 209–30. Marion Löffler discusses Welsh-language periodicals in terms of Enlightenment in *Welsh Responses to the French Revolution: Press and Public Discourse 1789–1802* (Cardiff, 2012), pp. 34–8.

45   R. T. Jenkins and Helen T. Ramage (eds.), *A History of the Honourable Society of the Cymmrodorion and of the Gwyneddigion and Cymreigyddion Societies* (London, 1951).

46   Gwyn A. Williams, 'Romanticism in Wales', in Roy Porter and Mikuláš Teich (eds.), *Romanticism in National Context* (Cambridge, 1988), pp. 9–36, here p. 16.

47   Ibid., p. 17.

48   Löffler notes that '"Wales", unlike "Scotland", "Ireland" or "America" only rarely appeared as a headline. News, letters and poetry were signed from Welsh counties, villages and towns, or, at best, from "north Wales" or "south Wales."' *Welsh Responses to the French Revolution*, p. 19.

49   Seward's 'Sonnet to France' was published in the *Gentleman's Magazine* in August 1789; see Bainbridge, 'Politics and Poetry', p. 192, for the text of the poem. Arline Wilson, *William Roscoe: Commerce and Culture* (Liverpool, 2008), reproduces Roscoe's 1789 'Ode to the People of France' (pp. 133–4). See Andrew Carpenter

(ed.), *Verse in English from Eighteenth-Century Ireland* (Cork, 1998), pp. 557–8, for the text of 'Liberty and Equality or Dermot's Delight'.

[50] Williams, 'Romanticism in Wales', p. 24. For discussions of Samwell, see Martin Fitzpatrick, 'The "cultivated understanding" and "chaotic genius" of David Samwell', in Jenkins (ed.), *Rattleskull Genius*, pp. 383–402; and Martin Fitzpatrick, Nicholas Thomas and Jennifer Newell (eds.), *The Death of Captain Cook and Other Writings by David Samwell* (Cardiff, 2007).

[51] *CIM*, I, p. 633, David Samwell to Iolo Morganwg, ?1794. 'Iorwerth' is Iolo, 'Dafydd Feddyg' and 'Dafydd Ddû' are Samwell.

[52] *CIM*, I, pp. 389–90, David Samwell to Iolo Morganwg, ?July 1791.

[53] Cathryn Charnell-White, 'Networking the Nation: The Bardic and Correspondence Networks of Wales and London in the 1790s', in Constantine and Johnston (eds.), '*Footsteps of Liberty and Revolt*'.

[54] Jon Mee has recently explained the difficulties for London reform clubs in the 1790s, when support for reform was so often taken to mean republicanism, illustrating the 'political energy and creativity that flourished under the umbrella of the LCS in these years when it had to deal with state repression as well as the contingencies of events to forge a space for itself in the public sphere'. See Jon Mee, 'Popular Radical Culture', in Clemit (ed.), *The Cambridge Companion to British Literature of the French Revolution*, pp. 117–28; here p. 127.

[55] Marion Löffler, 'Cerddi Newydd gan John Jones, "Jac Glan-y-Gors"', *Llên Cymru*, 33 (2010), 143–50.

[56] E. G. Bowen, *David Samwell (Dafydd Ddu Feddyg) 1751–1798* (Cardiff, 1974), p. 81. The debate on the 'Gagging Acts' took place in February 1797.

[57] Ibid., p. 83.

[58] For Wales as a mirror of France, see Davies, *Presences that Disturb*, pp. 64–6.

[59] Williams, 'Romanticism in Wales', p. 11.

[60] *Idem, The Search for Beulah Land: The Welsh and the Atlantic Revolution* (London, 1980), p. 22. Williams sees, for example, an unbroken line between radical sentiment in the 1790s and nineteenth-century Chartism in the growing industrial heartland of Merthyr Tydfil.

[61] The *Chester Chronicle*, a newspaper whose readership included north Wales and the northern reaches of mid Wales, as well as Cheshire, was an important forum for Welsh writers in the period. See Löffler, *Welsh Responses to the French Revolution*, pp. 134–67, for a selection of material relating to Wales in the *Chronicle*.

[62] J. G. A. Pocock, *Virtue, Commerce, and History: Essays on Political Thought and History, Chiefly in the Eighteenth Century* (Cambridge, 1985), p. 231.

[63] Alfred Neobald Palmer, 'John Wilkinson and the Old Bersham Iron Works', *THSC* (1899), 23–64. Wilkinson was also suspected of supplying guns to the French, under cover of 'iron piping', during the French and Revolutionary wars (p. 36).

[64] D. A. Farnie and W. O. Henderson (eds.), *Industry and Innovation: Selected Essays / W. H. Chaloner* (London, 1990), pp. 46–7.

[65] David J. V. Jones, *Before Rebecca: Popular Protests in Wales, 1793–1835* (Cardiff, 1973), extensively documents distress and disturbances in Wales in this period. See also Tim Jones, *Rioting in North East Wales, 1536–1918* (Wrexham, 1997).

[66] See, for example, the case of John Griffiths, a flax-dresser from Wrexham, who was prosecuted in 1795 for declaring that the king deserved 'weltering and rolling in his [own] blood'. See NLW, Great Sessions 4/64/6, no. 2.

[67] 150–160,000 emigrés fled France following the events of 1789. See Alan Forrest and Peter H. Wilson, *The Bee and the Eagle: Napoleonic France and the End of the Holy Roman Empire, 1806* (Basingstoke, 2009), p. 4. The best-known poetic response to the people displaced by struggles in Europe is Charlotte Smith's 1793 poem on the exiled French, 'The Emigrants'.

[68] See Hywel M. Davies, 'Loyalism in Wales, 1792–1793', *WHR*, 20, no. 4 (2001), 687–716.

[69] See Charnell-White, *Welsh Poetry of the French Revolution*, pp. 20, 39, for the use of Rhita Gawr in Welsh-language works.

[70] Sam Smiles, *The Image of Antiquity: Ancient Britain and the Romantic Imagination* (London, 1994), p. 41.

[71] Prescott discusses the 'combative motive for antiquarian recovery and memory' in *Bards and Britons*, p. 59.

[72] Smiles, *The Image of Antiquity*, p. 39.

[73] The poem was positively reviewed in 1793 by the *Critical Review* and the *Analytical Review*, which both printed long extracts from the poems. Anna Seward praised the poem's 'light of genius' in March 1793 in a letter that, not coincidentally, also reflects at length on recent events in France. See Anna Seward to Henry Cary, 9 March 1793. Archibald Constable (ed.), *Letters of Anna Seward: Written Between the Years 1784 and 1807* (6 vols., Edinburgh, 1811), III, pp. 213–14.

[74] George Richards, *Modern France: A Poem* (Oxford, 1793), p. 7.

[75] 'Llangollen' appeared in Sotheby's *Tour Through Parts of Wales, Sonnets, Odes, and Other Poems* (1794). The dating to autumn appears on the poem's title page – 'Written at the Close of the Autumn 1792' – and again at the head of the poem ('Autumn 1792').

[76] Roger Simpson, 'Building Arthurian Castles in Spain: William Sotheby's *Constance de Castile*', *Arthuriana*, 11, no. 4 (2001), 77–86.

[77] Marilyn Butler (ed.), *Burke, Paine, Godwin and the Revolution Controversy* (Cambridge, 1984), is the classic account of this subject. See also Jon Mee and David Fallon (eds.), *Romanticism and Revolution: A Reader* (Oxford, 2011).

[78] H. T. Dickenson, 'The Political Context', in Clemit (ed.), *The Cambridge Companion to British Literature of the French Revolution*, pp. 1–15.

[79] Mee and Fallon (eds.), *Romanticism and Revolution*, p. 8. Advertisements in the *Chester Chronicle* show that *Rights of Man* (the sixth edition in this case) was being sold in Chester, Wrexham, Holywell and Denbigh. See *Chester Chronicle*, 3 June 1791.

[80] Ffion Mair Jones discusses 'the voices of dissent' in the early 1790s in *Welsh Ballads of the French Revolution 1793–1815* (Cardiff, 2012), pp. 10–14.

[81] Mary Favret offers a brilliant exploration of this question in *War at a Distance: Romanticism and the Making of Modern Wartime* (New Jersey, 2009). For an account of Wales and war poetry in the 1790s, see Elizabeth Edwards, 'The Voices of

War: Poetry from Wales, 1794–1804', in Constantine and Johnston (eds.), *'Footsteps of Liberty and Revolt'*.

82 See John Barrell, *The Spirit of Despotism: Invasions of Privacy in the 1790s* (Oxford, 2006), for a wider account of this transformation.

83 Sarah Prescott, 'Anglophone Welsh Women's Poetry, 1750–84: Jane Cave and Anne Penny', in Jacqueline M. Labbe (ed.), *The History of British Women's Writing, 1750–1830* (Basingstoke, 2010), pp. 102–24. See also Catherine Brennan, *Angers, Fantasies and Ghostly Fears: Nineteenth-Century Women from Wales and English-Language Poetry* (Cardiff, 2003), pp. 23–41.

84 Aaron, *Nineteenth-Century Women's Writing*, pp. 42–3. Aaron further explains that 'when viewed through the prism of English-language culture, the egalitarianism of Welsh Dissent becomes more apparent. From conservative England's point of view, the picture of Wales afforded by the literature of the Romantic period was disturbing: the Welsh seemed extreme in their new-found enthusiasm, radical in their democratic control of their religious organizations, and prevented from joining the civilized world by their adherence to a primitive language' (pp. 45–6).

85 Damian Walford Davies, '"Sweet Sylvan Routes" and Grave Methodists: Wales in De Quincey's *Confessions of an English Opium Eater*', in *idem* and Pratt (eds.), *Wales and the Romantic Imagination*, pp. 199–227, here p. 220.

86 Misty G. Anderson, *Imagining Methodism in Eighteenth-Century Britain: Enthusiasm, Belief, and the Borders of the Self* (Baltimore, 2012), p. 3.

87 Davies discusses the pamphlet war around Welsh Methodism between 1797 and 1803 in '"Sweet Sylvan Routes"', pp. 217–24. Löffler describes efforts to refashion popular perceptions of Methodism in the wake of the Fishguard invasion in *Welsh Responses to the French Revolution*, p. 18.

88 See, for example, Cave's 'On the General Fast, April 19th, 1793', or 'A Poem occasioned by the late dreadful riots on Bristol Bridge [September 1793]', in *Poems on Various Subjects, Entertaining, Elegiac, and Religious, By Miss Cave, Now Mrs. Winscom* (5th edn., Bristol, 1794), pp. 142–4, 181–6.

89 See note 34 on colonial relations between Wales and border-lying cities like Liverpool and Bristol.

90 Aaron, *Nineteenth-Century Women's Writing*, p. 42.

91 Piozzi proudly refers to her 'Welsh blood' in her letters: see *PL*, II, p. 392, Hester Piozzi to Hester Maria Thrale, 25 October 1796, for an example.

92 See William McCarthy, *Hester Thrale Piozzi: Portrait of a Literary Woman* (Chapel Hill, 1985), pp. 38–9, for the 'universal hiss' that greeted her second marriage.

93 McCarthy suggests that Piozzi was 'turned into a politician' on reading Burke's *Reflections* in November 1790, a move that 'determined her public role for the rest of her writing career', ibid., p. 225.

94 For an account of Piozzi's Welshness read against her relationship with Helen Maria Williams, see Jon Mee, '"A good Cambrio-Briton": Hester Thrale Piozzi, Helen Maria Williams, and the Welsh Sublime in the 1790s', in Constantine and Johnston (eds.), *'Footsteps of Liberty and Revolt'*.

95 Hester Lynch Piozzi, *British Synonymy; or, An Attempt at Regulating the Choice of Words in Familiar Conversation* (2 vols., London, 1794), II, p. 338.

[96] See *PL*, II, pp. 198–9, Hester Piozzi to Sarah Siddons, 27 August 1794, for the full text of the poem, which was published (probably as a result of this letter) in *Songs, &c. in the Village Ghost. A Musical Entertainment. Performed at Sadler's Wells* (n.p., 1794), pp. 6–8.

[97] John Barrell, *Imagining the King's Death: Figurative Treason, Fantasies of Regicide* (Oxford, 2000), p. 657. Barrell also reproduces the text of 'Plant, Plant the Tree' (pp. 657–9).

[98] McCarthy, *Hester Thrale Piozzi*, p. 231.

[99] Hester Piozzi, *Three Warnings to John Bull Before he Dies* (London, 1798), p. 36.

[100] '[M]y honest wrath against the *Realities* of our present day, put it in my Head to make this Parody or Imitation or whatever you please to call it, of good Master Newbery's Chapter of Kings [Piozzi's 'Chapter of King-killers'] . . . give it Mr Siddons for Sadler's Wells, if he thinks it good enough.' *PL*, II, pp. 198–9, Hester Piozzi to Sarah Siddons, 27 August 1794. See also note 96.

[101] Katherine C. Balderston (ed.), *Thraliana: The Diary of Mrs. Hester Lynch Thrale* (2nd edn., Oxford, 1951), p. 902 (entry for 31 October 1794).

[102] In February 1794, Piozzi wrote to Penelope Pennington, 'My book is at Press, and I correct the Sheets very diligently – it will probably be devoured among other Lambs about Easter: I may then run to Brinbella myself, for if Sans Cullottism prevails here, my Neck will be one of the first to exercise the new Guillotine upon'. *PL*, II, p. 167. Reviewers of *British Synonymy* did not, however, see it as a political work, to Piozzi's disappointment.

[103] Edward Williams, *Poems, Lyric and Pastoral* (2 vols., London, 1794), I, p. xiii.

[104] For an account of the tensions involved in joining Jacobin ideology to the role of Welsh Bard, see Mary-Ann Constantine and Elizabeth Edwards, 'Bard of Liberty: Iolo Morganwg, Wales and Radical Song', in John Kirk, Andrew Noble and Michael Brown (eds.), *Political Poetry and Song in the Age of Revolution. Volume 1: United Islands? The Languages of Resistance* (London, 2012), pp. 63–76.

[105] Davies, *Presences that Disturb*, pp. 162–3, explains that the central principles of Iolo's Bardism 'amount to a template – indeed, a constitution – for a utopian republic, established on the principles of social equality, common property, public accountability and a bold, freethinking search after "Truth"'. See also Cathryn Charnell-White, *Bardic Circles: National, Regional and Personal Identity in the Bardic Vision of Iolo Morganwg* (Cardiff, 2007).

[106] Mary-Ann Constantine has shown how 'Winter Incidents' evolved from early drafts made in the 1770s into the poem as it appeared in *Poems, Lyric and Pastoral*. See '"This wildernessed business of publication: The Making of *Poems, Lyric and Pastoral* (1794)', in Jenkins (ed.), *Rattleskull Genius*, pp. 123–46.

[107] Mee, 'Popular Radical Culture', p. 126.

[108] Geraint H. Jenkins, *Bard of Liberty: The Political Radicalism of Iolo Morganwg* (Cardiff, 2012), p. 69. See pp. 15, 67–73 for accounts of Iolo and Milton, the place of Rational Dissent in his thought, and his reading of texts on natural rights.

[109] Jenkins, *Bard of Liberty*, p. 73.

[110] Cowper is the 'Sweet Bard of Humanity' in numerous draft prefaces to the 'Pruning Hook' ode, discussed below.

[111] Liam McIlvanney, *Burns the Radical: Poetry and Politics in Late Eighteenth-Century Scotland* (East Linton, 2002), p. 73.

[112] Three of these prefaces begin with Iolo's counter-claim: 'An unfallacious argument for going to war has not yet appeared; the most plausible is that adduced by M^r. Thomas Paine, i.e. "we may just apply the sword where the Law would apply the halter," but this is glaringly sophistical, the Halter is so powerfully and effectually controlled by the law that it is never applied but to its proper object . . .'. NLW 21401B, f. 16.

[113] NLW 21401B, f. 20.

[114] *CIM*, I, p. 558, Iolo Morganwg to Margaret Williams, 6 April 1793.

[115] NLW 21401B, f. 19. Iolo pushes the point further in f. 20: 'What in low life we call murder, is in the language of Royalty called War, it is the same I believe in the dialects of all Priests.'

[116] See, for example, NLW 21401B, f. 16: 'twenty thousand lie dead on the reeking gory plain, and a far greater number of innocent families, of both communities are involved in the most complicated misery and ruin: after all, the real aggressors are not amongst the slain, they have secured themselves from all dangers, they live, and are even protected, amongst us, "glorying in their shame".'

[117] Harriet Guest, 'The Consequences of War in the Winter of 1794–95', in Geoff Quilley and John Bonehill (eds.), *William Hodges: The Art of Exploration* (New Haven, 2004), pp. 61–70.

[118] See, for example, undated (and perhaps uncharacteristically violent) stanzas in NLW 21424E (f. 2) showing Iolo imagining himself cutting the king's throat:

> There is a man in Cowbridge Town
> A confirmed Sanculotte
> He would kill all clergy is well known
> And he wants to cut the king's throat . . .

[119] *CIM*, I, p. 648, Iolo Morganwg to John Walters, 21 January 1794.

[120] Ibid., p. 649. See *Poems, Lyric and Pastoral*, II, pp. 132–5 for 'God Save the King'.

[121] In the early 1790s Iolo was 'acting as chief promulgator of bardic, Druidic fantasies to the Jacobin circle of Joseph Johnson as well as to the Gwyneddigion society of the London Welsh'. See Franklin, 'The Welsh American Dream', p. 71.

[122] See also Constantine and Edwards, 'Bard of Liberty', pp. 67–8.

[123] Kenneth R. Johnston, 'Whose History? My Place or Yours? Republican Assumptions and Romantic Traditions', in Damian Walford Davies (ed.), *Romanticism, History, Historicism: Essays on an Orthodoxy* (New York, 2009), pp. 79–102.

[124] *CIM*, I, p. 672, Iolo Morganwg to Margaret Williams, 28 May 1794.

[125] Elizabeth Edwards and Marion Löffler, 'Iolo Morganwg and the "Lost Generation"' (unpublished research paper delivered at the 'Wales and the French Revolution' one-day forum, Aberystwyth, September 2011).

[126] Iolo captures this aspect of his character in a revealing letter of January 1794 in which he weighs up his aspiration to become a noted radical with his fear of the consequences of speaking out and his responsibilities to his young children. See *CIM*, I, pp. 648–9.

[127] Iolo experienced deep episodes of mental instability, here described in a letter of 27 October 1792 to his wife: 'a disorder in my head which alarms me very much has, for some time, prevented me from doing any thing . . . it is a perpetual pain and heat in my head . . . Laudanum gives me no relief, but rather increases the internal heat in my head'. *CIM*, I, p. 527.

[128] John Barrell, *Exhibition Extraordinary!! Radical Broadsides of the Mid 1790s* (Nottingham, 2001), p. ix.

[129] 'I have written several pieces in verse of late', Iolo wrote to his wife on 19 February 1794. *CIM*, I, p. 662.

[130] John Barrell, 'Radicalism, Visual Culture, and Spectacle in the 1790s', 'Romantic Spectacle', *Romanticism on the Net*, 46 (May 2007). See also *idem, Exhibition Extraordinary*, p. 4, for depictions of Burke and Reeves in a mock advertisement dating from summer 1793.

[131] See Charnell-White, *Welsh Poetry of the French Revolution*, pp. 154–61.

[132] Gavin Edwards, *Narrative Order, 1789–1819: Life and Story in an Age of Revolution* (Basingstoke, 2005), explores aspects of literary crisis in British literature following the French Revolution.

[133] NLW 6238A, ff. 123–5. Evans also copied the following anti-Pitt epigram, which he attributes to the *Cambridge Intelligencer* for 28 January 1797 (f. 120):

> Hope not for peace, while <u>Jehu</u> holds the reins,
> Or whilst a guinea in your purse remains,
> The Ministry, (if that blest hour you'd see)
> Must first be <u>Changed</u>, by leaving out the C.

[134] Löffler, *Welsh Responses to the French Revolution*, p. 32.

[135] Ibid., pp. 226–7.

[136] Geraint H. Jenkins, '"A Very Horrid Affair": Sedition and Unitarianism in the Age of Revolutions', in Davies and *idem* (eds.), *From Medieval to Modern Wales*, pp. 175–96. In an intriguingly parallel case, William Blake was accused by local soldiers of having uttered 'seditious expressions' in 1803: see Jon Mee and Mark Crosby, '"This Soldierlike Danger": The Trial of William Blake for Sedition', in Mark Philp (ed.), *Resisting Napoleon: The British Response to the Threat of Invasion, 1797–1815* (Aldershot, 2006), pp. 111–24. Blake's case suggests 'how tightly [reformers] felt themselves muzzled' during the invasion scare (p. 13).

[137] NLW 21401E, f. 34.

[138] See Marion Löffler and Heather Williams, *Translating the French Revolution* (Cardiff, forthcoming), for an account of literal/actual and cultural translation practices in Wales.

[139] Jones, *Before Rebecca*, p. 20.

[140] For an account of the Denbigh riots, see W. L. Davies, 'The Riot at Denbigh in 1795', *BBCS*, IV, part I (1927), 61–73.

[141] *PL*, II, p. 285, Hester Piozzi to Leonard Chappelow, 3 November 1795 – original italics.

[142] Ibid., pp. 285–6.

[143] It is worth emphasizing the political dimension of this project: as Katie Trumpener has explained, '[t]he material difficulties involved in recovering and reconstructing the national cultural legacy of an oppressed people brought home . . . the full effect of imperial occupation'. *Bardic Nationalism: The Romantic Novel and the British Empire* (Princeton, 1997), pp. 26–7.

[144] See Barrell, *Spirit of Despotism*, pp. 220–37, for a discussion of the significance of war in the mid-1790s.

[145] For an account of the Llywarch Hen saga, see A. O. H. Jarman, 'Saga Poetry – The Cycle of Llywarch Hen', in *idem* and Gwilym Rees Hughes (eds.), *A Guide to Welsh Literature, Volume 1* (Cardiff, 1992), pp. 81–97.

[146] Davies, *Presences that Disturb*, pp. 160–1.

[147] Joseph Hucks, *A Pedestrian Tour through North Wales, in a series of letters* (London, 1795), especially pp. 51–4.

[148] See Elizabeth Edwards, '"Iniquity, Terror and Survival": Welsh Gothic, 1789–1804', *Journal for Eighteenth-Century Studies*, 35, no. 1 (2012), 119–33, for a further discussion of the poem.

[149] Day's poem is set in 'a space haunted by political pariahs, masterless men and historical ghosts – in short, as one of the crucial, formative sites in which Romanticism came to terms with history'. Davies, *Presences that Disturb*, p. 2.

[150] See, in relation to this point, Claudia Kairoff Thomas's excellent discussion of Seward's 'war correspondence' – private letters revealing her strongly anti-war position – which appeared after this book went to press: *Anna Seward and the End of the Eighteenth Century* (Baltimore, 2012), pp. 98–116.

[151] Seward received numerous effusive poetic tributes for 'Llangollen Vale', among them Thomas Park's sonnet 'To Miss Seward', from his collection *Sonnets, and Other Small Poems* (London, 1797), which hailed Seward as 'SHE, who . . . by Deva's wave, / The deeds of elder Cambria gave / Again to fame!'

[152] William Bagshawe Stevens, 'Sonnet, on Miss Seward's Poem, Llangollen Vale', *Gentleman's Magazine*, LXVI (May 1796), 421.

[153] See, for example, Anna Seward to Henry White, 7 September 1795, *Letters of Anna Seward*, IV, pp. 98–109.

[154] Jill H. Casid, *Sowing Empire: Landscape and Colonization* (Minneapolis, 2005), p. 184.

[155] Ibid., pp. 188–9.

[156] Lynda Pratt, 'Southey in Wales: Inscriptions, Monuments and Romantic Posterity', in Davies and *idem* (eds.), *Wales and the Romantic Imagination*, pp. 86–103; here p. 87.

[157] Franklin, 'The Welsh American Dream', p. 84.

[158] Pratt, 'Southey in Wales', p. 91.

[159] See, for example, the papers of Elizabeth Baker of Dolgellau: a letter of 26 February 1797 describes 'the horrors, affrights of some of my neighbours . . . since two o' clock Friday morning, till midnight on Sunday last'. NLW Peniarth 416A, part 1.

[160] Roland Quinault, 'The French Invasion of Pembrokeshire in 1797: A Bicentennial Assessment', *WHR*, 19, no. 4 (1999), 618–42; here 619. See also Hywel M.

Davies, 'Terror, Treason and Tourism: The French in Pembrokeshire 1797', in Constantine and Johnston (eds.), *'Footsteps of Liberty and Revolt'*.

[161] Resisting the French, Quinault has argued, was primarily a matter of 'self-interest, rather than loyalty to "king and country"'. 'The French Invasion of Pembrokeshire', 628.

[162] Katie Gramich, 'Narrating the Nation: Telling Stories of Wales', *North American Journal of Welsh Studies*, 6, no. 1 (2011), 2–19, here 12.

[163] Quinault, 'The French Invasion of Pembrokeshire', 630.

[164] For an account of Gray's translation of the poem from Evan Evans's Latin version of the original, see Arthur Johnston, 'Gray's "The Triumphs of Owen"', *The Review of English Studies*, 11, no. 43 (1960), 275–85.

[165] *Chester Chronicle*, 5 May 1797.

[166] Ibid., 16 October 1801.

[167] Ibid. The song had earlier been published in the *Gentleman's Magazine*, in April 1800, where it is attributed to 'Mr. Braine' (i.e. Richard Braine) of Greenwich.

[168] Katrina Navickas, *Loyalism and Radicalism in Lancashire 1798–1815* (Oxford, 2008), discusses the place of ritual within public responses to developments in war and politics.

[169] *PL*, II, p. 451, Hester Piozzi to Leonard Chappelow, 20 October 1797; original italics.

[170] See *PL*, II, p. 411, Hester Piozzi to Hester Maria Thrale, 21 December 1796, for Piozzi's plans for a patriotic ballad that would become 'Written on the Spur of the Moment' (no. 32).

[171] *PL*, II, p. 470, Hester Piozzi to Robert Ray, 20 January 1798.

[172] Kevin B. Linch, '"A Citizen and Not a Soldier": The British Volunteer Movement and the War against Napoleon', in Alan Forrest, Karen Hagemann and Jane Rendall (eds.), *Soldiers, Citizens and Civilians: Experiences and Perceptions of the Revolutionary and Napoleonic Wars, 1790–1820* (Basingstoke, 2009), pp. 205–21; here p. 209.

[173] Austin Gee, *The British Volunteer Movement 1794–1814* (Oxford, 2003), p. 1.

[174] Bryn Owen, *History of the Welsh Militia and Volunteer Corps 1757–1908: Volume 3 Glamorgan (Part 2), Volunteers & Local Militia, 1796–1816, Yeomanry Cavalry, 1803–31* (Wrexham, 1994), p. 27.

[175] McIlvanney, *Burns the Radical*, p. 236.

[176] Gee, *The British Volunteer Movement*, p. 6.

[177] Davies, *Presences that Disturb*, p. 167.

[178] The opening up of the Continent meant that '[d]uring and immediately after the Peace of Amiens, the presses groaned with travellers' assessments of the changes between pre- and post-revolutionary manners throughout the theatre of war'. Benjamin Colbert, *Shelley's Eye: Travel Writing and Aesthetic Vision* (Aldershot, 2005), p. 11.

[179] See Jones, *Welsh Ballads of the French Revolution*, pp. 41–56, for an account of the news in the ballads.

[180] *Critical Review; Or, Annals of Literature*, 28 (1800), 299–305.

[181] Stuart Semmel, *Napoleon and the British* (New Haven, 2004), pp. 134–5.

[182] The radical Unitarian Joseph Fawcett was similarly drawing on the early–mid 1790s in poems published in his 1801 collection *War Elegies*. See, for example, 'War Elegy' in which a war widow, starving to death, murders her young child ('A mother gave it all she had − / Gave it a mother's blessing − DEATH!'), a scene reminiscent of the 1795 famine in north Wales (no. 26).

[183] For successive drafts of 'John Bull's Litany', see Constantine and Edwards, 'Bard of Liberty', pp. 72–3.

[184] Iolo probably continued to think in these terms in this period: see, for example, the regicidal imaginings contained in a manuscript travel diary written over the summer of 1802 (NLW 13174A). This notebook is discussed in Edwards, '"Iniquity, Terror and Survival"', 125–6.

[185] For examples see anon., 'An Ode', *Chester Chronicle*, 30 January 1801; 'T.L.', 'An Invocation to Peace', *Chester Chronicle*, 4 September 1801; anon., 'On the Peace', *Chester Chronicle*, 9 October 1801; John Thelwall, 'Ode to Peace', *Chester Chronicle*, 16 October 1801; Helen Maria Williams, 'Ode to Peace', *Chester Chronicle*, 1 January 1802 (earlier published in the *Morning Chronicle*, 17 November 1801).

[186] J. E. Cookson, *The Friends of Peace: Anti-war Liberalism in England, 1793–1815* (Cambridge, 1982), p. 173.

[187] Richard Braine, 'Serious Advice to Bonaparte', *Gentleman's Magazine*, LXXIII (August 1803), 763–4; anon., 'Stop to a Stride', *Gentleman's Magazine*, LXXIII (November 1803), 1060.

[188] 'Y. N. S.', untitled ['What's to be done to save the State?'], *Gentleman's Magazine*, LXIII (August 1803), 764.

[189] Frank J. Klingberg and Sigurd B. Hustvedt (eds.), *The Warning Drum* (Berkeley, 1944), pp. 173–4.

[190] Similar sentiments can be seen in the anonymous 'The Voice of the British Isles', published in the *Gentleman's Magazine* and the *European Magazine* in July and August 1803 respectively. This poem exhorting Britons to resist the French celebrates a British unity that nowhere mentions Wales: 'Now JACK, PAT, and SANDY, thus cordial agree, / We sons of the waves shall forever be free'.

[191] Anon., 'Stop to a Stride'.

[192] Compare, for example, 'On the Late Splendid Victory off Trafalgar' (no. 54) with 'Dirge, On the Death of Lord Nelson', anonymously printed in the *Morning Chronicle*, 8 November 1805.

[193] Richards's collected *Poems* (1804), which reprinted his poems from the 1790s, was positively received: see the *Poetical Register for 1804* (1806), 489. Llwyd's 1804 *Poems* was heavily criticized in the same periodical (510).

[194] For Welsh 'contributionism', see Prescott, *Bards and Britons*, pp. 71–2. It is worth pointing out that in 1803 'the proportion of volunteers was slightly higher in Wales than in Britain as a whole (Gee, *The British Volunteer Movement*, p. 69).

[195] See p. 299 for details of the publication of this poem.

[196] Llwyd's words are, of course, highly ironic in the light of the consequences of the Norman conquest for Wales.

[197] Mark Philp, 'Introduction', in *idem* (ed.), *Resisting Napoleon*, p. 15.

[198] *Cambrian*, 11 February 1804.

[199] *Ipswich Journal*, 2 June 1804.

[200] See, for example, 'Horrors upon Horrors; Or What are the *Hellish Deeds* that can surprise us, when committed by the *Blood-Hounds* of that *Arch-Fiend* of Wickedness, the CORSICAN BONAPARTE?' in Klingberg and Hustvedt (eds.), *The Warning Drum*, pp. 199–203.

[201] Reade's postscript playfully imagines the response of the critics to his poem:

> 'And who have we here,' they cry, 'what advent'rous Elf
> Who curses Invaders yet is just one himself
> Who invades out Territories, breaks thro' our Rules
> Respects not our Grecian nor our best Latin Schools
> What pile het'rogenous! what strange rancid Matter
> Does he thrust on our View and careless bespatter,
> A Poem he calls it, mere jumbled, jingling Words . . .
>
> *Invasion!* (Carmarthen, 1804), p. 23.

[202] Ibid., p. 24.

[203] The 'dual Welsh and British allegiances' of Welsh poets 'has yet to be fully resolved, even in this age of "four nations" or Archipelagic historiography.' See Charnell-White, *Welsh Poetry of the French Revolution*, p. 7.

[204] Aaron, *Nineteenth-Century Women's Writing*, p. 3.

[205] For William Pitt, insurrectionary Ireland at the close of the eighteenth century was 'a ship on fire, it must be extinguished or cut adrift'. See Iain McCalman (ed.), *An Oxford Companion to the Romantic Age: British Culture 1776–1832* (Oxford, 1999), p. 401.

[206] See Nick Groom, *The Union Jack: The Story of the British Flag* (London, 2006), pp. 202–10, for responses to the flag of 1801.

[207] This section of the poem was reprinted in *The Cambro-Briton: Volume III* (London, 1822), p. 294, suggesting the continuing relevance of Llwyd's point.

[208] See Marion Löffler, *The Literary and Historical Legacy of Iolo Morganwg, 1826–1926* (Cardiff, 2007), pp. 116–29.

[209] Morgan, *The Eighteenth-Century Renaissance*. Shawna Lichtenwalner, *Claiming Cambria: Invoking the Welsh in the Romantic Era* (Newark, 2008), pp. 11–24.

[210] See Elizabeth Edwards, '"Confined to a Living Grave": Welsh Poetry, Gothic and the French Revolution', in Marion Gibson, Garry Tregidga and Shelley Trower (eds.), *Mysticism, Myth, and 'Celtic' Nationalism* (London, 2012), pp. 87–98, for further discussion of this aspect of 'Ode of the Months'.

[211] Edward Griffith (ed.), *Correspondence, Relative to the Stationing of a Troop of the 4th Regiment of Dragoons, in the County of Carnarvon* (2nd edn., Chester, 1801). See Letter 11 for an account of the armed workers.

[212] John Barrell and Tim Whelan (eds.), *The Political Pamphlets of William Fox* (Nottingham, 2011), p. xxviii.

[213] 'I . . . prefer, whilst of rural employments I sing, / The life of a *Farmer* to that of a *King*'. *Poems, Lyric and Pastoral*, I, p. 169.

[214] Favret, *War at a Distance*, p. 29.

[215] Ibid., p. 101.

[216] *Chester Chronicle*, 20 January 1804. See David Carey, *The Pleasures of Nature; or, The Charms of Rural Life* (London, 1803), p. 48.

[217] Newspaper poems, surrounded by news items, advertisements and announcements, are 'subject to the material assertion of equality through juxtaposition on a single broadsheet', though the interactions between these adjacent pieces may be difficult to pin down. See Anne Jamison, *Poetics en Passant: Redefining the Relationship between Victorian and Modern Poetry* (New York, 2009), p. 66.

Texts

Editorial Principles

The aim of this anthology is convey the authentic voices of poems from the period 1789–1806 while also presenting readable texts. Original spellings, punctuation and capitalization have been retained except in the case of obvious misprints, which have been silently corrected. In the case of several manuscript poems, I have arranged the text as closely as possible to the manuscript source, including all cancellations and alternatives. These texts preserve poems that are unfinished and provisional, rather than attempt to fix a single version of the text where the source gives little clear sense of what a final version should look like. Extracts from longer published works are indicated by ellipses. Authorial footnotes will be found at the end of the poem to which they belong and all symbols used for footnotes in the source text (letters, asterisks, daggers etc.) have been retained. When authorial footnotes are only signalled by asterisks in the original, where they may have been placed at the end of successive pages rather than at the end of the poem, I have added line numbers in square brackets. Authorial marginal comments to manuscript poems that do not take the form of footnotes or endnotes to the poem will be found in the 'Notes to the Texts' section. The sources from which the texts have been taken are listed in the 'Notes to the Texts', as are alternative manuscript or printed versions of the poems. My explanatory notes will be found in a separate section after the poem texts.

1. David Samwell (Dafydd Ddu Feddyg), 'Ode for the New Year
MDCC,XC. As it was intended to have been
rehearsed this Day at St. JAMES's'

1.
BRITAIN, for arts, for arms renown'd
To this wide earth's remotest bound!
As time rolls on successive years,
With ev'ry blessing crown'd appears,
And claims th' admiring world's applause   5
For patriot chiefs, for equal laws
Whose influence, extended wide, displays
In man, the image of the great first cause.
    The center She from whence the sun
    Of Liberty his course begun,   10
And warm'd surrounding nations with his rays.
Favour'd of Heav'n, the queen of isles,
On freedom's glorious effort, smiles,
    To throw vile slav'ry's chains aside
    And crush the antique feudal pride   15
    Which cruel, desperate and bold,
    Long reign'd in Gallia uncontroul'd.
But reigns no more – at length the dauntless Gaul
Reclaims man's noblest right – the liberty of all.

2.
Like clouds before the rising day,   20
The gloom of slav'ry melts away,
And superstition fell and blind
Yields up her empire o'er the mind,
And bigot priests their crimes atone,
By bending at religion's throne,   25
Which he the Saviour of the world reveal'd
To breathe in man a spirit like his own.
    For lo! on Gallia, Belgia's plains,
    The radiant light of freedom reigns,
    From miserable man, alas! too long conceal'd.   30
        Primeval shades of tenfold night
        No more shall blind the mortal sight.

The darkened nations from afar,
Shall hail fair freedom's beautious star,
Which now ariseth in the west,   35
And soon shall gild the glowing east,
Where man debas'd by tyrant laws unjust,
Before his fellow man still bows and licks the dust.

3.
Thy age, blest freedom is begun!
Proceed thy destin'd course to run!   40
Till Europe's states, like Britain free,
And Asia's sons shall worship thee,
Till Afric's hords thy cause maintain,
And they beyond the western main
In groves profound, thy frequent shrines shall rear,   45
Where olive tribes delighted hear thy strain,
  Till virtue, peace and love abound,
  And science casts her beams around.
  To shew benighted nations how they err.
The muse's eye can pierce the gloom,   50
That hangs o'er ages yet to come.
And hail this Æra, first and best,
That bids futurity be blest,
Distinguish'd as the whitest age
Displayed on time's immortal page,   55
And hail to those, to whom 'tis given to see
This Year – the opening dawn of perfect liberty!

2. William Sotheby, 'A Tour Through Parts of South and North Wales' (extract)

From Book One

. . .

Now the soft murmurs, faint and fainter heard,
Die, while in contrast harsh from yon lone isle,   65
Loudly, with ceaseless revolution whirl'd,
Bursts the cogg'd wheel, and on the anvil blows,
Falling at measur'd intervals, and oft
More mark'd by casual interruptions, fling
Heavily forth their weight of sound. Soft falls   70
Upon the dewy earth descending eve,
And onward as I wander, wavering mists
Shadow the face of Nature, and diffuse
The thin blue veil, that half concealing adds
To the dim scene imaginary charms.   75

'Tis now the time, when from the narrow world
Withdrawn, and its close fett'ring care, the mind,
Swift as a prisoner from long bondage scap'd,
Exulting in its liberty, at will
Arrays its wild creation; yet the bard   80
That roams at eventide, through pathless woods,
His secret way, shapes not ideal scenes
More suited to the pensive range of thought,
Than yonder Castle,* 'mid the ruins vast
Lifting its hoary brow. The mellow tints   85
That time's slow pencil lays from year to year
Upon the ancient tow'rs, spread o'er the wreck
A grateful gloom, and the thick clouds that sweep
Along the darken'd battlements, extend
The melancholy grandeur of the scene.   90
Hail, solemn wreck! Thou silent hour, belov'd
Of fancy, hail! and thou, that o'er yon hill,
Mild orb, slow rising, with soft radiance gleam'st
Upon the Castle, while each varied shape
Of turret, and nich'd battlement that fronts   95

The light's full stream, its shadowy image casts
On the retiring walls.

. . .

Bold on the summit of the mountain brow
Frowns many a hoary tow'r, where *Cambria*'s chiefs
Waving the banner'd dragon dar'd to arms
The Norman host. Breathing his native strains,   220
There the descendant of the British bards,
Hoel, or lofty *Taliessin*, oft
At the dim twilight hour in pensive mood,
Amid the silent hall o'ergrown with bryars,
Recalls the festivals of old, when blaz'd   225
The giant oak, and chieftains crown'd with mead
The sculptur'd horn, while the high vaulted roof
Re-echo'd to the honour'd minstrel's harp.
O'er yonder crag, steep, lonely, wild, impends
The ruin'd fortress,* like th' aerial shape   230
Of battlement or broken citadel,
That when at eve autumnal gales arise,
Crowns the grey fleeces of the floating clouds.
Stranger! beneath yon tow'r a vaulted path
Down the steep mountain leads; with flaming torch   235
Amid the windings of the cliff descend,
Where, in its deep recess, the hollow'd rock
Catches the gather'd damps, that drop by drop
Fall through the porous stone. Gilt by the blaze,
The radiant cave, the dews that gem the roof   240
Shedding around from long pellucid points
The mimic diamonds, veins of sparry ore,
That glittering down the arches' crystal sides
Their interlacing fret-work weave, renew
The visionary scenes to childhood dear,   245
Of subterranean palaces, the haunts
Of Genii brooding o'er their secret wealth.

   . . . O'er the sunny lawns
The scatter'd groves of graceful foliage bloom,   260
Mingling with sweet variety: The hills
Sink softly melting to the plain beneath,

Lost gradual in its level, as the stream
That glides into the bosom of the sea:
High low'r the wilder steeps, darken'd with oaks   265
Majestic, as bold nature unconfin'd
Spreads in his forest range; and at the base
Of yon wood-waving cliff, where the proud wreck
Of ancient *Dinevawr* sublimely lifts
Its ivied battlements, swift *Towy* winds   270
Voluminous, in many a lucid fold
Wildly meand'ring; while beyond arise
The verdant heights that guard the shelter'd vale
And fade away, dim'd by the distant clouds.

[Line 84] * Caerfily Castle
[Line 230] * *Caraigcennin*, the remains of a British fortress.

From Book Two

                    . . . O thou who seek'st
Yon rude coast's verge extreme that o'er the flood   50
Projects its craggy brow, cautious explore
The solitary path; no print appears
Of human step, save where thy stranger mien
Scares the shy wildness of the lonely child,
Who with her lean flock creeps for warmth beneath   55
The wither'd hedge. She knows not to direct
Thy doubtful way, alone the narrow bound
Of her rude range she knows, nor dreams of worlds
Beyond the limits of the barren waste.

. . .

Thee, *Snowdon!* king of *Cambrian* mountain hail!
With many a lengthen'd pause my ling'ring feet
Follow th' experienc'd guide; a Veteran maim'd   155
With glorious wounds, that late on *Calpe*'s height
Bled in his country's cause; though time has mark'd
With graceful touch his silver hair, yet health,
The child of temperance, has fix'd the rose
Of youth upon his cheek; keen beams his eye   160

Beneath his hoary brow, and firm his foot
Springs upon the steepness of the rough ascent.
Proud of his native land the Veteran points
To every mountain, wood, and winding stream,
That by tradition sacred made records   165
His great forefathers' deeds: for not deriv'd
Of simple lineage the brave warrior boasts
Hereditary blood of British chiefs,
Cadwallader or *Roderic*'s ancient stem.
Tremendous *Snowdon!* while I gradual climb   170
Thy craggy heights, tho' intermingled clouds
Various of wa'try grey, and sable hue,
Obscure th' uncertain prospects, from thy brow
His wildest views the mountain genius flings.
Now high and swift flits the thin rack along,   175
Skirted with rainbow dyes, now deep below
(While the fierce sun strikes the illumin'd top)
Slow sails the gloomy storm, and all beneath,
By vaporous exhalation hid, lies lost
In darkness; save at once where drifted mists,   180
Cut by strong gusts of eddying winds, expose
The transitory scenes. Here broken cliffs
Caught at long intervals, anon a sea
Of liquid light, dark woods, and cities gay
With gleaming spires, brown moors, and verdant vales,   185
In swift succession rush upon the sight.
Now swift on with side the gather'd clouds,
As by a sudden touch of magic, wide
Recede, and the fair face of heaven and earth
Appears. Amid the vast horizon's stretch,   190
In restless gaze the eye of wonder darts
O'er th' expanse; mountains on mountains pil'd,
And winding bays, and promontories huge,
Lakes and meand'ring rivers, from their source,
Trace'd to the distant ocean: scatter'd isles   195
Dark rising from the watery waste, and seas
Dividing kingdoms, and *Ïerne* crown'd
By Wicklowe's lofty range. Thou who aspir'st
To imitate the soft aerial hue,
Flung o'er the living scenes of chaste *Lorraine*;   200
Here, when the breath of autumn blows along

The blue serene, gaze on th' harmonious glow
Wide spread around, when not a cloud disturbs
The mellow light, that with a golden tint
Gleams through the grey veil of thin haze, diffus'd   205
In trembling undulation o'er the scenes.

3. Anon., 'An Ode to Commerce. Inscribed to John Wilkinson, Esq.
the distinguished iron master'

Maid of multifarious form,
Perhaps without a parent born,
Unless we trace thy lineage high,
And find a father in the sky,
Denizen of ev'ry clime,   5
It must be from a source divine!

Once, and thou wert then a child,
Wandering o'er the woodland wild,
Gleaning from the thieving thorn
The wool from passing fleeces torn,   10
Ere the shuttle knew to go,
Ere the waters knew the prow.

O'er the river's rapid way,
Plenty bade the plain be gay;
Want and thou, with head and heart,   15
Mother, nurse, of many an art,
Gave the young, expanding thought,
Now with many a project fraught;
Hence the forest's tallest oak
Fell beneath the steady stroke;   20
Hence the deep incision sunk,
And sound proclaim'd the hollow trunk;
Hence thy trod the pathless isle
That severs still the streams of Nile.

The tail that steers the eagle's way   25
Bade the boat the helm obey;
The stately swan's impelling feet
Bade the oar the current meet;
The wing unsullied taught the sail
To spread and grasp the growing gale.   30

Wider as thy charms expand,
    Other regions court thy smiles,
Cities crown the sinking strand,
    Arches bind Venetian isles;
Pleas'd the Adriatic tide   35
    O'er the Crescent* cast a shade,
Roll'd its wealth, and taught his bride
    To triumph in the power of trade.

Let by thee to objects new,
Columbus spurn'd the narrow view,   40
Creator like, a world he gave
Beyond the wide Atlantic wave;
Hence, with gems to deck thy throne,
Rolls the pearly Amazon;
Hence, to heap thy growing stores,   45
The wealth of Peru, de la Planta pours.

And Kiang,† Ocean's eldest child,
    With orient treasure gay,
Loud rolling from the summits wild,
    Still wafts the tribute to its parent sea.   50

Freedom and thine equal law,
    Brav'd the tyrant's iron paw,
Bade the Belgic bogs display
    An empire – stolen from the sea!
Bade the daring sons of gain,   55
    Ere their name as yet was known,
De Ruyters, Tromps, assert their claim,
    And grasp the naval trident as their own!

Hence, beneath thy liberal smiles,
    Expiring freedom saw,   60
And bade her native, envy'd isles
    Adopt her son Nassau!
To hurl destruction on her foes,
    Now indignant Britain rose –
Commercial freedom, William, join –   65
    Theirs La Hogue! and theirs the Boyne!

Contest gave that credit birth,‡
The wonder now that proves thy worth,
That bade the gradual glory rise,
That nations, leagu'd in arms, defies!   70
That Europe's pending balance guides,
And leads the car of triumph o'er the tides!

Grateful Britain, commerce joins
    With honour's wreath to bind
The patriot head, whose purpose proves   75
    The welfare of mankind:
Awhile to war and heroes dumb,
    The silver trump of Fame,
Thy country, Wilkinson, employs
    To sound thy worthier name!   80

Scotia far, thy works§ display,
And Cornwall rushing to the sea,
Where Cumbria spreads th' extended shore,
And Cambria's hilly summits soar,
Where'er thine eye exploring bends,   85
Teeming plenty still attends,
While industry with busy glee,
Finds her thousands fed by thee.

Still load¶ with wealth, and lead the stream,
    And bid th' eternal arch expand;   90
Cherish still th' effective flame,
    While art applauds thy fost'ring hand;
King of Commerce, coin a mine,
    And let a deathless name be thine!

* Alluding to the war of Candia, and the annual ceremony of throwing a
ring into the Adriatic.

† A river of China.

‡ The National Debt. It is a fact that the present prosperity, and extensive commerce of this country, is in a great degree owing to this enormous burthen.

§ The extensive works carried on by Mr. Wilkinson are situate [*sic*] in every part of Britain. The iron-works in Scotland, at Bradley in Staffordshire, Snedshill and Wisley in Shropshire, Bersham in Denbighshire, copper-works in Flintshire, his concerns in the Cornish tin-mines, coal-mines in different places, his manufacture of patent lead pipes, and his concerns in Westmoreland, are parts of a whole which is almost beyond comprehension.

¶ This stanza has a reference to the iron bridge, iron boats, and conveyance by canal; his princely patronage of the arts will appear in his having, at this time, at different places, twenty-two fire engines, upon the improv'd plan of Messrs. Bolton and Watts, of Birmingham, at an expence to Mr. Wilkinson of near a hundred pounds. His elegant and useful coinage, by its extensive circulation, is well known; while he expends a considerable part of a splendid fortune in the acquisition of experimental knowledge and improvements, which will benefit posterity rather than himself; that posterity will gratefully place his name among its benefactors, and Britain and human nature among their ornaments.

4. Richard Llwyd, 'An Ode for the New Year [1791],
Inscribed to Paul Panton, of Plasgwyn, Esq.'

Genius of freedom's favour'd isles!
Lo, on yonder cliff she smiles;
Smile, as spreads the bright'ning blaze,
Lucid reason's liberal rays!

The tomes that wasting times defy,   5
And fancy's retrospective eye,
Still forms the phalanx firm and free,
When listening on the rock's rough side,
As dulcet, on the ærial tide,
From oaken groves, that distant rung;   10
As inspiration's minstrel sung
    The loud prophetic strain,
The bliss that freedom's hand bestows,
The gen'rous flame, that awes her foes,
    And pour'd it not in vain.   15

Such as o'er the trackless heath,
Unharass'd yet in fields of death,
    Unfetter'd freedom ran;
Ere yet the moated rampart knew
Oppression's callous steel-clad crew,   20
    Her foes, and those of man!

'Twas now, by dread contention drest,
The fair assum'd the hostile crest,
    The pointed spear, the shield,
Now taught the gen'rous breast to glow,   25
Assert its right, direct the blow,
    And dare the tented field.

Awhile to desolation doom'd,
As either* rose alternate bloom'd
    In discord's hated hue;   30
And freedom, Britain, pining, saw
Progressive slaughter's iron paw,
    The fatal field bestrew.

Yet peace again her reign renews,
And commerce op'd her boundless views,   35
   Hence the blissful union broke
The feudal despot's galling yoke,
Fair freedom's dome Britannia's offspring grace,
   And hail a chieftain† from her genuine race.

Hence the glorious theme was sung,   40
Hence her fields and vallies rung,
The sounds her torrents still retain,
And tell it to the ambient main!
Triumphant Thames proclaims it far,
Responsive roars the Delawar: 45
Old Ocean pleas'd returns the strain,
And pours it on the polish'd Seine.‡

Hail, all hail, the godlike ray
That sparkles, kindles into day;
Gallia feeds the gen'rous flame,   50
Soars, to raise the human name,
Spurns a tyrant's mad decrees,
Nor rears a myriad for one fiend's caprice.

The breast that boasts the beam benign
Exalts the social to divine,   55
Where love of public virtue glows,
From private worth the blessing flows;
This constitutes the general good,
As confluent streams compose the flood.

Yet, Panton, tho' the shield be thine,   60
   Where Britain's regal§ roses bloom,
And Emlyn, ‖ Cowryd's¶ patriot line.
   That brav'd awhile their country's doom;
For these, beyond the domes of death,
   The braided laurel Cambria** leads   65
Her happier hour entwines a wreath
   For virtues that adorn the shades.

* The white and red roses, badges of the contending houses of York and Lancaster.

† Henry the Seventh, whose accession to the Crown restored the British blood in the family of Tudor.

‡ A river of France, running thro' Paris.

§ Gules a chevron, between three roses argent, barbed and seeded proper; the armorial bearing of Roderick the Great, sovereign of all Wales, and who divided it between his three sons, called *Y tri thywysog talaethog*.

‖ Trehairne Cock o Emlyn. The daring intrepidity of this hero is aptly expressed by his shield and motto – argent, six bees Volant, en arriere sable. The motto, *Dial os daw*. Its meaning and pointed allusion to the figures are exactly the same as that of Scotland – *Nemo me impune lacessit* – encircling the order of the thistle.

¶ Cowryd ap Cadfan of Dyffryn Clwyd, a British Chieftain. He bore argent three boars' heads, couped sable, armed or.

** To Mr. Panton's fine taste this country is, and posterity will be, indebted for the preservation of the late Rev. and ingenious Mr. Evan Evans's fine collection of British antiquity; the good, while they applaud his humanity, in rescuing this wayward child of genius, in the evening of his days, from penury and wretchedness, admire the liberality with which the amateur is admitted to his researches.

5. Richard Llwyd, 'Ode, for the Anniversary
of St. David [1792]'

BRITONS! Brothers! yours the lay
That hails your country's festal day;
And be with pride the symbol* shewn,
That marks its triumph as your own.

'Twas thus Menevia's† shepherd sung,   5
When heav'n on ev'ry accent hung –
When, op'ning prospects bright and new,
He sprinkled Hermon's holy dew.

The pages of eventful store,
The muse of retrospective lore,   10
Can weary'd Britain's warlike race
Thro' time's envelop'd foldings trace.

While Europe from each crowded shore
Pour'd her savage outcasts o'er,
Oppression stalk'd her blood stain'd way,   15
And urg'd a woman's‡ arm to slay.

Alternate theirs – on death-fraught plains –
The victor's triumph – captive's chains;
Yet Britons§ vanquish'd – Rome could awe –
Rome, that gave the world its law!   20

Harrass'd by the hydra foe,
Cambria shew'd her cliffs of snow,
And bade her native offspring be,
To time's remotest period, free;

Nurtur'd in the British isles,   25
On other realms, lo, Freedom smiles;
Nor be to these the bliss confin'd,
But grasp the boon – all human kind.

* The leek.

† St. David's bishoprics. He was one of the early preachers of Christianity in this island.

‡ Boadicea, Queen of the Iceni, wearied out at length with the insulting barbarity of the Roman soldiery, satiated her revenge by putting 70,000 of them to the sword.

§ Vide the speech of Caractacus before Claudius.

6. David Thomas (Dafydd Ddu Eryri),
'The Banks of the Menai. An Ode'

Inscribed to the Druidical Society of Anglesey.
Recited at the Meeting of the Welch [*sic*] Bards on Primrose Hill, September
22nd, 1792.

    BEHOLD the fair testaceous shore,
    Which oft was stain'd with human gore,
    Methinks aerial forms surround,
    As guardians of this fairy ground;
Loth to disturb the Druid's solemn shade,   5
I softly glide along the verdant glade.

    Here inspiration's tribe, before
    Excel'd in deep prophetic lore,
    In yonder antiquated cell
    The white rob'd virgins lov'd to dwell;   10
There ancient bards consum'd their midnight oil,
Enrapt in thought, or bent on mystic toil.

    Surprising beauties strike my eyes,
    From land and water, earth and skies;
    The rural scene, the prospect bright,   15
    Rush now spontaneous on my sight:
Here nature's works, how beauteous and how great,
Where the wise patriots find a sweet retreat!

    Here Gwalchmai tun'd his nervous lays,
    And sung the conquests of his days;   20
    Here liv'd Caradog, bold and brave,
    Who spurn'd the terrors of the grave;
Heroes of old, who wore the martial wreath,
And gain'd true honour in the fields of death.

Let all who in the paths succeed,   25
    Excel in every godlike deed.
Ye men, who claim the honour'd line,
The spark of genius cause to shine,
Transfer young merit's fairest bloom
To regions far beyond the tomb;   30
Let Britons, of the Tudor's race,
Enjoy the philosophic blaze,
Each bosom warm in freedom's cause,
And yet obedient to the laws;
Then shall your fame extend from pole to pole,   35
Your well-known worth to distant ages roll.

7. David Samwell (Dafydd Ddu Feddyg), 'The Resurrection of Rhitta Gawr'

A Chief at the time of King Arthur, who destroyed so many despots, that he made himself a Robe with their Beards, being the subject given at a meeting of Welsh Bards on Primrose Hill, near London Sep.ʳ 22. 1792.

Ode.

Deep in the shadowy realm beneath,
The silent dark domain of death.
Let mortal voice for once resound,
And echo from her choral cave
Pass thro' the portals of the grave
And wake the Heroes under ground.

Let us to the work proceed,
Bards I do a potent deed,
That shall strike the world with dread,
That shall rouse the slumb'ring dead,
[illeg.]
Look above and mark how soon
Yonder cloud shall ride the moon,
Then the boiling cauldron bring,
To this consecrated ring,
Now the moon is gone, and hark!
Bursting thro' the pitchy dark,
Spirits throng around us fast,
Tell the future shew the past,
Heard ye thro' the awful gloom,
Bradshaw seal a monarch's doom,
Saw ye on the scaffold fall,
The owner of the purple pall,
'Tis done, the elder Charles is dead,
To the Cauldron give his head,
Heard ye Tudor's son depart,
To the Cauldron give his heart
The eighth Henry fiercer far
Than the Libyan Tygers are

Than hungry wolves that prowl for food
Than sharks the terror of the flood.

For the cauldron next prepare
The bowels of the Russian bear,
[illeg.]
Barbarian he of wretched mind,
Who fights for pay t' enslave mankind,
Bring her,* who with a demon's smile
Could point infernal bombs at Lisle,
Give the priests and prelates tongues
That would varnish Gallia's wrongs
With them to the cauldron fling
All of Prussia's faithless King,
And the German Emp'ror's head,
Then the charm will raise the dead,
Add the whiskers of the Turk,
Now the spell begins to work.

1.

Bravest of those brave souls who dwell
In heav'ns confines or depths of hell,
Old <u>Rhitta Gawr</u>, with joy we hear
Thy dread voice sounding thro' the gloom,
We see thee burst thy iron tomb,   5
And see thee in thy ancient garb appear.

2.

'Tis thee with songs the Bards invoke,
Dark Hero of the hairy cloak,
From proud infernal faces torne,
Thou mad'st the despots for their sins   10
Resign the honours of their chins,
Close as when pigs by Lucifer are shorne

3.

[lines 1–3 illeg.]   15
"If Europe still with lawless despots swarms
I'll make them prove the prowess of my arm,
And tax their whiskers for another cloak.

4.

If right I read, in you I trace,
A remnant of the tuneful race,   20
Round Arthur's board his victories who sung,
When thro' the lofty sounding hall
Attuned to Love and glory's call,
The joyful harps of British Minstrels rung.

5.

I've heard <u>Taliesin</u> pour his strains,   25
O'er Cambria's echoing hills and plains,
He knew the mysteries of druid lore,
Could tell how matter different forms assumes
How the great sun the earth opake [*sic*] illumes
And whence the moon her silver aspect bore.   30

6.

Oft have I listened with delight
To hear the learned Bard recite,
The various changes which to man belong
Arthur to hear of Nature's laws
From War's terrific work would pause   35
And listen to the gentle Minstrel ['s ?song]

7.

The sons of slaughter crowding round,
I've heard the harps of <u>Llywarch</u> sound
To martial strains he swept the rapid strings,
The clash of arms, th' ensanguined plain,   40
Where mercy pleads, but pleads in vain,
While horror o'er the scene extends her raven wings.

8.

[lines 1–2 illeg.]
Today's the ardor of the warrior's breast,   45
And mournful notes slow-sounding tell,
How twice twelve sons in battle fell,
In blood of youth, all sunk to endless rest.

9.

I've known Aneurin's tuneful skill.
Command the passions to his will,   50
And mark'd his breast with youthful ardour ^{transport} glow,
As wild he sung of Cattraeth's field,
Where Saxon hosts were doomed to yield,
And Britain triumph'd o'er her deadly foe.

10.

Devote to freedom's glorious cause,   55
The ancient Bards maintain'd her laws,
And spread their mighty influence round,
The flowing verse thro' Britain ran
And taught the sacred Rights of Man,
While Awe-struck tyrants trembled at the sound.   60

11.

Descendents of those favour'd few,
O keep their noble aims in view,
And liberty with manly strains defend
So shall the bard preserve his fame,
In every clime and ev'ry age the same,   65
Mankind's instructor and the general friend."

Chorus of Bards

Hail Liberty! enthron'd in heav'n's own light,
Whose beams now cheer long injur'd Gallia's plains,
Thee we adore, and hail with ⁱⁿ druid strains,
Indulgent smile upon the votive rite,   70
With joyful songs we greet the opening day
And [illeg.] hour of perfect triumph nigh,
[illeg.] tyrants flee the rising [illeg.]
[illeg.] eye,
And hideous ruin to their impious views,   75
Have heap'd their Camps with mountains of the dead,
The princes of the Earth in ashes mourn
The proud are humbled and the lowly rise,
We see the kingdom of just men return,
More temp'rate seasons, and serener skies,   80
The sabbath of the good and triumph of the wise.

Oct.ʳ 20. 1792.

David Samwell

* Her who with a demon's smile
Could point infernal bombs at Lisle

i.e. The Princess Christiana sister to the Duke of Saxe Teschen Comʳ. in chief at the siege.

8. George Richards, 'The Captivity of Caractacus' (extract)

Thick rose the lances dyed in British gore;
With scar-entrenched limbs and shining mail,
Their blood-stain'd plumage nodding to the gale,
The lords of empire darken'd Albion's shore.
His dreary conquest shaggy, waste, and rude,   5
High from the prow the imperial eagle view'd:
  Beneath the proud bird's hateful shade
  Siluria's captur'd prince was laid
Silent and still and stern; the conqueror foe
Shook at the savage firmness of his brow.   10
While as the broad keel plough'd the briny way,
  O'er the pale cliffs, that lessen'd to the sight,
  The bearded Bards, in robes of radiant white,
With harps that glitter'd to the orb of day,
  Along the calm cerulean main   15
  Pour'd a bold inspiring strain;
And bade their monarch's towering soul
Proudly upborn disdain a foe's controul,
As Penmanmawr uplifts its awful form,
Assail'd by ocean-waves and Cambria's mountain storm.   20

. . .

O Prince, when loos'd from mortal clay
Thy spirit mourns the aerial way,   60
And joins our fathers' armed shades,
Brandishing their gleamy blades,
Tell them the cause in which they died,
Is Albion's buckler, Albion's pride:
Tell them each spot, whereon they bled,   65
With life-blood of the foe is red:
Tell them our babes are taught to wield
The curtled axe and bloody shield:
Though Rome's aerial eagle, streaming gore,
Sails darkly shadowing Britain's naked shore;   70
Though frowning from the cliff's projected height
Her haughty battlements our plains affright;

Yet tell them, their own dauntless zeal,
To guard and dignify our country's weal,
Glows in their faithful sons: and when again   75
They draw the morning gale on Sarum's plain,
Their limbs shall move unshackled, and their veins
Wander through sinews undebas'd by chains.
    That holy spark of freedom's flame,
They struck with life into our moulding frame,   80
    Tell them, deep in northern snow,
    On stormy hills, in mossy bogs,
    'Mid sickly marshes, blue with fogs,
On many a shiver'd cliff's dark-hanging brow,
Whose fearful fragments fill the vale below,   85
    Pure, vigorous, glowing, we maintain;
To prove our high descent from freeborn sires;
And, when their souls are veil'd in earth again,
To warm them in the womb with their own generous fires.

    That flame, O patriot Prince, shall glow   90
In native lustre on thy martial brow,
When thou return'st, beneath the beam of day
    To animate a kindred clay.
Then, when thou goest all terrible to wield
Trisingis' blazing faulchion o'er the field   95
When from thy aweful port the hosts retire,
Like stars before the sun's ascending fire;
When thy tall plumes in all their terrors rise,
And flame, like lightening, flashes from thy eyes;
Then shall our scythed chariots, as of yore,   100
    Wheel round the giddy steep,
    That overhangs the deep,
And headlong roll our foemen to the shore;
Again shall Druids look superior down
On mortal kings, and awe them with a frown;   105
The potent wand shall wave its magic round;
Through holy groves the golden axe resound;
    And altars, bright with flames, illume
    Another Mona's solemn gloom.

Then to the silent midnight orbs of fire,   110
    On moonshine banks of haunted streams,
'Mid grey oaks mellow'd by the night's wan beams,
    The Bard shall touch his silver wire,
And soothe the sleeping wanderer's fairy dreams:
While, as the soft suspended numbers sail,   115
Through the tall pines, that up the cavern'd steep
    Rise midway waving o'er the deep,
    In each soft murmuring gale
A warrior's troubled spirit seems to moan,
Or Misery's wasted form to pour her feeble groan.   120

Go then, O Albion's pride, and dauntless stand
At Cæsar's throne: think on thy native land,
Thy long illustrious line of freeborn sires,
And the proud blood that circles through thy veins.
    Though low debas'd by chains,   125
Though pale and wasted by the tyrant's hand,
'Tis thine to glow with thy fam'd father's fires:
    To bear unconquer'd the high mind;
    Thy dignity of being to revere;
What great souls own, what generous warriors feel,   130
    In simple boldness to reveal;
Through their own Jove, with red right arm uprais'd,
    In which the forked lightning blaz'd,
Sat, as to prepar'd to strike, and bent his brow severe.

So Claudius, laid on Tiber's viny mounds,   135
    Beneath Campania's sunny skies,
    And lull'd by music's tenderest sounds;
Whose eagle meets the morn on Ganges' stream,
And travels with the day, till eve's mild beam
Illumes the wave in Gallia's western bays;   140
    He, to whom marble temples rise,
    And altars, rich with perfumes, blaze;
    Who, number'd with the immortal gods above,
Hurling the bolts of fate, moves only less than Jove:

Ev'n he shall glow   145
With generous envy toward a captive foe;
And blushing wish, that far from shady bowers,
    Imperial domes and spiry towers,
His infant limbs had roll'd in Cambrian snow;
That Freedom, near romantic Vaga's tide,   150
Had hung her gleaming faulchion at his side;
    While the keen northern blast
Harden'd his manly sinews, as it pass'd;
    And the steep mountain hoar,
    And the wild torrent's roar,   155
Maintain'd that inborn nobleness of mind,
Which lifts and dignifies our common kind,
Firm as Plinlimmon's base, and free as ocean-wind.

    Such was the lofty strain,
Which, mingled with the murmur of the shores,   160
And melancholy sound of dashing oars,
Came, soft by distance, o'er the heaving main
From Albion's cliffs: – on whose romantic brow,
High o'er the world of waters towering grey,
Yet faintly linger'd the pale gleams of day,   165
While fearful darkness veil'd the waves below:
    Till deepening gradual, the dim night
Gains on the topmost disappearing height;
And all the starry skies with fires unnumber'd glow.

[Line 8] *Siluria's captur'd prince.* Caractacus, king of the Silures.

[Line 81] *Deep in northern snow.* The Britons, when defeated by the Romans,
retired into the north-west parts of the kingdom, and there remained un-
conquered.

[Line 90] *That flame.* This whole paragraph is founded upon the idea of
transmigration, and the return of the soul of Caractacus to reign again over
Britain.

[Line 121] *Go then, O Albion's pride.* The two following paragraphs are
founded upon the behaviour of Caractacus at the throne of Claudius Cæsar,
as described by Tacitus.

9. *William Sotheby, 'Llangollen. Written at the close of the Autumn 1792' (extract)*

Inscribed to the Honourable Robert Fulk Greville.

THOU that embosomed in the dark retreat
Veilest from profaner gaze thy hallowed seat,
Genius of wild Llangollen! once again
I turn to thy rude haunts, and savage reign:
'Mid the grey cliffs that o'er yon heights impend,   5
O'ershadowing mountains that the vale defend,
Woods whose free growth the gloom of midnight spreads,
And torrents foaming down their flinty beds,
Within thy sheltered solitudes confined,
At distance from the murmur of mankind,   10
I sooth to peace the cares of life awhile,
And woo, lone Nature's long-forgotten smile.

    Loved vale! when o'er thee beamed the spring-tide ray,
And from thy heights slow sunk the summer day,
From thy delightful scenery restrained,   15
Far off by fond solicitude detained,
I watch'd where pain's wan eye sad vigils kept,
Or hung upon the couch where languor slept:
Bright Autumn fading, ere my footstep came,
On the illumined forest ceased to flame.   20
But now while waning to his mournful end
He sinks from sight like a departing friend,
Swift let me trace the varied views around
Spread o'er the range of thy enchanted ground;
While yet upon the leaf pale hues appear,   25
And the last tint yet lingers on the year,
That like the flush of the faint hectic strays
Wan-gleaming as the bloom of life decays.

. . .

Dinas!* more beauteous thus in late decay
Thy castle, cloathed with pensive colors grey;   50
Bleak mountain! yet more beauteous thus thy head
Untraced but by the stranger's lonely tread,
Than in thy gorgeous day, when tyrant power
With trophies hung thy far-resplendent tower.
The British bard, at thy unhonored name,   55
Points to the wreck, a monument of shame.
"So fall the towers, by vengeful time defaced,
That stood when rebel arms their strength disgraced;
Moulder the walls that hid the traitor's head,
When freedom to the field her Britons led.   60
Wretch! that expired'st within yon rocky mound,
By solitude and terror circled round,
Vain was thy hope on EDWARD that reposed,
Vain the last wish thy dying breath that closed.
Yet ere the requiem bad thee peaceful rest,   65
Scarce cold the lip that uttered the request,
A stranger's hand usurped thy ancient power,
A stranger's banner glittered on thy tower.
Lo! the defenders grateful EDWARD gave
To sooth thy spirit hovering o'er the grave.   70
Stern avarice and murder stalk around,
Sole guardians thy forsaken infants found.
No parent on their death-bed drops the tear,
No parent strews with flowers their honoured bier.
But the rude hinds their fate obscure bewail,   75
Traced in the strange traditionary tale;
And village girls point weeping to the wave
Where fairies floated o'er their watery grave."

  So fly the dreams deluded youth recalls,
So fade the glories of the Gothic halls!   80
Where'er the castle reared its stately head,
Oppression prowled around, by murder fed.
Above the banquest foamed, and unrestrained
Riot's swoln lip the o'erflowing goblet drained;
While in the dungeon's gloomy cave beneath   85
Lurked famine, listening to the cry of death.

. . .

As bending o'er the bank, in pensive mood,
I gaze upon the swift-descending flood,   110
Torrents from crag to crag that ceaseless thrown
Wear the rough rocks, and smooth the polished stone;
Then whirled in eddies round the echoing cave,
Silver with fleecy foam the distant wave:
Visions of ancient glory swarm around,   115
And the dark glen becomes enchanted ground.
Warm inspiration views the wizards hoar
That listened to the floods prophetic roar,
And as the wave its changeful* current rolled,
The fate of nations, fall of kings foretold.   120
Bold lour at intervals the heights around,
Orb within orb, by Druid temples crowned,
Half hid beneath the earth huge CROMLECHS bend,
And the tall CARNEDDS lessening piles ascend.
Dark on the mountain's tempest-beaten head   125
Rude British forts their massy bulwarks spread.
And oft when time has battered down the piles,
And peace on the forgotten station smiles;
Though long the summer sun and winter snow
Has mellowed the deep soil that turfs their brow,   130
The rich grass spiring o'er the sheep-fed heath,
Points out the levelled turrets sunk beneath.
. . .

[Line 49] * "The remains of Dinas Bran, one of the primitive Welsh castles, nearly cover the summit of a vast conoid hill, steeply sloped on every side. The founder is unknown. In the reign of Henry III. it was the retreat of Gryffyd ap Madog, who traitorously confederating with the English against his countrymen, was obliged to secure himself from their vengeance in this aërial fastness.

On the death of Gryffyd, Edward I ungratefully bestowed on John Earl Warren the wardship of the eldest son of his old ally; as he did that of the second, on Roger Mortimer. These lords caused their wards to be drowned under Holt-Bridge; and took possession of their estates. An obscure tradition of this murder was current in the country under the fable of two young fairies, who had been there destroyed, in that manner."
          PENNANT's Tour in Wales.

[Line 119] * Drayton's Poly. Song X

10. Edward Williams (Iolo Morganwg), 'Winter Incidents, Written in 1777'

Bleak Winter comes with wrathful roar.
Exclude the tyrant! shut the door,
And let us blunt his nipping gale
With blazing hearths, with sparkling ale,
And lead the sullen hours along   5
With tale of old and mirthful song.
      No feather'd songster tunes a lay,
To cheer the short, the joyless, day;
Yon mournful blackbird mopes alone,
Has quite forgot his mellow tone;   10
How mute yon linnet on the thorn!
No joyous lark salutes the morn:
The screech-owl tells her doleful tale
Where warbled once the nightingale;
Wild geese with clamours fill the sky,   15
Their clank proclaims the tempest nigh;
Swans, fearful of the polar gales,
Seek shelter in *Silurian* vales;*
The sea-gull in the meadow screams,
And wood-cocks haunt lone thicket-streams;   20
Rude winds from hills *Brigantian*† blow,
And from their pinions shake the snow;
Whilst trembling stars, intensely bright,
Pour all their fulgence on the night;
The breeze with gellid rigour teems,   25
And turns to rock the languid streams,
Whilst, from its fount on yonder hill,
Unfetter'd runs the rapid rill.
The village boys with morn awake
To trace the surface of the lake,   30
And, thoughtless, run at passion's call
In slipp'ry paths, where many fall:
The just resemblance let me scan;
The *rash desire*, unthinking man;
Though seeming joy thy wish attends,   35
The fell deceit in ruin ends.

Observe yon prattling lisper strain,
To roll the snow-ball o'er the plain;
So misers heap, with sore turmoil,
What never can re-pay their toil.   40
  As trudging home beside the brook,
With health redundant in his look,
Yon sturdy farmer blows his nails,
And his unlucky lot bewails,
Not destin'd like the drunken 'squire,   45
To lounge before the parlour fire;
Man, discontented with his fate,
Ne'er sees the folly till too late.
  Now village curs, with echo'd howl,
Scare from her haunt the plaintive owl.   50
Foreboding billows loudly roar,
And cloath in foam the rocky shore;
We guard against the pelting rain,
'Twill soon with fury sweep the plain.
  Wise Industry, thou canst defy   55
The terror of a wintry sky;
When storms are fierce, and billows rude,
Thou canst with ease their force elude;
With smiling plenty store thy shed;
In warmth repose thy pillow'd head;   60
Pile high thy crackling hearth, and tune
A cheerful song to *rosy June.*
  Important in his elbow chair,
The village sage, in silver'd hair,
With self-applauding glee, repeats   65
His well-known tale of youthful feats:
He was a very *blade*, he says,
Not like your *louts* of modern days;
He won at wrestling many a prize;
Could nicely box a neighbour's eyes;   70
And, 'twas allow'd by all the town,
Could fairly drink a *Parson* down.
Thus, oddly thus, we grasp at fame,
Puff to the world an odious name.
How little is it understood,   75
That, to be *great*, we must be *good.*

Hark! from yon dell what frightful sound
Spreads thund'ring horror all around!
Sweet thrush! first herald of the Spring,
Joy warm'd my soul to hear thee sing;   80
What time appear'd the primrose pale,
Near my lone arbour in the dale;
Where warbled wild thy carols gay,
Prophetic of the lovely May;
Now, bleeding from thy mortal wound,   85
I view thee, flutt'ring, on the ground;
But cruelty could ne'er appal
The ruthless heart that doom'd thy fall.
    Thou, that in blood canst thus delight,
Steel well thy soul, court fame, and fight,   90
With well-directed cannon balls,
Knock down ten thousand harmless Gauls,
Drink human gore, and laugh thy fill
At Him who said, "*Thou shalt not kill.*"
I, who for *Britain*, *France*, and *Spain*,   95
Crave peace from Heav'n, and crave again,
Unmindful of the puffs of Fame,
Weep, and detest the warrior's name.
If, in life's road, it be my chance
To meet a *brother* born in *France*,   100
A stranger in the fangs of grief,
Where no kind hand affords relief;
He, though *contending cannons* roar,
Shall open find my friendly door;
And, spite of all that *Kings* command,   105
Find in my cot his *native land*,
My peaceful cot, secluded far
From Hell-born rage of ruthless war.
    Nature each cruel thought repels,
Rare is that heart where nature dwells;   110
Where soft compassion is combin'd
With ev'ry motion of the mind;
Where genial feelings form the man
On fearless *Love's* eternal plan.
    What midnight horrors, raging high,   115
Assemble in the stormy sky!

The forky lightening now descend;
But rest in peace, my foreign friend;
They thunder harmless o'er thy head,
Not level'd at this humble shed: 120
No dread we feel, an anger'd God
Finds here no vile *Oppressor's* rod:
Though 'tis thy lot awhile to part
From each dear object of thy heart,
All Nature, at *one* Great Command,   125
Shall guard them with parental hand;
Thou shalt behold again with joy,
Thy prattling girl, thy lisping boy;
And, doom'd in grief no more to roam,
Enjoy through life thy native home.   130

* *Seek shelter in* Silurian *vales*. In hard Winters the Vale of *Glamorgan* (part
of the ancient *Siluria* is frequented by many swans, from whence, I believe,
is unknown. They always depart when the frosts are over.

† *Hills* Brigantian. *Brigantium* was the ancient name of the Northern parts
of England.

11. Edward Williams (Iolo Morganwg), 'Solitude. From the Welsh. Written in 1789'

*From the Welsh.** Written in 1789.

Say, why, my friend, would'st thou persuade
Thy Bard to quit his tranquil shade?
He dwells contented with his lot,
Hid from the world in humble cot;
And, heedless of the glare of wealth,   5
Finds all he wants in peace and health;
With hopes, when well-matur'd by age,
To find himself a rural Sage.
    Sweet Solitude has peerless charms,
Where Virtue's glow the bosom warms;   10
Where waken'd Conscience feels no pain,
And Reason breaks dull Folly's chain;
Where Taste informs th' observant eye,
That can bright Nature's charms descry;
And where the strong, enlighten'd mind   15
Can in itself sweet converse find;
Can talk with Truth, too little known,
That in the Conscience rears her throne.
    He, that avoids the jar of strife,
Spends here unknown his quiet life;   20
The *Muse*, with *Fancy's* plastic pow'r,
Will visit oft his lonely bow'r;
Instruct him in the tuneful art,
Illume his mind, refine his heart;
And *Wisdom* shall his thought expand,   25
His soul is all at her Command:
His breast, where once wild Passion storm'd,
Is by Adversity reform'd;
Bless'd in th' event, his grateful mind
Adores the rod, and stands resign'd,   30
Submits, with reverential awe,
To gracious Heav'n's unerring law.
Restor'd by this to mental ease,
He feels the lore of Nature please;

And lays his head in downy rest,   35
Meek Innocence, upon thy breast;
Yet hears, with sorrow, from afar,
The madden'd world's eternal war;
Sees where the blameless heart is broke
By dire Oppression's galling yoke;   40
Where *Kings*, that *fiends incarnate* reign,
With human carnage load the plain;
For this his bosom heaves the sigh;
For this the tear streams from his eye.
O! when shall man from discord cease?   45
Rul'd by thy laws, thou *Prince of Peace*,
Obey thy mandates from above,
And own thy reign of endless *Love*.
     Behold, on *Afric's* beach, alone,
Yon sire that weeps with bitter moan;   50
She, that his life once truly bless'd,
Is torn for ever from his breast,
And, *scourged*, where *British Monarchs* reign,
Calls for his aid, but calls in vain;
His sons, on *Slav'ry's* shameless land,   55
Now bleed beneath a *Villain's* hand;
Their writhing frames how sorely gall'd!
Still *Britons* must be *Christians* call'd –
Their groans the wide horizon fill!
Vile *Britons!* 'tis your *Senate's* will –   60
I cease – those cruelties affright
A Muse that shudders at the sight.

* From the Author's own Welsh; and it is always so where no other name
is given.

*12. Edward Williams (Iolo Morganwg), 'Ode; Imitated
from the Gododin of Aneurin,* an ancient British
Bard, who wrote about the Year 550'*

1.

War's ireful havoc roll'd along,
    Its fury blaz'd with rapid flame;
She led the death-denouncing throng,
    Daughter of *Eudaf*, glorious name:
Her breast, more white than driven snow,   5
Feels, rending deep, the deathful blow;
    Aim'd well the *Saxon* flung his dart:
Her faithful heroes weep around,
View BRADWEN, breathless, on the ground!
    See the last blood stream from her heart!   10
We madden'd at the rage-inspiring sight;
Her eyes untimely clos'd in Death's eternal night.

2.

Fair leader of th' embattled host,
    Of BRITAIN's high-born soul possess'd,
In Youth's high-bloom for ever lost,   15
    We drench with tears thy lovely breast:
Now, stamping wild, we tear the ground,
Bid kindled Anger's trump resound,
    And meditate th' avenging blow
Burns in the soul resentment's fire,   20
We ruminate resistless ire,
    And hurl its horrors on thy foe:
Soon shall the piercing steel, th' unerring dart,
In search of sweet revenge explore that *Saxon's* heart.

3.

True, BRADWEN, to thy deathless name,   25
    We chace thy foes with wrath profound;
Fierce as the desolating flame,
    When heather'd* mountains blaze around.
Struck with Distraction's wild amaze,
We on thy blood-stain'd beauty gaze,   30

Whilst thy great soul ascends the sky;
We whet the blade, we grasp the lance;
Bid War's indignant rage advance;
    Thy death demands, their thousands die:
They fall, they load th' obstructed fields of war,   35
And Vengeance, true to thee, mounts her triumphant car.

4.

O! BRADWEN! 'twas a woful [*sic*] day,
    We gave to thee the trophied urn,
Whilst to supernal realms of day,
    Bright myriads hail'd thy blest return: 40
Long shall the glories of thy name
Stand foremost on the rolls of Fame,
    The Bard's high song for ever grace;
'Twas *this* reliev'd each aching breast!
We, with the soothing thought imprest,   45
    Kiss'd thy dead lips, our last embrace:
Till time expires, through distant ages far,
Thy tale shall rouse to life th' avenging soul of War.

5.

Again return illumin'd skies,
    Your task, ye Sons of Death, resume!   50
Britons! dead BRADWEN calls! arise,
    Revenge! revenge! her hapless doom!
With potent mead high fill the horn!
Bid songs of death hail up the morn!
    Loud raise the warrior's ancient lay!*   55
'Tis noon – proclaim the dire event!
How through fierce ranks on carnage bent,
    Stern Havoc tore his rapid way;
The Saxons fall, we view their mingled blood
Stream down the rugged brink, and swell the crimson'd flood.   60

6.

From toils of death we sought repose,
    Sleep chain'd us to th' unfeeling dead;
Till, wrapp'd in gloom, chill morn arose,
    And rous'd us from the gory bed;

O'er *Cattraeth's** field we wander far; 65
Trace, anxious trace, the track of war;
    Shroud in cold earth our honour'd slain;
Lost in th' astonishment of life,
We view the dreadful scene of strife,
    The slaughter'd legions heap the plain. 70
Terrific Monarch of the dreadful place,
Exulting Horror shews his heart-benumbing face.

      7.
One peaceful Sun again appears,
    No battle treads the mangled ground;
Afar no weeping mother hears 75
    Of clashing steel the dreadful sound.
Yon aged sire! – his wishes burn,
Hoping to see, with joy, return
    A darling son: but hopes are vain; –
Far, far, he lies depriv'd of breath; 80
Trod by th' exulting heel of death,
    That stalks a giant o'er the plain; –
Abhorring Nature, struck with wild affright,
Flies from the reeking field, and shudders at the sight.

      8.
At *Madoc's* tent the clarion sounds, 85
    With rending clangor hurried far;
From echoing dells each note rebounds,
    But when return the Sons of War?
Thou, sprung from dire necessity,
Dumb Peace, the desart yields to thee; 90
    Owns now thy melancholy sway;
Loud sounds the trump, and loud again, –
What trump can rouse th' unheeding slain? –
    What call awake the breathless clay? –
One, only *one,* hears the continued blast, 95
And, bleeding, crawls along the slaughter-mangled waste.

9.

One tent contains our living few,
  Each in fierce conflict sadly torn;
Uncheer'd we taste, with anguish view,
  Sad Victory's replenish'd horn;   100
See traversing the track of death,
With wilder'd look, with panting breath,
  New throngs possess'd of wretched life;
What doleful moans! what piteous cries!
Of wailing mothers rend the skies,   105
  Of orphan'd babe, and widow'd wife;
They tear their locks, and view the trampled host,
Where died their only joys, where all their hopes are lost.

10.

Struck dumb with grief, yon beauteous fair,
  Beside her clay-cold lover weeps;   110
Sweet maid! thy sighs are spent in air,
  On Death's eternal bed he sleeps.
He wakes no more to bless thy charms,
To glad thy soul with circling arms,
  With love in raptur'd looks confess'd: 115
O! turn away thy woful eyes,
They drench in vain the cheek that lies
  Unconscious on thy lovely breast,
Thy Bard's pierc'd heart sore feels thy rankling grief,
Can mingle tears with thine, but what can yield relief?   120

[Title] * ANEURIN was called *Myd-ym Beirdd*, i.e. Monarch of the Bards. He was brother to the celebrated GILDAS, author of the epistle, *De Excidio Britanniæ*. His *Gododin* [*sic*] is a noble poem; the first for poetical sublimity in the *Welsh* language; it is equally distinguished for the fine pathos of numberless passages, and is of considerable length; the subject of it is the battle of CATTRAETH, fought by the *Britons* under MYNYDDAWC EIDDIN against the *Saxons*. *Gildas* was, like his brother *Aneurin*, a Bard; and there are some fragments of his works still extant: There were two more of their brothers who were Bards; their names CEIAN and AVAN; and, in a manuscript in my possession, their brothers and sisters, to the number of twenty-four in the whole, sons and daughters of CAW O BRYDYN, are said to have been *Bards*;

and, what is more wonderful, *Attend, ye modern Bards!* they were SAINTS: — so *Monks* were called, in those times, in WALES. This CAW O BRYDYN was a petty prince of the OTTADINI, in *North Britain*; and having been driven out of his territories by the *Saxons*, he retreated into WALES with his sons and daughters, who thereupon entered on a monastic life; *Gildas* and *Aneurin* were of the monastery of ST. ILLUUS; and so, probably, were the others; or of the neighbouring monastery of ST. CADOC, in LLANCARVAN *(Carbani vallis)*, it would be natural for them to keep together as much as possible.

[Line 28] * *Heather.* in some parts of Wales, and in the North of England, is the same as heath or ling.

[Line 55] * *The warrior's ancient lay.* The *ancient Britons* had their *war-songs*, and a variety of them, adapted to various occasions; of these we have many still extant in manuscript: they are, for the most part, in *triplets*, which kind of verse if called *triban milwr*, i.e. the *warrior's triplet*.

[Line 65] * *Cattraeth.* Probably *Caturactonium*, in *Yorkshire*; for the battle was fought near the river *Derwenydd*, or *Derwent*.

13. Edward Williams (Iolo Morganwg), 'ADDRESS TO THE INHABITANTS OF WALES. Exhorting them to emigrate, with WILLIAM PENN, to Pennsylvania' (extract)

Written at Sea by an Anonymous Emigrant, about the Time of the first Settlement of that Colony, to which many Welsh Families went.

Translated from the Welsh.

1.

YE, sprung from BRITAIN's ancient race,
Whilst Tyranny, with shameless face,
  Enslaves your native plains;
Attend my tale, nor, with the crowd,
Mean vassals of the selfish Proud,   5
  Despise my friendly strains.

2.

A guiltless land involv'd in grief,
Your country mourns, and craves relief,
  With noblest claim to peace;*
Much injur'd land! for still in vain   10
Of treatment hard thy sons complain,
  Of wrongs that never cease.

3.

We daily feel the wrathful rod:
What is the crime? – we seek our GOD
  Where Conscience leads the way;   15
The *Priest* our bitter draught supplies,*
This we must bear, or shut our eyes
  To *Truth's* meridian ray.

4.

Oft as we fall, with piteous moan,
Before the great eternal throne,   20
    Th' *informer's* at our side;
Law quickly plies the leaden stroke,
We faint beneath the galling yoke
    Of Anti-Christian Pride.

5.

Pale Want on harmless brows appears,   25
Our thorny paths are drench'd with tears,
    Excessive ills we feel;
All *Hell* assails the batter'd head,
That's mangled by th' insulting tread
    Of stern Oppression's heel.   30

6.

The bread our industry supplied,
Is to the famish'd lips denied,
    Though feeble babes complain;
This bids thy soul, fond parent, bleed,
Thy scanty stores are all decreed   35
    The filching *Proctor's* gain.

7.

Whilst thus, in dire Affliction deep,
By villains dogg'd we sorely weep,
    And drag th' enslaving chain;
We fall a prey to gnashing Spite,   40
That listens, whilst in depth of night
    To Heav'n we dare complain.

8.

Conscience! thy call we must not hear,
But turn to thee the deafen'd ear,
    And violate thy laws;   45
Tyranic fiends we then may please,
And live with Hypocrites at ease,
    And gain the World's applause.

9.

But whilst, in thy determin'd way,
We name our God, and humbly pray,   50
　　For his illuming grace;
Persisting still in selfish views,
The soul-enslaving PRIEST pursues,
　　With HELL's unwearied pace.

10.

The prison gate soon opens wide,   55
In loathsome cells we must abide,
　　So *Laws infernal* doom;*
Till, from our lov'd relations torn,
In woful banishment we mourn,
　　And fill an early tomb.   60

11.

O! thou, possess'd of BRITAIN's Crown,
Is gratitude for ever flown
　　From thy relentless heart?
Hast thou forgot how CAMBRIA bled*
For thee, when at thy trampled head   65
　　The Rebel flung his dart?

12.

No plot, but for thy safety form'd,*
In Wales appear'd, when highly storm'd
　　Rebellion through the Land:
Yet, if to TRUTH we turn the mind,   70
Our blameless limbs thy fetters bind,
　　'Tis thus thy laws command.

13.

I saw, for thee, my *Father* slain,
Where on SAINT FAGAN's reeking plain,*
　　Glamorgan pour'd her blood: 75
Did with my widow'd mother weep,
Whilst in old ELY's channel deep,
　　Swell'd high the purple flood.

14.

Ye, that in War's wide grave were laid,
Your orphan'd sons are ill repaid   80
   For loyal blood you lost;
They seek their GOD, for this pursu'd,
By vile decrees – on billows rude
   Of Persecution tost.

15.

We'll drag no more this heavy chain,   85
No more in *Slavery's* realm remain,
   Where hell-born codes increase:
Though, tow'ring high, rude billows roar,
We'll cross them to yon distant shore,
   Where hide the Sons of Peace.   90

. . .

24.

Here, number'd with the truly great,
Rejoicing in the calm retreat,   140
   To Truth's black foes unknown;
The free-born mind, th' unfetter'd thought,
With sacred lore of *Conscience* fraught,
   He, fearless, calls his own.

25.

To slavish Doubt let others yield,   145
And fly, like dastards, from the field,
   When Truth her standard rears;
I scorn the Tyrant's rude controul,
Confide in HEAV'N that nerves my soul,
   And banish all my fears.   150

26.

Chains that enslave Britannia's isle
Long held my feet in durance vile,
   But sorrow soon will cease;
Kind PROVIDENCE unbars the den,
Gives me to 'scape, with bounteous PENN,   155
   To distant *Realms of Peace.*

27.

Led there by HEAV'N in woful times,
First were these far-sequester'd climes
　　To British worthies known;
These, from no native of the land   160
By conquest wrench'd with murd'ring hand,
　　We fairly claim our own.

28.

Boast, CAMBRIA, boast thy sceptred Lord, –
'Twas HE, thy MADOC, first explor'd*
　　What bounds th' Atlantic tide;   165
He, from the tumults of a Crown,
Sought shelter in a *world unknown*,
　　With HEAV'N his only guide.

29.

He soon, with joyful tale, return'd
To CAMBRIAN hills, where thousands mourn'd,   170
　　Scourg'd by fell Discord's hand;
Now, loos'd from HELL, she there appear'd,
With brother's blood her front besmear'd,
　　She triumph'd in the Land.

30.

At LUNDY's Isle what numbers meet;   175
All throng with joy to MADOC's fleet,
　　That first subdu'd the main;
They quit the gory sod of WALES,
Proud SNOWDON's height, SILURIAN vales,
　　And MONA's ravag'd plain.   180

31.

Fled from Contention's ireful crew,
To native cots they bid adieu,
　　Returning there no more;
But, through rude storms at endless war,
With PROVIDENCE their friendly star,   185
　　They seek the peaceful shore.

32.

We heard of late astonish'd Fame
Declare that still our MADOC's name*
    Bids Glory's trump resound
Where still, amid the desart wild,   190
A free-born race, of manners mild,
    Old *British* tribes are found.

33.

I thither fly with anxious haste,
Will brave all dangers of the waste,
    Range 'tangled woods about;   195
Pierce ev'ry corner, like the wind,
Till Death forbids, or surely find
    My long-lost brethren out.

34.

I'll teach them all the truth I know,
To them extol the lively glow   200
    Of soul-retaining grace;
And, heedless there of worldly gains,
Will glide through life with these remains
    Of BRITAIN's injur'd race.*

35.

Haste! and forsake your meagre hills,   205
Their woful rounds Oppression fills,
    O! think of no delays:
Where *Madoc's* offspring still abides,
Or in the Land where PENN presides,
    Will end our tranquil days.   210

36.

Adieu, GLAMORGAN, from whose vales
I'm driven far through stormy gales,
    O'er foamy billows wide;
Mayst thou, though fiends afflict thee sore,
Still thy *forbidden* GOD adore,   215
    Whatever ills betide.

[Line 9] * *With noblest claim to peace.* The lash of intolerant laws that were enacted about this time, and had been, it must be confessed, in some degree, justly provoked, fell with equal severity on the peaceful and the turbulent, on many of the most loyal as well as the seditious; and drove out of the Principality of *Wales* considerable numbers of people, who, for their loyalty as *subjects*, and their pacific principles as *Christians*, were entitled highly to the protection of their country, and even to a degree of indulgence, to which, perhaps, no other party could possibly support any claim.

[Line 16] * *The* Priest *our bitter draught supplies.* The Church of England, in those days, under the influence of one of those mistakes that are incidental to every thing that originates in *Human Nature*, was, it must be confessed, of a persecuting spirit; but this error it has, long ago, seen, acknowledged, and reformed; its present moderation is but little short of exemplary: *qære*, can so much be said of some of its opponent sects?

[Line 57] * *So laws infernal doom.* See the 16ᵗʰ Car. II. cap. 4.

[Line 64] * *How* CAMBRIA *bled.* The *Welsh*, one would have imagined, had, during the Civil Wars of *Cromwellian sanctity*, give the most unequivocal proofs of loyalty, but many of them dissented from the Church of England, which was then inspired by the true spirit of *Popery:* the Tigers of *Religious Persecution* were called up from their native *Hell*, their talons fastened in-discriminately on the *innocent* as well as the *guilty*, if any guilt could possibly exist in following the dictates of a tender, though, perhaps, mistaken, con-science; dissention was *absurdly*, or, more probably, *maliciously* considered as the grand characteristic of sedition; so, without the least reference to any other consideration, the *Welsh* Non-conformists were included amongst the supposed criminal: but the origin of dissention in *Wales* was very different from what it was in *England*. The Scriptures had in the days of ELIZABETH been translated into the *Welsh language*, but soon after it was, I know not for what good reason, though necessary to bring the *Welsh* over to the use, in common conversation, of the *English tongue*; to accomplish this, the Church service was performed every where in *English*, though not one in fifty, in most places, understood it. The *Welsh* companied that the *Church of England*, like that of *Rome*, with-held from the common people the Scriptures in their own language; a *Welsh Bible* could not be purchased; it was not in print. *Itinerant*, and many of them *lay* preachers arose, and formed numerous con-gregations; they, after many difficulties, obtained an edition of the Welsh Bible. This execrable policy, of attempting to force the *English language* on the *Welsh*, first occasioned the dissention amongst them, which, as the original

cause does still, in a great measure, exist, will in all probability end in their
total defection from the Established Church. *Truth* itself, when heavy loaded
with the armour of *Human Policy*, will sink to the ground; and the weapon,
that is by absurdity put into its hand, is the only one that can wound it.

[Line 67] * *No plot but for thy safety form'd.* This is strictly true: during the
Cromwelian Civil wars (and the same may be said of the rebellions of 1715 and
1745) not a single party was formed in *Wales* but in direct opposition to them.
Yet steadfast loyalty could not screen the poor injured *Welsh* from the scourge
of offended *Priestcraft*, whose infallibility they had presumed to dispute.

[Line 74] * *St.* FAGAN's *reeking plain. St. Fagan's* is a village on the banks of
the *Ely* river in the vale of *Glamorgan*. When the second Civil War broke
out in the year 1648, the Welsh were the first that took up arms in favour
of Charles the Second. Sir *Edward Stradling*, of *St. Donat's Castle*, Sir *Nicholas
Kemyss, of Keven Mably*, and Colonel *Powel*, raised, armed, and cloathed,
each of them, a thousand men within their own county of *Glamorgan*. These,
commanded by Major General *Stradling*, Sir *Nicholas Kemyss*, and Colonel
Powel, joined Major General *Langhorne* and Colonel *Poyer*, whose men had
been raised chiefly in the countics of *Brecon, Carmarthen,* and *Pembroke*; their
collected forge amounted to about eight thousand. *Oliver Cromwell*, hearing
of this, sent Colonel *Horton* before him with three thousand horse, and two
thousand foot, to *Wales*, and followed himself with what forces he could
spare: the two armies met at *St. Fagan's* on Monday May 8, 1648. Colonel
Horton, engaged by *Langhorne* and *Stradling*, was forced to give way; but,
being soon joined by three thousand more, dispatched by *Cromwell* to his
assistance, with a heavy train of artillery, such as had never been before seen
in *Wales*, he charged the van of the *Welsh* forces, who were all undisciplined
and raw, with much resolution. Having withal the great advantage of the
horse and artillery, and calling out all the while to his men to reflect on the
danger they were in, the country being full of enemies, the Royal army
after a bloody conflict of two hours was entirely routed: about three thousand
were slain, and as many taken prisoners. Sir *Nicholas Kemyss* and his men,
having been cut off by an ambuscade, retired to *Chepstow Castle*, which
they, for about three weeks, very manfully defended; but Colonel *Pride*,
arriving with his heavy artillery, made a breach, and carried the castle sword
in hand. Sir *Nicholas Kemyss* was there put to death in a manner so horribly
barbarous and cruel, that no less a genius than that of *Cromwell* could ever
have suggested. The battle of *St. Fagan's* gave, it is said, sixty-five widows to
the single parish of *St. Fagan's*, and upwards of seven hundred to the county
of *Glamorgan:* when harvest came, the hay was mown, and the corn reaped,

chiefly by women; for of men there were not a number half sufficient for these purposes left by the slaughtering sword of war. See Brotherton's "Life of Oliver Cromwell," edit. 1743; from which, and some Welsh memorials, this account has been collected.

There were living in *Glamorgan*, about thirty years ago, several old people that remembered the battle of *St. Fagan's:* one of them assured me, that the river *Ely* was actually reddened by human blood; yet, with all its sufferings, with all its unimpeached loyalty, so harassed were the inhabitants of *Glamorgan* by the scourge of *Parsoncraft*, that great numbers of them were obliged to fly, during the reign of *Charles* the Second, from the ruin that their native country had unjustly heaped on them, to the wilds of America.

[Line 164] * *Thy Madoc*. Many of our Welsh historians assert, that America was discovered, about the year 1170, by *Madoc*, son of *Owain Gwynedd*, Prince of *Wales*. We have manuscript accounts of this discovery that were written before the birth of *Columbus*. Dr. *David Powel*, in Queen *Elizabeth's* time, says, in his History of Wales (on the authority of *Guttyn Owain*, who wrote in *Welsh* in King *Edward* the Fourth's time), that *Madoc*, in hopes of discovering the lands that lay beyond the *Atlantic* (of which there were ancient manuscript accounts, as well as traditions, in *Wales)*, and of finding there a retreat from the horrors of intestine wars which then deluged all *Wales* with blood, resolved on a voyage of discovery, and, sailing westward, arrived in less than two months on the coasts of a fine fertile country, destitute of inhabitants: leaving about one hundred of his men behind, he returned to *Wales*, and as soon as possible set about preparing another fleet for a second expedition; telling his countrymen what a fine country he had dis-covered, where they might, uninterrupted, enjoy liberty, peace, and plenty, representing to them, on the other hand, what barren rocks his brethren and nephews were, with hands of murder, contending for: so having prevailed on many to go with him, he set sail from from *South Wales* with a fleet of ten ships, full of such persons of both sexes as preferred peace to discord. This second voyage occurred in the year 1195, according to Sir *Thomas Herbert*, who wrote about the year 1635, and, having free access on all occasions to the noble collection of *Welsh* manuscripts in the library of *Ragland Castle*, had better opportunities of tracing the history of this remarkable event than any other person living. The total destruction, by fire, of this library has not yet been brought into the list of *Oliver Cromwell's* glories; it is time, however, that it should. Long! very long! to time's remotest period! shall the curse of *Welsh literature* attend the detestable name of *Oliver Cromwell*. For farther accounts of Prince *Madoc's* discovery of *America*, see the History of Wales, by *Wynne*, p. 195, &c. and *Warrington's*, p. 309; *Herbert's* Travels, &c.

[Line 188] * *We heard of late, &c.* Very soon after the settlement of *Virginia* and other parts of *North America* by the *English*, accounts were received of a tribe of *Welsh Indians* in the interior part of the Continent; and at this time there are, in *Wales* and *America, Welshmen* living who have conversed with these people, who are now, as it appears from numerous and well-authenticated accounts, seated on the river *Missouri*, about five hundred miles above its junction with the *Mississippi*. See Gent. Mag. vol. LXI. part I. pp. 329, 386, 534; part II. pp. 612, 693, 795, 800; Dr. Williams's Enquiry concerning the first discovery of America; and his Farther Observations on the Discovery of America.

[Line 204] * BRITAIN's *injur'd race.* The *Welsh* still retain a lively sensibility of the numerous injuries that they have, through a long succession of ages, experienced from the *Coritani, Beligians, Scots, Picts, Romans, Saxons, Danes, Normans,* &c. &c. and complaints of this nature are, to this day, the frequent themes of the *Ancient British* Muse.

14. Edward Williams (Iolo Morganwg), 'The Horrors of War, a Pastoral'

Written in Answer to a Soldier's Request, about the Time when the News arrived
of General ELLIOT's *Achievements at Gibraltar.*

AMYNTOR. CORYDON.

1.
AMYNTOR.

Still, CORYDON, still on the plain,
In joyless obscurity wasting thy days;
   Unheedful, an insolent swain,
Whilst honour invites, and lays open her ways!
   This life of a shepherd forsake,   5
More brilliant employments of glory pursue;
   To nobler conceptions awake,
Keep deathless renown, a sole object, in view;
   Thou, known to the nations around,
Shalt live, with bright Fame's immortality crown'd.   10

2.
CORYDON.

Contented I live on my farm,
And all the proud sons of Ambition despise;
   Thy soul feels a constant alarm,
Is toss'd in a storm, on a shadow relies.
   Where cheerful tranquillity reigns,   15
And Virtue's true joys are more valued than wealth,
   O! give me the peaceable plains;
The pleasures that flow from Contentment and Health:
   Unknown to the vultures of Pride,
I'll humbly, through life, a meek shepherd abide.   20

3.

AMYNTOR.

But thou canst the musical verse
Energic, attune to the trumpet of Fame;
    Canst Valour's atchievements rehearse,
The glories, unrival'd, of heroes proclaim.
    Then bid thy bold numbers resound,   25
And give all thy soul to the rapture of song;
    With bright Immortality crown'd,
Thy Muse shall be led in her laurels along:
    See the fields where her enemy lies,
And Victory's shouts are ascending the skies.   30

4.

CORYDON.

And hast thou no bosom to feel
The weapon of Death in that enemy's heart;
    Oh! how can the slaughtering steel
Such horrible warmth to thy wishes impart!
    Let harden'd Brutality raise   35
Her shout to the skies, and with misery jest,
    Deep Sorrow shall mourn in my lays;
I warriors abhor, and their fame I detest,
    Who, drowning Humanity's voice,
Can, wading through blood, with Infernals rejoice.   40

5.

AMYNTOR.

For valour and conquest renown'd,
All ages, all nations, the hero revere;
    Whilst beaming effulgence around,
He walks like a giant in Glory's career;
    When home he returns from the war,   45
What songs of applauses resound in his ways!
    He triumphs in Victory's car,
And voices imperial are loud in his praise;
    The world shall its warriors adore,
When monarchs entomb'd are remember'd no more.   50

6.

CORYDON.

No cries of weak orphans avail,
Whilst calling on fathers that never return;
    Sad widows, unpity'd, bewail,
See thousands, unheeded, in misery mourn;
    War's fell desolation extends,   55
O'erwhelming the land like a hurricane wide:
    Whilst gladden'd Ferocity rends
The glittering domes of tyrannical Pride;
    Where, class'd with the merciless great,
The warrior at soul is a demon complete.   60

7.

AMYNTOR.

I now to the battle repair,
No dangers of death can my bosom appall;
    I'll hurl through the thundering air
The lightings of death on the treacherous GAUL:
    A scourger of insolent SPAIN,   65
At BRITAIN's command like an eagle I fly;
    I'll wade through the blood of her slain,
A son of renown, I will conquer or die;
    Thus, ranking with heroes of old,
Shall the fields that I won through long ages be told.   70

8.

CORYDON.

The GAUL and the SPANIARD I deem
Friends, innocent neighbours, and brothers to me:
    More warm in my peaceful esteem,
When slander'd by despots, and worried by thee;
    When roars thy rude cannon aloud,   75
And utters thy soul in its horrible breath;
    Despising thy sycophant crowd,
I mourn, sorely mourn, for those victims of death.
    Talk no more of thy pupil of Fame,
I've a soul that abhors his detestable name.   80

9.

AMYNTOR.

I frighten away from the land
Each insolent foe that would sorely molest;
   And guard with my death-dealing hand,
The peace and the plenty by shepherds possess'd.
   The rustic, at ease in his cot,   85
May startle, when roars the loud cannon afar;
   But all that can charm in his lot,
Stern Valour protects and the terrors of war:
   Then join in the dignified song,
That rolls the bright glories of heroes along.   90

10.

CORYDON.

Would princes, like shepherds in peace,
The dictate of innocent NATURE obey,
   AMBITION's wild ravings would cease;
The kindlers of discord would vanish away;
   Then WISDOM, ineffably bright,   95
Would o'er the wide world in BENEVOLENCE reign;
   And LOVE, that meek angel of light,
With happiness crown'd would inhabit the plain;
   With laws on BENIGNITY's plan,
Would REASON preside in the dwellings of man.   100

11.

AMYNTOR.

Then still in oblivion remain,
Thou shepherd, ignobly regardless of praise;
   With cowardly sheep on the plain,
In stagnant rusticity wasting thy days:
   I live the support of a crown,   105
That centers in valour its ultimate aim;*
   Consigning my deeds of renown,
To nations unborn that shall honour my name:
   Whilst blended with glories of kings,
My fame in the trump of loud ecstacy rings.   110

12.

CORYDON.

 I see thy detestable heart,
To slav'ry subdu'd by the demon of Pride;
 But nought of sophistical Art
Can the tinge of thy soul, and its villainies hide:
 Go combat those insolent foes,   115
The passions malignant that rule in thy breast:
 Where humble BENEVOLENCE glows,
The vot'ries of PEACE are eternally blest:
 True glories await them above,
Where life never ends, in the mansions of LOVE!   120

* *That centers in valour, &c.* War and conquest are, generally speaking, the *aim* and *ambition* of monarchs in all ages; to them the slaughtering of 40 or 50,000 subjects, whose families are thereby reduced to misery and ruin, is a thing of no moment, though this answers no other end but that of gratifying the pride, resentment, or avarice, of a very few individuals. It is obviously certain that *Christianity*, with its inseperably-attendant Arts and Sciences, has (notwithstanding the vices that still too much prevail) so far civilized its own part of the world, that the art of *war is learned no more*; *swords* have long since been *beat into ploughshares*, and *spears into pruning-hooks* by all, except our still *unchristianized* RULERS, and their *minions*. Were only the governments in this respect quiescent, it is absolutely certain, that in no country in Europe could any set of men, however ferocious and unprincipled, so assemble and embody themselves together as to be able to commit public declarations on any neighbouring people; not the least disposition to any outrage of this nature remains amongst those who constitute the great majority of the BRITISH nation; and the same may be said of every other *Christian* nation. When *Church and State* are equally civilized with those those Communities, over whom they still *rule with rods of iron,* the *Christian world* will no longer see *nation lift upward against nation.*

15. Edward Williams (Iolo Morganwg), 'Ode on Converting a Sword into a Pruning Hook'

Recited on Primrose Hill, at a Meeting of ANCIENT BRITISH BARDS, Resident in London, Sept 22, 1793, being the Day whereon the Autumnal Equinox occurred, and one of the four grand solemn Bardic Days.*

Gwir, yn erbyn y Byd
          Motto of the *Ancient Bards of Britain.*
In English – *Truth, against all the World!*

"And they shall beat their swords into plough-shares, and their spears into pruning-hooks; nation shall not lift up sword against nation; neither shall they learn war any more." ISAIAH, ch. ii. ver. 4.

1.

Fell weapon, that in ruthless hand
          Of warrior fierce, of despot king,
Hast long career'd o'er ev'ry land,
          Hast heard th' embattled clangors ring;
Wrench'd from the grasp of *lawless Pride,*   5
With reeking gore no longer dy'd,
          I bear thee now to rural shades,
          Where nought of Hell-born War invades;
Where plum'd AMBITION feels her little soul;
          And hiding from the face of day   10
          That dawns from HEAV'N, and drives away
          Those fiends that love *eternal Night,*
She, with rude yell, blasphemes the SONS of LIGHT,*
That bid her deathful arm no more the world control.

2.

I saw the *Tyrant* on her throne,   15
          With wrathful eyes and venom'd breath,
Enjoy the world's unceasing groan,
          And boast, unsham'd, her fields of death;
When through the skies her banners wav'd,
When, *drunk with blood,* her legions rav'd,   20
          Her *Priest* invok'd the *Realms above,*
          Dar'd at thy throne, thou GOD of LOVE,

Call for the thunders of thy mighty will,
    To storm around the guiltless head,
    To strike a *peaceful brother* dead;*   25
Whilst blasphemies employ'd his tongue,
The gorgeous Temple with loud echoes rung;
I felt my shudd'ring soul with deepest horror chill.

             3.

I saw the *Victor's* dreadful day,
    He, through the world, in regal robe,   30
Tore to renown his gory way;
    With carnage *zon'd* th' affrighted globe:
Whilst from huge towns involv'd in flame
The *Monster* claim'd immortal fame,
    What lamentable shrieks arose,   35
    In all th' excess of direst woes!
Loud was the *Sycophant's* applauding voice:
    Together throng'd the sceptred band,
    Hymn'd by the *Fiends* of ev'ry land:
    How mourn'd my soul to hear the tale   40
Of sad Humanity's unpity'd wail!
And each *Imperial dome* with horrid shouts rejoice!

             4.

But hear from HEAV'N the dread command,
    It gives to speed that awful hour,
When from OPPRESSION's trembling hand   45
    Must fall th' *insulting rod of pow'r,*
Long vers'd in mysteries of war,
She scyth'd her huge triumphant car;*
    Her lance with look infuriate hurl'd;
    Bade fell Destruction sweep the world;   50
She wing'd her CHURCHILL's name* from pole to pole:
    Now brought before th' *eternal throne,*
    Where *Truth* prevails, all hearts are *known,*
    She, self-condemn'd, with horrid call,
Bids on her head the rocks and mountains fall,   55
To shield her from the wrath whose venging thunders roll.

5.

Thou, *strength of Kings*, with aching breast,
    I raise to Thee the mournful strain;
    Thou shalt no more this earth molest,
    Or quench in blood thy thirst again.   60
Come from rude *War's* infernal storm,
And fill this hand in alter'd form,
    To *prune the peach, reform the rose*,
    Where in th' expanding bosom glows
With warmest ardours, ev'ry wish benign: 65
    Mine is thy day so long foretold
    By HEAVEN's illumin'd Bards of old,
    To feel the rage of Discord cease,
To join with Angels in the SONGS OF PEACE,
That fill my kindred soul with energies divine.   70

6.

Dark ERROR's code no more enthrals,
    Its vile infatuations end;
Aloud the trump of Reason calls;
    The nations hear! the worlds attend!
Detesting now the craft of Kings,   75
Man from his hand the weapon flings;
    Hides it in whelming deeps afar,
    And learns no more the skill of war;
But lives with NATURE on th' uncity'd plain:
    Long has this *earth* a captive mourn'd,   80
    But *days of old** are now return'd;
    We PRIDE's rude arm no longer feel;
No longer bleed beneath Oppression's heel;
For TRUTH to LOVE and PEACE restores the world again.

7.

The dawn is up, the lucid morn,   85
    I carol in its golden skies;
The Muse, on eagle-pinions borne,
    Through Rapture's realm prophetic flies;
The battle's rage is heard no more,
Hush'd is the storm on ev'ry shore;   90
    See *Lambs* and *lions* in the mead
    Together play, together feed,

Crop the fresh herbage of perennial Spring:
   From eyes that bless the glorious day
   The scalding tears are wip'd away;   95
   Raise high the song! 'tis HEAV'N inspires!
In chorus joining with seraphic lyres,
We crown the PRINCE OF PEACE, he reigns th' ETERNAL KING!

Duw a phob Daioni.

[Subtitle] * The four grand solemn Bardic days are, of ancient usage, the two equinoxes, and the two solstices: the *new* and *full moons* are also, subordinately, solemn Bardic days: these are the conspicuous days, we may say *holidays*, of NATURE, and were, doubtless, observed long before the institution of any other *solemn, sabbatical,* or *festival,* days: this, and many other usages of the *Ancient British Bards*, bear the stamp of, and are obviously retained from, remotest antiquity; these customs are not known to have been discontinued or suspended in any age whatever, but have always, to the present day, been observed. This is a matter of no less *curiosity* than of *wonder* that it should not have been long ago noticed; but the *Ancient British Bardism* has for ages been in the hands of those who ranked not with the higher classes, and is retained only in those very sequestered and mountainous places that are seldom, if ever, visited by literary men. *Bardism* has also been for time immemorial under some degree of persecution; its regular professors are known in *Glamorgan* by the nick-name of *Gwyr Cwm y felin,* and generally supposed to be *infidels, conjurors,* and we know not what. The *North Walian* BARDS, as they call themselves, but improperly, of whose meetings we sometimes of late meet with accounts, know nothing at all of the *ancient* and *genuine Bardism.*

[Line 13] * *Blasphemes the Sons of Light.* The renovated state of religion, and of every thing else, promised to the world in the *Christian prophecies,* is entirely subversive of all the present establishments in *Church and State,* and will, of course, whenever any thing of it appears in the world, if it is to be a thing of this world, be opposed with might and main by the *priesthoods,* &c. of every country; for this reason, the morning of the glorious day will be overcast with clouds, and very stormy.

[Line 25] * *Strike a peaceful brother dead.* What can we conceive so horrid as the blasphemous idea of *wheedling* the ALMIGHTY to become a party in the *diabolical* contentions and *throat-cutting matches* of the great men of this, little less than, *infernal* world.

[Line 48] * *Scyth'd her huge triumphant car.* Alluding to the war chariots of the *Ancient Britons*, that were on all sides armed with long and sharp *scythes*, as history tells us, which made terrible havoc, when they were furiously driven into the ranks of their enemies.

[Line 51] * *Her Churchill's name. Churchill*, the warring *Duke of Marlborough*, was, in private life, a most execrable character; and such are the characters of too many *great warriors*.

[Line 81] * *Days of old are now returned.*] The *Ancient of days* in the *Prophet Daniel* may, with some plausibility, be supposed to mean no more than the restoration of the primeval state of *Innocence, Peace,* and *Benevolence.*

16. Jane Cave, 'THOUGHTS On the PRESENT TIMES; Written some Time after the PROCLAMATION for the late General FAST'

A FAST proclaim'd! another Fast!
    Nature recedes with dire alarms;
We dread the future, – mourn the past; –
    And all the world repairs to arms!

When times are big with great events!   5
    When empires rise, or *Monarchs* fall!
When famine, plague, or war torments!
    And horror fills this earthly ball!

When thousands undistinguish'd bleed,
    And mingle in one common gore;   10
When falls the rider and his steed,
    And life's bright day of hope is o'er!

To *this* or *that* misguided man,
    No more impute the wond'rous cause;
What mortal can reverse the plan   15
    Of sacred Heaven's unerring laws?

If e'en a sparrow cannot die,
    'Till God the fatal mandate send;
Shall *Kings*, yea *kingdoms* bleeding lie
    By *chance's* weak uncertain hand?   20

Great potentate whom hosts adore,
    How vast thy infinite designs!
What human thought can e'er explore
    The depth of thy unfathom'd mines?

When Isr'el lost his fav'rite son,   25
    By jealous brethren sold away;*
Which brother thought the deed was done
    To give them bread some future day?

And when the youth in prison lies,‡
    By Woman's false infernal word;   30
What sage philosopher descries
    'Twou'd lead to make him Egypt's lord?

Who e'er conceiv'd the infant found,†
    As tho' on chance's billows tost!
Was destin'd by his GOD to drown,   35
    Great Pharaoh and his mighty host?*

All Israel's children long had sigh'd,
    Beneath oppression's iron rod;
And long had for redemption cried;
    At length their suit ascends to GOD!   40

The Lord by Moses thus applies:
    "Let all my captive people go;"
But ah! the King his suit denies,
    And hence unheard-of judgments flow!

Locusts, lice and frogs prevail,   45
    Plagues of every kind abound!
Thunder roars, and fiery hail;
    Death in ev'ry house is found!

Thus GOD by vengeance cloth'd in blood,
    Set Is'rel's suff'ring captives free;   50
And delug'd in the mighty flood,
    All who deny'd that liberty.

How long the sons of *Christian* lands,
    Or rather lands which bear that name;
Have bound with dire oppressive bands,   55
    Let *Afric's* hapless race proclaim!

Shall not their groans like incense rise?
    And mercy plead their injur'd cause;
Till vengeance through the nations flies,
    Which sanction murder by their laws!   60

Great *Wilberforce*,* – soft pity's friend!
   Go on, – pursue thy grand design!
Till horrid slavery shall end,
   And *Afric's* sons with freedom shine!

Descend thou bright celestial Dove!   65
   Haste with the olive branch of peace;
Deluge a sinful world in love,
   And bid the floods of discord cease!

Conduct the hand which guides the helm,
   Fair freedom's foes convince, – annoy;   70
May *truth* and *justice* sway the realm,
   And each opposing voice destroy.

Our Sov'reign and his royal train
   Preserve, and be their constant guide;
Let *mercy* triumph thro' his reign,   75
   And be the King his people's pride!

* Gen. xxxvii. 28.

‡ Gen. xxxix. 20.

† Exod. ii. 3.

[Line 36] * Exod. xiv. 27.

[Line 61] * Member for Yorkshire, who has repeatedly exerted his influence in Parliament for the Emancipation of the Slaves.

17. *Hester Piozzi, Untitled ['Can impious France, though frantic grown']*

Can impious France, though frantic grown,
Drag her pale VICTIMS from the throne
    While royal blood is spilt!
Yet think conniving Heaven will spare
To hurl down thunder-bolts, and share   5
    In such gigantic guilt?

No; tardy-footed Vengeance stalks
Round her depopulated walks,
    And waits the dreadful hour
When desp'rate Wretchedness shall rave,   10
And hot Contagion fill the grave,
    And Famine bid devour.

Rise warriors, rise! with hostile sway
Accelerate the destin'd day,
    Revenge the royal cause;   15
Exerting well-united force,
Tear those decrees that would divorce
    True liberty from laws.

18. Edward Williams (Iolo Morganwg), 'Church and King
rampant or Satan let loose for a thousand years'

Tri Dyn a fynnant fyw ar eiddo arall Brenin offeiriad a lleidr.

This piece was occasioned by a blasphemous Song that appeared lately (1794)
in a newspaper, its chorus Church & King.

1.
Now loosed from his mighty chain
Old Satan comes with man to dwell,
Thrives here for ever to remain,
Aided by all the Pow'rs of hell
See from his <u>pitt</u> infernal hurld,   5
Comes what this earth with horror fills
In whelming ravage o'er the world
A pouring flood of countless ills.

2.
Gigantic ills, too lately known
The canting priesthood first we name,   10
With Kingship on a tyrants throne
Whose flinty bosom feels no shame,
In these all other ills abound
Hark o'er the land their titles ring,
In slavish phrase that's bray'd around   15
The _{madden'd} rant ^{cant} of Church and King.

3.
Attorneys that no conscience feel
Drive on the pettifogging trade
The man of blood with heart of steel
In war employs the murd'ring blade   20
In lordly pomp adored by fools
Dwells honour that infernal thing
All these come tutor'd from the schools
Of hellish pride of Church and King.

4.

See fashion tricked in tinsel'd plumes   25
Walk forth with ideots [*sic*] at her tail
To check what her <u>vile</u> ^{low} <u>Tribe</u> assumes
No pow'rs of reason can prevail
At fashion's call to take your purse
Yon pistol'd robbers on the wing,   30
How patronized this dreadful curse!
By Tawdry courts by Church and King.

5.

He from the dirt of rapine sprung
The rich monopolist appears
With insult on his boastful tongue   35
He battens on the paupers tears.
More baneful venom o'er the land
A pestilence could never fling
Than rude monopoly's fierce band,
The vulture brood of Church and King.   40

6.

What lawless mobs along the street
Roll tiger-like with savage roars
Hurl brutal rage on all they meet
Demolish windows, break our doors,
They brandish high th' assassins knife   45
These <u>pitt</u> and <u>reaves</u> together bring,
To burn your house to take your life
In worship _{homage} due to Church and King.

7.

Religion flies our fetter'd land
From persecution speeds away   50
For shelter seeks a foreign strand
Where dawns of truth a summer's day.
'Tis Freedom's woful doom to see
Fiends in our Isle together cling,
To rule by spies and perjury   55
Enslaving all to church and King.

8.
Our feet are every where beset
By wily spies an odious clan
How lies conseald [*sic*] th' informer's ^{oppressor's} net
for those who claim the rights of man,   60
On all that seek the paths of peace
What vollied slanders Villains fling,
What ireful shouts that never cease,
For wars, for murders, church and King.

9.
Deluded sons of Britain's Isle   65
Obey the swindling minion's voice
Nor see what fraudful arts beguile,
But, madden'd, in their shame rejoice,
Idolatry from shore to shore
Bids Blasphemous responses ring   70
Enacts her laws, and bids adore
The infernal God of Church and King.

10.
Sorely complains degraded man
Of ills that ^{powers that} would his reason blind,
Of Laws meant only to trepan   75
But not to form the virtuous mind.
Words are too feeble to relate
What horrid ills forever spring
From maxims of tyrannic state
From perjured clubs of church and king   80

11.
With naked limbs, a ghastly form
unceasing groan and tearful eye
exposed amid the wintry storm,
Behold despairful poverty.
Say, mourner, why thy bosom bleeds   85
What woes thy soul with anguish wring
Alas! thy wretchedness proceeds
From grasping claws of church and king

12.

Hard is our fortune to remain
Where evil's mighty deluge rolls;   90
Where principles despotic reign
Infernal as monarchic souls:
Vice glories in her mountain'd mass
Corruption takes unbounded swing
and with a shameless front of brass   95
Concenters all in Church and King.

13.

O Let us to some desert wild
Haste o'er the stern atlantic wave
There live with freedom self exiled
From realms where bloody Tyrants rave   100
and, thanking heav'n, there shall we thus
In strains of joy together Sing
"Good Lord! thou hast deliver'd us
From <u>Pitt</u> and <u>Spies</u>, from <u>Church and King</u>"

14.

Thou that by Nature nobly blest   105
Hast view'd her charms from earliest youth
and, of an eagle's eye possess'd
Canst bear th' effulgent blaze of truth:
Haste! thy devoted head conceal!
Fly to the Pole on speedful wing,   110
Or thou shalt soon unpitied feel
Th' infuriate fang of Church and King.

19. Edward Williams (Iolo Morganwg), 'John Bull's Litany'

Translated from the Ancient British of Iolo Morganwg, A Mad Welsh Bard, With Notes, and a Key, &c &c, Anything to please the Critics, By one of the Swinish Multitude.

Pandæmonium, printed by Edmund and Teague, and sold by Paddy Macdonald, at the sign of Burke's Head, in Quibble Court, All-fools Alley, in the year one thousand seven hundred and nine o' clock.

John Bull's Litany, to be sung or said in all churches and chapels in England and Wales and the Town of Berwick upon Tweed, and all the people shall say <u>amen</u> so be it.

1.
Thou, truly Majestic, on heaven's high throne,
Our oppressors are strong, a fierce multitude grown,
For mercy we call and to thee make our moan.
   Have mercy upon us.

2.
Oh! spare us a while from the vultures of Law,   5
That feed on man's blood with insatiable maw,
Till to some foreign desert we in safety withdraw, **a**
   Spare us good Lord.

3.
Deliver us all from the Tygers of Pow'r
That seek ev'ry moment our souls to devour   10
Oh! guard us from these in this ~~dangerous~~ perilous hour,
   Good Lord deliver us.

4.
From Falshood canine, that runs, madden'd, around,
~~Who~~ that strives to give Truth an incurable wound,
And exults to see Liberty bleed on the ground,   15
   Good Lord deliver us.

5.

From <u>blood-thirsty K——gs</u>, ^{blockheads enthroned} who make slaughter their sport,
And, shameless to lies, for pretences resort
From the ravings, the Pride and punctilios of Court, **b**
       Good Lord deliver us.   20

6.

From <u>Edmund</u> O Paddy, that bull-making dolt,
Who cannot _{ne'er could} distinguish a pig from a colt, **c**
From all Fools of his cast that shoot rashly the bolt,
       Good Lord deliver us.

7.

From conspirating Courts, and their infamous work,   25
The Russian she Bear, the Pope, Emp'ror, and Turk,
The scandal of Reeves, and the daggers of Burke, **d**
       Good Lord deliver us.

8.

From frivolous Pomp, of no follies ashamed,
From the meanness of Pride, still to reason untamed,   30
From <u>Capitals</u> rude that <u>Corinthian</u> are named, – **e**
       Good Lord deliver us.

9.

From things without meaning called Garters and stars,
From Religion a Trade that all Piety mars,
And from ~~Monarchs~~ _{Tyrants} whose thrones are supported by Wars,   35
       Good Lord deliver us. **f**

10.

From pack'd special Juries, a rascally crew, **g**
From addresses of slaves that bid _{freedom} Reason adieu
And from his <u>W–nch–lfa</u>'s nonsense misnomer'd <u>True Blue</u>
       Good Lord deliver us. **h**   40

11.
From Archy MacBlunder, that gribbler in grain, i
From Placemen who faint at the name of <u>Tom Paine,</u>
And from Sycophant knaves who take God's name in vain,
          Good Lord deliver us. k

12.
From Tyranie's [*sic*] frown, stifling Freedom's debate,   45
From brazen-faced Parsoncraft's infidel prate,
And from making the Church a vile Engine of state, l
          Good Lord deliver us.

13.
From the broods of self-interest with dagger in hand,
That drive humble Reason away from the Land,   50
From these Journey-men K—s, a detestable band, m
          Good Lord deliver us.

14.
From high-titled Villany, fleecing the Poor,
From Peers that bark merit away form the door,
From a Church that on Earth reigns an infamous whore   55
          Good Lord deliver us.

15.
O! Monarch of Heaven! thou King of all Kings!
From thy Laws, whilst obey'd, all felicity springs,
Defend us from all these detestable things.

16.
Let Reason once more to the World be restored,   60
Uniting Mankind in its peaceful accord,
We, Britons, beseech thee to hear us good Lord.

a <u>Till to some foreign desert we safely withdraw.</u> Such is the great expense of obtaining Justice in England, that to a Poor man, it is absolutely true that <u>there is no law in England</u>, the writer of this can in his own case strongly evince this, for this and other good reasons, it is recommended to as many as are oppressed in this Country, to withdraw to the American states, that invite with <u>Liberty</u> in one hand and <u>Wealth</u> in the other, to do this in peace, is much better than to join with any seditious (as it must be termed) Party whatever. It is a dictate of Religion, of Reason, and of Nature, that Governments and Laws, tho' Tyrannical, should be obeyed so far as not to oppose any thing to them but Reason and Argument, no other force or violence. To emigrate from a Country where there are either no <u>laws</u> or they are <u>oppressive</u>, is not forbidden by any law of God, Man, or Nature.

b <u>The punctilios of Court</u>. To <u>these</u>, it appears that some thousands of British lives must be sacrificed, we are to see our tender parents, dear Sons, Brothers, and friends, set up on end to be shot at, <u>O! shame, where is thy blush?</u>

"Perhaps, indeed, the Ambassador of that (the French) Republic would not be fine enough in his appearance to figure in our Drawing-room, and therefore we must not endure the thought of a negociation [*sic*]. If that is the case, Ministers should say so, in order that the good people of England might know the <u>important reason</u> why their blood should be spilled, and their treasure squandered." <u>FOX</u>.

"Governments being yet in an uncivilized state, are almost continually at war, – apart from all reflections of morality and Philosophy, it is a melancholy fact, that more than one fourth of the labour of Mankind is annually consumed by this barbarous system." <u>TOM PAINE</u>.

c <u>cannot distinguish a pig from a colt</u>. This is in fact the case with poor <u>Burke</u>, but we must <u>pity</u> not <u>laugh</u> at him, we may ourselves have Children that will be Ideots [*sic*] – <u>ecce homo!</u>

"The Legislator would have been ashamed, that the coarse husbandman should well know how to assort and use his sheep, horses, and oxen, and should have enough of common sense not to abstract and equalize them all into animals – whilst he the œconomist, disposer, and shepherd of his own kindred, subliming himself into an airy metaphysian, was resolved to know nothing of his flocks but as men in general."

Burke's Reflections, 12th edit 8[vo] p. 272.
<u>A fool's Bolt is soon shot</u>, said Solomon.

So it seems that a lamb and a colt are not to be distinguished at their birth from each other, any more than a <u>Lord</u> and a <u>hangman</u>, and were it not that the farmer brings up one an <u>aristocratic horse</u>, and another a <u>Peasant Ram</u>, they would no more differ from each other than would the children of a <u>King</u> and a coal-heaver when left to nature. <u>Insult! Impudence.</u>

d <u>Daggers of Burke</u> The sporting club rant of Burke and his dagger in the house of Comons is well known.

e "Nobility is a graceful ornament to the civil order, it is the Corinthian Capital of civil Society."
    Burke's reflections, p. 206.

No! Paddy. No! The Corinthian Capital of civil Society is, what thou hast never been, nor ever will be.
    An <u>honest Man</u> – the honest work of God.

f <u>Monarchs, whose thrones are supported by Wars</u>
    "<u>Peace</u>, which costs nothing, is attended with infinitely more advantage, than any <u>Victory</u> with all its expence. But this, tho it best answers the purpose of Nations, does not that of Court – Governments; whose habited policy is pretence for taxation, places, and offices."
    Tom Paine.

"War is harvest to such Governments"
    ib.

g <u>Packed special Juries &c</u> To the Attorney General.
How does a <u>special</u> differ from a <u>pack'd</u> Jury?

h <u>misnomer'd True Blue</u>. A production very worthy of a <u>Lord</u> called <u>True blue</u> has lately been handed to the Public. All in the <u>Black-guard</u> Dialect of <u>New-Market</u>, the reasoning worthy of <u>Burke.</u> Enquire of all the <u>Ballad singers</u>.

i <u>Archy Macblunder</u>. This <u>Macblunder</u> was, according to our <u>Welsh Bard</u>, a Fellow that lived about three hundred years ago, in the time of <u>Owen Glyndower</u>. He was an <u>Atheist</u>, and made very light of <u>morality</u> and <u>Religion</u>, which puts me in mind of the following passage, from a recent publication.

    "Gentlemen of the Jury – It is held out to a community consisting of ten or twelve millions of people, that there was no law that bound them except those obligations which/that arose from <u>morality</u> and <u>religion</u>. According to this defendant, we had no law to defend our lives, our property, or our reputations; but were reduced back to a state of Nature." – what horrid falshood [*sic*], to assert that Tom Paine had said any such thing! – what horrid Atheism, that makes light of morality and religion!

k who take God's name in vain. The very frequent braying of God save the King, by the most brutish of all the Blackguards over their cups and draughts in pot-houses. – It seems that this vile murdering bloodthirsty song is used as a kind of charm to lay the spirit of the times which is that of rational enquiry, and greatly dreaded by some, who think that Truth and Reason are not proper weapons [*sic*] for the Vulgar, as they must be abusedly called, but this Vulgar, or as Burke will have it, Swinish Multitude, have now a great number amongst ^{them} that know more than pleases the Great ones of this, by them, unjustly monopolized, World, – but the word is gone forth, and it will not return, Learning, Good Sense, Philosophical, and Political Knowledge are vigourously [*sic*] spreading amongst the lower classes, who at last see that Ignorance is the mother, not of Devotion, but of Slavery, and that knowledge is the only weapon that will break the galling chain. – Hear this ye – ! ye – ! &c&c

l making the Church a vile engine of state "My Kingdom is not of this world" said one. That's a da––d lie, answers the modern Parson, who claims a property in a man's Conscience.

m 'Journey-men K––s. It is not very clear what the Welsh Bard means by K––s, it may possibly be Knaves, the word in the original Welsh is Brenin, which anciently signified K––g, synonymous to Knave. In its modern acceptation it signifies any Officer that executes the Law, from the Monarch up to the Hangman, this may be wrong, tho' it does not yet appear to be so, for the Welsh Bards and their language are very barbarous things. I asked the old Celtic Rhymer what he meant by the word Brenin, Why said he, I mean a Journey-man K––, that is a Bumbailiff, Hangman, Informer, Attorney general, or, in short a place-man of any description whatever: – what an ignorant old fellow! that he is so in the extreme, will appear from the following particular: I asked him what he meant by the Welsh Term Rheithwyr-anudon, why said he, I mean a Pack'd Jury or which is the same thing a special Jury. Now having myself some knowledge of the language, I am able to assure the reader that Rheithwyr-anudon signifies literally Forsworne Juries. So let every loyal Englishman say
From Welsh Bards, Good Lord deliver us

20. Joseph Hucks, 'On the Ruins of Denbigh Castle, in North Wales'

Now sad and slow, borne far on dusky wing,
Sails the still Eve – Night from her ebon throne
Slow rising, scatters wide her mystic spells
O'er the tir'd world; and from yon murky cloud
Gleams the pale moon, diffusing holy light   5
Thro' many a midnight Isle and silent scene.

  Much musing on this mimic round of life,
And all its strange vicissitudes, I view
Proud Pile! thy tempest-beaten towers, that rear
Their heads sublime, and to the angry storm   10
Bid bold defiance, tho' their aged brows
Bear visible the marks of stern decay;
While superstition, with a phrenzied eye,
And wildering fear, that thro' the shadowy gloom
Kens many a horrid form and spectre pale,   15
Affright the lonely wanderer from thy walls.
Proud Pile! engraven on thine aged front,
In deep but time-worn characters, I trace
The stern feudality of antient years:
Ambition reared thee in an evil hour,   20
To cover its dark doing – many a tear
Thy walls have witness'd! – many a tortur'd groan
Appall'd the silence of thy midnight gloom!
Is there a heart that sorrows at thy fall?
Ye patriot few; who arm'd with fortitude,   25
E'er while have sought for freedom! whom the force
Of England's proud usurpers, nor their threat
Could ever bend from virtue's stern resolve!
For what ye have done, ev'n with tears of joy
Now do I thank ye; 'tis the only meed   30
I have to offer, humble, but sincere.
I thank ye for that lesson, which your deeds,
Bright as the richest gem in virtue's crown,
Have taught me – deep engraven on my heart
In life's ingenuous spring, 'twill never die.   35

Far hence thou busy world! nor here intrude
Thy sounds of uproar, arguing much of care,
Of impotent alarms and deep dismay,
Of hateful contests, hopes, and sickly fears.
Stop traveller! and with mournful eye behold   40
This feeble monument of pride and pow'r,
Which time and desolation have assail'd
With widest havock – O'er the solemn scene
In silence pause – It is the pictur'd tale
Of man's brief hour; ev'n as this mouldering pile,   45
That yet lifts high its forehead to the storm,
Till the wild winds shall tear it from its base;
So flies the date of poor mortality;
For while man journeys, heedless, thro' the vale
Of many-colour'd life; with silent tread   50
Time, yet unknown to pity or to spare,
Steals on his path, and sweeps him from the earth.

21. Edward Williams (Iolo Morganwg), 'Song.
Bella! horrida Bella! Written in Novr 1794'

1.
Bard of Wars and desolations
Bid the ^{Raven} muse of kings,
Bear thee to their conflagrations,
Where their dreadful tumult rings.

2.
Speed thee to the field of battle   5
Give its air thy baleful breath
Bid augmented furies rattle
Glad _{Glut} thy soul with groans of death.

3.
Tell the world it must not mention,
Cursed humanity no more,   10
But the sharks of place and Pension,
Kings, and swords of death adore.

4.
^{Thus in} song aloud proclaiming
What rejoice'd thy fereful eyes
Nations Legions murder'd, cities burning ^{flaming}   15
Havoc's roars that rend the skies!

5.
Sing of desolated Regions
Sword and famine hurried far,
Hell and kings with all their legions,
In th' imperial cause of war.   20

6.
From the Camp to Courts returning
Tell it there in sounding song.
Orphans, Widows, Millions mourning,
How the Kingdom'd world they throng.

7.
These are joys to Sons of Murder,   25
Extacy to Courts and Kings
Monarchy this grand disorder
O'er the World with rapture flings.

8.
But I see thy phiz distorted,
Wears no more the sanguine smile   30
News to Monarch's ears ill-sorted
Brings thy songs _{Comes alas} to Britain's Isle.

9.
<u>Liberty's</u> bold sons advancing
Drive their kingly foes away,
<u>Liberty</u>, with vigour prancing,   35
Strikes the <u>Tyrant</u> with Dismay.

10.
On the gory plains of Flanders
Now the fight becomes a chace,
Foremost of her bold commanders
Britain's <u>Fred'rick</u> wins the race.   40

11.
While the Democratic sweater
Stalks, indignant o'er the Land
Of good heels one pair is better
Than five hundred pairs of hands.

12.
Hark how fame proclaims our glories ^{relates our stories} 45
Of the British scamper sings
Gives the world our peerless stories ^{glories}
Chapter'd in the <u>Book of Kings</u>.

22. David Samwell (Dafydd Ddu Feddyg), 'Ode, Written on
a long and uncommonly tempestuous cruise with a
Squadron of Men of War in about 63° North
Latitude, Dec' 24 1794'

1.

On <u>Norway</u>'s bleak and rugged shore
In concert with old ocean's roar
I strive to wake the Lyre,
Although these dark and frozen skies
Forbid the <u>Man of Rhime</u> to rise   5
And catch celestial fire.

2.

Thou gloomy Genius of the North
Let all thy shaggy bears come forth
From out their drear abode,
And let thy wolves at midnight's noon   10
Forbear to howl yon rising moon
But listen to my ode.

3.

Around the <u>Scald</u>, who rudely sings,
The half-year's night her mantle flings
And wraps him in the dark   15
The sun is gone his southern rout,
Our Purser's candles are burnt out
Extinguish'd to a spark.

4.

While thus forsaken by the sun
We cruise for <u>Frenchmen</u> or for <u>fun</u>   20
And dance the hays together
The sport of waters and the wind,
No <u>Sans culottes</u> or <u>fun</u> we find
But winter and rough weather.

5.

Ye Hags in Lapland caves who dwell   25
And boast propitious gales to sell
To seamen for their riches,
Give us a wind for England fit,
We'll give ye drafts on Billy Pitt
Ye sacrilegious <u>Bitches</u>.   30

6.

We'll give besides the <u>murd'rers fat</u>,
And <u>finger of birth-strangled brat</u>,
Untimely doomed to die,
But if with more regard ye view
The <u>liver of blaspheming Jew</u>,   35
<u>Dukes Place</u> shall that supply.

7.

Oh grant us then to leave this coast
Where we have long been tempest tost
In peril and alarm
We seem enchanted in this round   40
Or by some spell terrific bound
Till you dissolve the Charm.

8.

Thus sorrowing on the troubled Main
Our Prayers are oft proffered in vain
At dawn & setting day   45
The gallant Sailor's Spirits flag
And not a foul infernal Hag
Will speed him on his way.

9.

Then hail <u>new moon</u>! the Poet's friend,
Our wearied hopes must now depend   50
On thy renascent light
O! calm the ocean and the air
Convert this adverse wind to fair,
And gild our Polar night.

10.

So may <u>Endymion</u> faithful prove   55
On <u>Latmos</u>, and return thy love,
Soft regent of the main,
And long unrival'd mayst thou keep
The sov'reign empire of the <u>deep</u>,
And ev'ry <u>Poet's brain</u>.   60

11.

For me of <u>Cambrian</u> lineage sprung
Soon as I see thy bow unstring
I bless the light divine,
And the first offering that I bear
Confesses thy material care,   65
This moon-struck ode of mine.

12.

And obedient to thy will
Fair winds our swelling canvas fill,
Of which the sailor brags,
Divining, as he quaffs his grog,   70
Those breezes, unprophetic fog,
We're sent by Lapand <u>Hags</u>.

13.

But thy propitious aid alone
Chaste Cynthia, shall thy vot'ry own
Who like a Seer espies   75
(When seamen's vision, over-cast,
Can soar no higher than the mast)
The secrets of the skies.

[Note to stanza 12] On Christmas day the wind, which had blown almost a constant gale from the South, for above six weeks, changed in our favour, and continued so till the Squadron arrived in the <u>Downs</u>: and let me add that, this fair wind proved, in such a situation, as sumptuous a treat to us all (down from the admiral, who had only <u>salt beef</u> on his Table, to the common sailor who had <u>nothing better</u>) as to our jovial friends in England, were the <u>Turkies</u>, <u>Chines</u> &c smoking that day on their Tables. Few ships have experienced such a long continuation of unwearied stormy weather; and none, perhaps, ever cruised in such high latitudes in the depth of Winter.

23. Hester Piozzi, 'See, see the mad Marauders come!'

See see the mad Marauders come
    Let loose to kill and plunder;
They hope to find our Senates dumb
    Our Soldiers struck with Wonder
        But let them shun this hostile Shore   5
        Or back again we'll bang 'em
        And of this Tree of Liberty
        A Gallows make to hang 'em.

Nor Crown nor half a Crown they'll get
    We'll never be such Ninnies;   10
To feed the Starving Mounseers fat
    With our bright English Guineas.
        Then let them shun this happy Shore &c.

No Palace here was ever built
    With poor Men's blood or Tears Sir   15
Like proud Versailles pollute with Guilt
    Which finds a Lot severe Sir.

        Then let Mounseer,
        Not venture here
        Or back again &c.   20

We'll fight till Death for Church & King
    And firmly fix'd we'll see 'em
The merry Bells around shall ring
    And grace a grand Te Deum.

Those who to plot w.th France combine   25
    Old England shall disown 'em
Our Brunswic [sic] sinks their Jacobine
    As Howe has lately shown 'em
        Then let them shun our hostile Shore.

24. *Edward Williams (Iolo Morganwg), 'Newgate Stanzas'*

In the year 1794, when there were many State Prisoners in Newgate, none were permitted to see them without previously writing their names ^{and places} ^{of abode} in a book kept for that purpose, <u>Edward Williams</u> going there, with a friend, one evening to see the <u>Rev^{d.} Mr. Winterbotham</u>, wrote, in addition to his name and place of residence, <u>Bard of Liberty</u>, as he had several times before done, but this had been at length noticed, orders had been given to keep a <u>Watchful eye</u> on every one, and admittance was now refused in the following words, "<u>We admit no Bards of Liberty here, the only Liberty here</u> <u>allowed them is that of walking out</u>". This was complied with, with a wish that all Bards of <u>Liberty</u> might in future meet with no rougher treatment, or greater misfortune, than that of being turned out of a jail; going home to his lodgings he that evening wrote the following stanzas in imitation of <u>Horace</u>, Lib I. Ode 22. <u>Integer Vitæ</u> &c.

1.
Dear <u>Liberty</u>, thy sacred name
O! let me to the world proclaim,
Thy dauntless ardour sing:
Known as thy son, nor <u>Knaves of State</u>,
Nor <u>Spies</u> I fear, nor <u>placeman's hate</u>,   5
Nor * <u>Mobs of Church and King</u>.

2.
Nor <u>jails</u> I dread, nor <u>venal Court</u>,
And where <u>belorded fools</u> resort,
I scare them with a frown:
J <u>Reeves</u> and all his crew defeat;   10
And, if a <u>Tyrant King</u> I meet,
Clench fist, and knock him down.

3.
Of late, as at the close of day,
To Newgate cells I bent my way,
Where Truth is held in thrall;   15
'twas to scorn a Tyrant's claim,
Wrote <u>Bard of Liberty</u> my name,
And Terror seized them all!

4.
Poor <u>Kirby</u> trembled, struck with fear,
A form uncouth, like shaggy bear   20
On Russia's frozen plain;
Nor would he for one moment's space
The Bard of Liberty's bold race
Within his walls detain.

5.
Of such queer phiz and awkward mien,   25
No stupid ass was ever seen:
Whilst oddly mutter'd he;
"Danger immense to Church and State!
We dare not trust within this Gate,
A <u>Bard of Liberty</u>."   30

6.
Should I be doom'd, o'er burning sands,
To traverse <u>Afric's</u> desart lands,
Where <u>hungry Tygers</u> roar;
There, <u>Liberty</u>, shouldst thou the Muse
Bless with thy soft refreshing dews;   35
Thou that the Worlds adore!

7.
Or am I to the Pole exiled;
To glooms where Nature never smiled,
Since <u>Earth</u> or <u>Heav'n</u> began:
Warm'd by thy flame, bright <u>Liberty</u>,   40
With fervent ^{ardent} soul shall sing to thee,
And sing the <u>Rights of Man</u>.

* Alluding to the renown'd Church and King mob of Birmingham in 1791.

25. Edward Williams (Iolo Morganwg), 'TRIAL BY JURY,
The Grand Palladium of BRITISH LIBERTY'

A SONG,
SUNG AT THE CROWN AND ANCHOR, FEB. 4, 1795.
In CELEBRATION of the Late TRIALS for HIGH TREASON,
And TRIUMPHANT ACQUITTALS of
THOMAS HARDY, JOHN HORNE TOOKE,
AND
JOHN THELWALL;
AND IN HONOUR OF THEIR COUNSEL
THOMAS ERSKINE, and VICARY GIBBS.

By EDWARD WILLIAMS,
Author of POEMS, *Lyric* and *Pastoral*, lately published.

HERE, Brothers, we meet in th' abundance of joy,
    Prepar'd with our festival strain,
The storms, tho' severe, did but little annoy,
    Their thunders exploded in vain:
See how firmly the mountain sustains ev'ry shock,   5
    Tho' lightenings fly, raging, around,
And INNOCENCE, like an immoveable rock,
    Is ever invincible found.

Come hither! ye S*pies* and *Informers of State!*
    With Consciences offer'd for sale;   10
Come hither! and all your atchievements relate!
    Whilst Ridicule joys in the tale!
Or will ye, disgrac'd, to your PERJURER throng,
    Nor *Memory* wish to possess;
Then haste! gnash your fangs! whilst we call for the song   15
    Of Triumph's exulting excess!

Th' ASSERTORS OF TRUTH that were trampl'd awhile,
    That *Villany* fiercely pursued,
Claim the song of our gladness – true Sons of our Isle,
    With virtues gigantic endued.   20

What joy to the world! these to MAN and his CAUSE,
     The JURIES OF BRITAIN restor'd:
Our JURIES – our themes of eternal applause!
     Let their names be forever ador'd.

Boast, BRITAIN, thy JURIES! thy glory! thy plan!†   25
     They treat the *stern Tyrant* with scorn!
O! bid them descend, the best Guardians of Man,
     To millions of ages unborn;
Far and wide as the light, of true FREEDOM the soul,
     Be thy BLEST INSTITUTION proclaim'd;   30
With ERSKINE, with GIBBS, on Eternity's roll,
     In the language of glory be nam'd.

† The principle of Trial by Jury originated in Britain.

26. Anon., 'For the Chester Chronicle'

Dum hæc in animo mea revolvo, effundo Lacrymas

Oft to old Neptune's briny deep,
    From worldly sorrows free,
The man of pity walks to weep,
    And sings, O Want! of thee.

Thy pallid mien, and ghastly form,   5
    Have sought our northern shore;
For here the herdsmen droops forlorn,
    Here starves the humble poor.

For want of bread the infant cries;
    The father hangs his head;   10
The mother fills the air with sighs,
    And wou'd her child were dead!

Rather than see its infant form
    Become a prey to thee,
"I'd hurl it headlong to the storm,   15
    And die in misery!"

Such, haughty War, thy poignant woes,
    To thee such scenes belong,
The painful Muse wou'd thee disclose
    In simple, artless song.   20

But yesterday I saw, with dread,
    A sight that drove me wild,
A mother gathering chaff for bread,
    To feed her hungry child:

Around her knees the trembling babe,   25
    Its eyes uplifted high,
The mother bade its form to save
    From grim-ey'd Poverty.

Oh God of mercies! loud I cry'd,
    From whence can this arise?   30
From War, from War, I deeply sigh'd,
    From War, that rends the skies.

Pity 'tis, then, that such a curse
    Shou'd hurt our happy isle;
Shou'd drain the nation's thread-worn purse,   35
    Or drown the fair one's smile.

Oh! soon again may Peace appear,
    And Concord's milder beam;
To glad each swift, revolving year,
    To cherish and redeem.   40

May Gallia's plains, and Albion's shore,
    No jarring discord prove!
May distant nations live once more
    In kind and mutual love!

Denbigh, Aug. 14. 1795.

27. Thomas Ryder, 'Introductory Ode for the Cambrian Register'

> Darogan Merddin
> Dyvod breienin
> O Gymru werin
>   O gamwri;
> Dywawd Derwyddon,
> Dadeni haelon,
> O hîl eryron
>   O Eryri.   LLYWARCH AB LLEWELYN.

> Prophetic Merddin erst did sing
> The advent of an omen'd king,
>   Of Cambrian race subdued;
> And white-rob'd Druids too have said,
> That grace new-born should rise display'd
>   From Snowdon eagles' brood.   MEIRION.

BY the hallow'd rocks and shades,
Woods embrown'd, and darksome glades;
By the mountain's shaggy head,
By the ocean's murmuring dread,
By th' horizon's awful sight,   5
By Plymlumon's hoary height;
While clouds condensing o'er his brow,
Speak the threat'ning tempest's vow;
By – hark! – see – the scouling steep,
Ranging wildly o'er the deep;   10
Earth – air – sea – skies – assume terrific form,
And Cambria's genius rides amidst the storm.

Hark! hark! hark! the chord is struck;
Heard ye the air with fervor shook?
What means that solemn throb of woe,   15
Yielding to the minstrel slow?
What means that touch – the eye of fire,
Glittering o'er the trembling wire?
Passion in a phrenzy moves,
The chords fall lifeless to the loves.   20

Fancy wakes another string,
   In airy tunes the mountains ring:
Through the vast concave – sound is form'd on sound,
And rude magnificence is heard around.

   Daughter of dark – of fearful brood,   25
   Ideas fondest, earliest food!
   That calls the embryo genius forth,
   While wisdom smiles on native worth,
   That on the golden tip of day
   Marks *Cader Idris'* rising way,   30
   While young creation's bursting light
   Gives snow-clad *Snowdon* to the sight;
   And, opening with a purple stream,
   Bids the wide way lambent gleam,
Till the proud bard the highest praise may share,   35
And in the height of conquest – gain the air.

   Say can you bid the curtain glide,
   And cast your jetty locks aside?
   Around the ebon canvas throw
   Thoughts that speak and lights that glow?   40
   Bring *bardic numbers* forth to view,
   Of bards who sang – of bards who drew?
   While many a mail-clad chief around
   Joyous list'ned to the sound:
   Or rous'd – indignant grasp'd the steel,   45
   And doom'd the caitif [*sic*] wretch to feel;
While lofty passion wak'd the welcome guest,
Till strains of softer tone inclin'd to rest.

   Lo, Arthur moves; the soul-struck lay
   Opens widely to his way;   50
   Inferior bards behind him move:
   Himself the honors of the grove.
   Imagination's powers are rais'd,
   Nymphs forewarn'd, or hero's prais'd.
   See yon dame – tread gently – slow,   55
   Indulging solitary woe.
   Behold the chief that bleeding lies;
   For him she gives – to heav'n her sighs.

What, shall the son of Owain yield his breath?
Fierce gleam his eyes – he grasps his sword in death.   60

    Cadwallon's airs persuasion drew,
    Along the muse of pity slew.
    Ah! stop the winged shaft of death,
    And longer keep the fleeting breath.
    Behold the piteous numbers flow,   65
    Round the sacred mistletoe;
    Sighs that seize upon the heart,
    Nor fruitless call for mercy's part.
    The feeling warrior felt the strain,
    And rais'd his vanquish'd foe again;   70
While heav'n applauding, heard the poet's prayer,
That taught the hand of conquest how to spare.

    Who comes, in flowing garb array'd,
    Measured steps, and feebly made?
    Hoary locks and trembling head   75
    Age's blossoms – of the dead?
    'Tis Coel's son – high Lywarch moves,
    The ambient air with joy approves.
    His harp beneath his arm was hung.
    Around his waist a belt was slung;   80
    His right hand moving to and fro,
    Gave notice e'er the tongue should flow;
While with a graceful air and form inclin'd,
He touch'd the trembling string and woo'd the list'ning wind.

    "A father o'er sons has wept,   85
    While many a moon has o'er them slept.
    A father's grief has rent the air
    With piteous cries of sad despair.
    With jetty chord the harp was strung,
    When the parent painful sung;   90
    And many a sob and many a sigh,
    Accordant to the care dimm'd eye,
    Burst in sad concert to the lay,
    That mourn'd the proud – the painful day'
While echo to the sound gave cold return,   95
And own'd, with quiv'ring lip, herself to mourn.

Have I not struck the warrior chord?
Have I not charm'd the festive board?
Has not the maiden heard the strain?
Did she not wish to hear again?   100
The children round my knees were press'd,
And, touching of the strings, were bless'd;
The old men turning from the fire,
Bade deafness for a while retire;
And, welcom'd by the sounding lays,   105
Renew'd the thoughts of former days.
Thus Lywarch sung – the thrilling touch is o'er,
And Cambria's minstrel falls, to rise no more.

E'er yet these eyes are clos'd in death;
E'er yet the fates demand my breath;   110
The harp once more shall vibrate forth
Sounds of joy to real worth.
I see thy genius, Cambria, rise,
Blest and protected, to the skies.
A future *George* shall glory give,   115
And Cambria's fame immortal live.
Ye bards attend the sounding chords;
Ye scribes indite the flowing words:
Once more shall Learning round her Snowdon rise,
Beam o'er his head, and blossom to the skies –   120
On Truth's bright winds, to fame eternal soar,
Till time shall fail, and record be no more.

28. 'Eliza', 'Sketched on a Party down the River Wye, from Ross to Monmouth'

With gentlest gales our vessel bears away,
Smooth flows the Wye, and cloudless breaks the day;
The cheerful rowers brisk their oars enlave,
And the bright sunbeams dance from wave to wave;
The pure, transparent, glittering mirror's seen   5
Reflecting silvery tints, and woodlands green;
The ready pilot, as we glide along,
Points the sweet views to animate my song.
Close by the helm we take our gazing seat,
Whilst the wild scene reminds of Paraclete;   10
The mouldering ivy'd pile that's rear'd on high,
The rocks, the woods, the stream that murmurs by;
The moss-grown abbey Pope's own pencil drew,
And Eloisa, weeping to the view:
These retrospective visions will appear,   15
And check gay fancy in her blithe career.

To Monmouth's far fam'd bridge we steer our course,
And leave behind the rural shades of Ross:
Who can behold, and, seeing, not admire
Its neat churchyard, and heaven directed spire;   20
The winding river meandering through its views,
The grass green sod, mark'd by th' unletter'd muse:
Ah, who can quit these scenes without a sigh,
Worth long entomb'd, and history in our eye;
Who sweetly wandering, mourns not o'er the loss   25
Of Kyrle the good, the noted man of Ross?
Pope's flowing verse his memory shall prolong,
Pure as Wye's stream, and as its current strong;
Yet tell it not, in this enlighten'd age,
When thou hast read the philanthropic page,   30
When thou hast view'd each noble generous plan,
That not a stone erst told, – Here lies the man; –
That not one grateful stanza erst to say,
Or point where his respected relicks lay: –
Tell it not strangers, as they eager gaze   35
O'er Wye's pure stream led through his shadowy ways,

Lest its own willows from the watery wave
Recoil inverted, weeping o'er his grave.
Alas! like Cambria's mouldering piles his lot,
The world forgetting, – by the world forgot;   40
Till Kinnoul,* blushing for his country's fame,
Rear'd to the gazing world his honour'd name.

Ye blue ey'd Naiads of these crystal floods,
Nymphs of the coral caves, and sylvan woods;
Ye rocks majestic, round whose echoing bounds   45
We wind our way, and raise the plaintive sounds!
Lorn echo murmuring lengthens out the song,
"Which like a wounded snake drags its slow length along."
Ye green rob'd mountains, rich in nature's dress,
Small by degrees, and beautifully less;*   50
Ye pending woods, whose deep embowering shade
The Druid bards their choice asylum made,
Whose varied tints, reflected by the sun,
Nature's own sweet and cunning hands laid on;
Where, whilst th' enchanted spirit fondly clings   55
"She plumes her feathers, and lets grow her wings:"
Hills of the muse, on whose soft flowery brows,
The nine Aonian Sisters oft repose;
All hail! – hail, sweet attractive scenes to me,
Whose soul delights to meditate on thee.   60
Ah, could I touch thy own seraphic lyre,
Ah, could I catch a spark of native fire,
Here, humbly gazing, at thy feet reclin'd,
Here, as I lingering, longing, look behind;
Here, whilst the liquid lapse translucent flows,   65
And whilst the summer breeze so mildly blows,
Here would I range 'midst fancy's wide controul,
And give to breathing thought my active soul;
"Whilst Vaga echoes through her mazy bounds,
And rolling Severn hoarse applause resounds."   70

Sweet minstrels – and wild as sweet th' extempore song,
Which yet amid thy mountains flows along,
Around their harps in soft Penillion verse,†
At festive scenes they yet their feats rehearse;

Like fam'd Italia form the endless lays,   75
And wind the lengthening song an hundred ways!
As the fam'd phœnix, so their sounding lyres
Rise yet more brilliant through time's mouldering fires.
Ye moss grown towers, whose turrets intervene,
Where many a flower now blooms to blush unseen!   80
Where many a mouldering pile, with sculpture rare,
Here wastes its grandeur in the desert air;
"For dark oblivion lowering lurks before,
And covers with her dusky wings the door."
Where many a bard, warm'd with poetic fire,   85
Once tun'd his voice and swept the sounding lyre;
Arms, and the men they sung, whom conquering fate
Victorious gave to save a sinking state!
Ere yet the Roman legions roll'd their powers,
And gave to ruin Cambria's cloud-cap'd towers;   90
Her sacred groves to fire and sword consign'd
Left, like a vision, scarce a wreck behind;
Still, still, the valiant race inur'd to toil,
Bold as their rocks, and hardy as their soil,
Like the fam'd serpent Cadmus conquering slew,   95
Whose buried fangs an armed phalanx grew:
Or as the wounded hydra's many a head,
Fell but to rear another in its stead;
So Cambrio-Britain's conquest may be view'd;
Their sources powerful, – though their cause subdu'd.   100

[Line 41] * Lady Kinnoul.

[Line 50] * Sugar loaf mountains, so called from their spiral shape.

† Penillion verse, or ancient style of minstrelsy among the mountains, like
the modern Improvisatore of Italy, they continue singing extempore, without
intermission, through the night, never repeating the same stanza.

29. Anna Seward, 'Llangollen Vale, Inscribed to the Right Honourable Lady Eleanor Butler, and Miss Ponsonby' (extract)

Luxuriant Vale, thy Country's early boast,
    What time great GLENDOUR gave thy scenes to Fame;
Taught the proud numbers of the English Host,
    How vain their vaunted force, when Freedom's flame
Fir'd him to brave the Myriads he abhorr'd,   5
Wing'd his unerring shaft, and edg'd his victor sword.

Here first those orbs unclosing drank the light,
    Cambria's bright star, the meteors of her Foes;
What dread and dubious omens* mark'd the night,
    That lour'd, ere yet his natal morn arose!   10
The Steeds paternal, on their cavern'd floor,
Foaming, and horror-struck, "fret fetlock-deep in gore".

PLAGUE, in her livid hand, o'er all the Isle,
    Shook her dark flag, impure with fetid stains;
While "DEATH,* on his pale Horse," with baleful smile,   15
    Smote with its blasting hoof the frighted plains.
Soon thro' the grass-grown streets, in silence led,
Slow moves the midnight Cart, heapt with the naked Dead.

Yet in the festal dawn of Richard's† reign,
    Thy gallant GLENDOUR's sunny prime arose;   20
Virtuous, tho' gay, in that Circean fane,
    Bright Science twin'd her circlet round his brows;
Nor cou'd the youthful, rash, luxurious King
Dissolve the Hero's worth on his Icarian wing.

Sudden it drops on its meridian flight! –   25
    Ah! hapless Richard! never didst thou aim
To crush primeval Britons with thy might,
    And their brave Glendour's tears embalm thy name.
Back from thy victor-Rival's vaunting Throng,
Sorrowing, and stern, he sinks LLANGOLLEN's shades among.   30

Soon, in imperious Henry's* dazzled eyes,
 The guardian bounds of just Dominion melt;
His scarce-hop'd crown imperfect bliss supplies,
 Till Cambria's vassalage be deeply felt.
Now up her craggy steeps, in long array,   35
Swarm his exulting Bands, impatient for the fray.

Lo! thro' the gloomy night, with angry blaze,
 Trails the fierce Comet, and alarms the Stars;
Each waning Orb withdraws its glancing rays,
 Save the red Planet, that delights in wars.   40
Then, with broad eyes upturn'd, and starting hair,
Gaze the astonish'd Crowd upon its vengeful glare.

Gleams the wan Morn, and thro' LLANGOLLEN's Vale
 Sees the proud Armies streaming o'er her meads.
Her frighted Echos warning sounds assail,   45
 Loud, in the rattling cars, the neighing steeds;
The doubling drums, the trumpet's piercing breath,
And all the ensigns dread of havoc, wounds, and death.

High on a hill as shrinking Cambria stood,
 And watch'd the onset on th' unequal fray,   50
She saw her Deva, stain'd with warrior-blood,
 Lave the pale rocks, and wind its fateful way
Thro' meads, and glens, and wild woods, echoing far
The din of clashing arms, and furious shout of war.

From rock to rock, with loud acclaim, she sprung,   55
 While from her CHIEF the routed Legions fled;
Saw Deva roll their slaughter'd heaps among,
 The check'd waves eddying round the ghastly dead;
Saw, in that hour, her own LLANGOLLEN claim
Thermopylæ's bright wreath, and aye-enduring fame. 60

. . .

Now with a Vestal lustre glows the VALE,   85
 Thine, sacred FRIENDSHIP, permanent as pure;
In vain the stern Authorities assail,
 In vain Persuasion spreads her silken lure,

High-born, and high-endow'd, the peerless Twain,*
Pant for coy Nature's charms 'mid silent dale, and plain.   90

Thro' ELEANORA, and her ZARA'S mind,
    Early tho' genius, taste, and fancy flow'd,
Tho' all the graceful Arts their powers combin'd,
    And her last polish brilliant Life bestow'd,
The lavish Promiser, in Youth's soft morn,   95
Pride, Pomp, and Love, her friends, the sweet Enthusiasts scorn.

Then rose the Fairy Palace of the Vale,
    Then bloom'd around it the Arcadian bowers;
Screen'd from the storms of Winter, cold and pale
    Screen'd from the fervors of the sultry hours,   100
Circling the lawny crescent, soon they rose,
To letter'd ease devote, and Friendship's blest repose.

Smiling they rose beneath the plastic hand
    Of Energy, and Taste; – nor only they,
Obedient Science hears the mild command,   105
    Brings every gift the speeds the tardy day,
Whate'er the pencil sheds in vivid hues,
Th' historic tome reveals, or sings the raptur'd Muse.

How sweet to enter, at the twilight grey,
    The dear, minute Lyceum* of the Dome,   110
When, thro' the colour'd crystal, glares the ray,
    Sanguine and solemn 'mid the gathering gloom,
While glow-worm lamps diffuse a pale, green light,
Such as in mossy lanes illume the starless night.

Then the coy Scene, by deep'ning veils o'erdrawn,   115
    In shadowy elegance seems lovelier still;
Tall shrubs, that skirt the semi-lunar lawn,
    Dark woods, that curtain the opposing hill;
While o'er their brows the bare cliff faintly gleams,
And, from its paly edge, the evening-diamond† streams.   120

. . .

What boasts Tradition, what th' historic Theme,
    Stands it in all their chronicles confest
Where the soul'd glory shines with clearer beam,   135
    Than in our sea-zon'd bulwark of the West,
When, in this Cambrian Valley, Virtue shows
Where, in her own soft sex, its steadiest lustre glows?
. . .

[Line 9] * *Omens*. According to the records of Lewis Owen, the year 1349 was distinguished by the first appearance of the Pestilence in Wales, and by the birth of Owen Glendour. Hollingshed relates the marvellous tale of his Father's Horses, being found that night in their stables, standing up to the middle in blood. The Bard, Iolo Goch, mentions a Comet, which marked the great deeds of Glendour, when he was in the meridian of his glory. *See Mr.* Pennant's Tour.

[Line 15] * Isaiah.

† Richard the Second.

[Line 31] * Henry the Fourth.

[Line 89] * *Peerless Twain*. Right Honorable Lady Eleanor Butler, and Miss Ponsonby, now seventeen years resident in Llangollen Vale, and whose Guest the Author had the honor to be during several delightful days of the late Summer.

[Line 109] * *Lyceum*, – the *Library*, fitted up in the Gothic taste, the painted windows of that form. In the elliptic arch of the door, there is a prismatic lantern of variously tinted glass, containing two large lamps with their reflectors. The light they shed resembles that of a Volcano, gloomily glaring. Opposite, on the chimney-piece, a couple of small lamps, in marble reservoirs, assist the prismatic lantern to supply the place of candles, by a light more consonant to the style of the apartment, the pictures it contains of absent Friends, and to its aerial music.

[Line 119] † Evening-Star.

30. Anon., 'The False Alarm'

Swift as lightning through the Heavens,
And as Tremendous too,
The Cry of Landing spread around
And o'er the Country flew.
The Sea Coast all is lin'd with Ships   5
Of huge enormous size;
Unnumber'd Frenchmen fill the Decks,
With hideous heads and eyes,
The French have too – cry'd every Man,
The Guillotine on Board;   10
They'll roast our Children, steal our wives,
And put us to the sword;
Cold Horror seiz'd each Britain's heart;
And froze his Ancient Blood;
Caractacus wou'd then have turn'd aside,   15
And sought some friendly Wood;
In every Hall along the shore
Confusion strange arose;
The Men they hid their plate or Gold,
The women pack'd their Clothes   20
The Men of Conway look'd in Vain
Upon their Ancient Walls:
For what avails an old Castle
Against such furious Gauls;
Stout Abergella rung with Cries   25
Of Terror and Dismay;
St. Asaph too, (with her Cannons)
Trembl'd for the coming fray,
The news o'er Denbigh threw a gloom,
And dash'd their cups of Joy;   30
The toast they pledg'd to Jervis health,
Was mingled with Alloy.
The Children cry'd the Ladies scream'd:
E'en Dowagers shed tears;
In Phrensy lost sweet Mrs Griffith   35
Tore her curls and ears

A troop of Scots, then quarter'd there,
Were order'd to prepare,
Who march'd next morning with the dawn
All through the Streets so rare   40
While all thus fear'd a word Arrived –
O: Sweet word of Comfort
That all this Bustle, Stir, and Cry
Was but a false report.
So back again the Scots return'd   45
Who Denbigh town had sent;
Return'd again with perfect limbs
As wise as when they went
Let <u>Green</u> then lay his Balls aside,
And spare your Tears ye fair;   50
And Mrs Griffith, now replace
Your fine dishevell'd Hair.

31. Cæsar Morgan, 'The Victory of Fishguard. A favorite Song'

The words by the Rev'd Dr. Morgan, whose Countrymen were forward
to repel the French Invaders, who very lately made a Descent in Wales.
Set to Music by H. Skeats.

1.
Restless Frenchmen, sail not under
Yonder Cliff's Impending height,
Cleave not yonder Waves asunder,
With your boats and oars so light,
With your boats and oars so light;   5
Those blue Hills sustain a Nation
Fam'd of yore for feats of Arms.
Britons there maintain'd their station,
Nor declin'd the Wars alarms,
Nor declin'd the War's alarms.   10

2.
Ev'ry breast with rage is swelling,
Fury beams in ev'ry eye,
Cambrian Heros, fear dispelling
Know to conquer or to die;
Dare you yet forsake your Shipping?   15
Dare you press the fatal Sand?
With presumptuous footsteps, skipping
On fair Freedom's sacred Land?

3.
See the Mountain's side portending
Storms and Tempests soon to rise;   20
See the glittering bands, descending,
Flash like Lightning from the Skies:
Gallant Barons, proudly riding,
Hardy Yeomen, Peasants bold,
Arts of Peace, and War dividing,   25
Arm'd with Scythes like them of old.

4.
Hark, how strokes on strokes resounding,
Through the distant Vallies ring.
Britons, o'er the rock rebounding,
On their Foes with ardor spring;   30
O'er their trackless sands pursuing,
Round they deal the vengeful Steel,
Vanquish'd Frenchmen, humbly suing,
Low, before the Victors kneel.

5.
Britons, bold in facing dangers,   35
'Midst encounters, fierce of Soul,
Spare the conquer'd, suppliant Strangers,
Owning Pity's soft controul;
While with Mercy, Valour mixes,
British Warriors shine compleat   40
In their bosoms honour fixes,
Her sublime and spotless seat.

32. Hester Piozzi, 'Written on the Spur of the Moment, to be Sung at the Crown and Anchor'

Ye British Seamen list to me
And scorn the Democratic Tree,
They'll hang you on't, not make you free.
    If thus for Fools you hanker;
Then scorn their soft seducing Tongue   5
And sing with us a loyal Song
Nor do your Country so much Wrong
    To part the Crown & Anchor.

Our Royal Master mild and good
Has made it clearly understood   10
That in his Ancient Patriot Blood
    Lives neither Fear nor Rancour
Then haste on Shore his Pardon crave
And gain his Leave to catch the Waves
From Foreign Foes our Realm to save   15
    To save both Crown & Anchor.

Those men that hate both Church & Throne,
Old England ever will disown
They're not her real Flesh & Bone
    They're but an eating Canker;   20
Then quickly haste oh haste I pray
To lop the poyson'd Limb away,
Then lend one Royal loud Huzza
    Huzza for Crown & Anchor.

33. *Edward Williams (Iolo Morganwg),*
'Song for the Glamorgan Volunteers'

Un ac oll cyfoll cyfun
Gyda nerth i gyd yn un
      Iolo Morganwg

Yn undawd undid Frodorion
      Cynddelw

By Edward Williams
      Bardd wrth fraint a defawd
      Beirdd Ynys Prydain

1.
Whilst war pours around all its terrible storms
And dangers appear in their numberless forms
We mid those wild uproars that spread their alarms
Volunteer'd for our Country fly boldly to arms
At Liberty's call ev'ry soul is awake   5
We the field to crush tyranny cheerfully take
And oppose the sharp steel or the death-pinion'd ball
To barbarous foes that would Britons enthrall,
One and all!
One and all!   10
Fly at Liberty's call,
To vanquish all foes that would Britons enthrall.

2.
We, Sons of Glamorgan, of Britain's old Race
Eye with filial affection our dear native place,
No nation before us this region possess'd,   15
To this day 'tis our own, in its plenty we're blest.
The Saxon, the Dane, and the Norman, in vain
Strove to bind our forefathers in tyranny's chain,
Or if we one moment experienced a fall
Soon we sprang from his grasp that would Britons enthrall,   20
One and all!
One and all!

Never long in our fall,
We sprang from his grasp that would Britons enthrall.

3.
The <u>Norman</u> invader, a while with success,   25
Once trampled our plains, dared their Natives oppress,
But <u>Ivor</u> and <u>Morgan</u>, those Chiefs of renown,
Assail'd the fierce <u>despot</u>, soon humbled him down,
Their Sons, undegenerate, form a throng band
To die or repel evry [*sic*] foe from the Land,   30
Whether <u>faithless Batavian</u> or <u>insolent Gaul</u>,
Death awaits ev'ry Soul that would Britons enthrall.
One and all!
One and all!
Whether <u>Dutchman</u> or <u>Gaul</u>   35
Death awaits every Soul that would Britons enthrall.

4.
Our Country to free from all painful alarms
On the shores of Sabrina we meet under arms,
Sprung from Ancient <u>Silurians</u> who gloriously bled
In Liberty's cause, by <u>Caractacus</u> led,   40
To his standard how throng'd an invincible host
When Rome's mighty legions insulted their coast,
In us they revive to repulse the fierce <u>Gaul</u>
And all his Allies that would Britons enthrall.
One and all!   45
One and all!
We'll repulse the proud <u>Gaul</u>,
And all his allies that would Britons enthrall.

5.
From Rapine's <u>mad</u> Soul what oppressions are hurl'd!
What huge devastations that deluge the world   50
See whelming wide regions the rancours of Hell
Haste! grasp the keen blade! and those furies repel!
With all his high threats and his Gasconade boast,
Let him dare set a foot on one inch of our coast,
Before our bold onset th' invader shall fall,   55
We'll crush ev'ry foe that would Britons enthrall.

One and all!
One and all!
Each invader must fall
Destruction his doom that would Britons enthrall.   60

6.
For the Fair one, we love, for our children and wives,
For friends that have brighten'd the joys of our lives,
We take up the Sword and with Ardour advance
To humble the pride of unprincipled France,
And rather than yield to her haughty <u>controll</u>   65
All the blood from our veins in one torrent shall roll,
Like true British souls in the contest we'll fall,
Or defeat ev'ry foe that would Britons enthrall,
One and all!
One and all!   70
In the contest we'll fall!
Or vanquish all foes that would Britons enthrall.

7.
Sweet Girls of Glamorgan whose frowns we more fear
Than the fiercest of foes tho' their millions appear,
We fly to the wars, bid all pleasure adieu   75
British rights to secure and protection to you
O smile on your heroes that toil under arms
By nothing subdued but the force of your charms
At your feet we cry quarter, the victors o'er all
Those insolent foes that would Britons enthral,   80
One and all!
One and all!
At your feet we now fall,
The triumphant o'er foes that would Britons enthrall.

8.
Return, lovely Peace, with thy banners unfurl'd,   85
And, from our loved isle, give thy laws to the world,
O terminate ireful hostility's jars!
Bid hide in their Hell the fomentors of wars!
May brutal resentments that hunger for blood
Domestic and foreign be nipp'd in the bud   90

Whilst Freedoms true Sons for this sentiment call
Confusion to those that would Britons enthrall,
One and all!
One and all!
Fill the glass to their fall!   95
Confusion to those that would Britons enthrall.

Syrth y Ffranc is dranc dyn drwg, ystyried!
Os tiria'n Essyllwg,
Awr derfyn gelyn yw gwg
Aerguniaid Bro Morganwg.
      Iolo Morganwg ai cant.
         1797

Stanza III.
Ivor, Lord of Upper Senghenydd in Glamorgan, with a handful and resolute
and determined men, took the Castle of Cardiff, with its usurping possessor,
Robert Fitzhamon, his only daughter and heiress Mabelia and her husband
Robert Earl of Glocester [*sic*] whom he detained in their own Castle as
prisoners till they restored to the Welsh their ancient Laws and Privileges.
He was called Ivor Bach, i.e. Ivor Petit [see Camden in Glamorgan].

Morgan Lord of Avan the direct descendent of Iestin ap Gwrgan Prince of
Glamorgan, sided with our last Natural Prince Llewellyn ap Gruffudd against
Edward the Bardicide and after the Prince had been treacherously slain, or
more properly murdered, Morgan and his men held out manfully for their
national rights and ancient Laws, nor would they submit to the usurper till
these had been confirmed to the men of Glamorgan and of other resisting
parts of Wales. and what was very particularly insisted was upon were the
ancient modes of holding courts of Justice. [see Wynne's History of Wales,
and, in numerous Manuscripts, the genealogies of the Line of Iestin ap
Gwrgan, hence it was that the Laws of Hywel Dda prevailed in Glamorgan
till the time of Henry the 8th, and even in some instances to this very day in
[illeg.], Coetty &c Lordships]

Batavian. a Dutchman.

Stanza IV.
Sabrina. The Severn along the estuary of which, called the Bristol Channel,
the Country of Glamorgan extends upwards of 50 miles.

Silurians, or Silures (in Welsh Essyllwyn and their Country Essyllwg & Bro
Essyllt) the name anciently given to the Inhabitants of Siluria that included
the modern counties of Glamorgan, Brecon, Monmouth, Radnor, that part
of Caermarthenshire eastward of Tywi, Herefordshire, and the Forest of
Dean side of Glocestershire. A Sovereign state or Principality in ancient
British ages, and for the greatest part of it continued so under its own Princes
of the Line of Morgan Mwynfawr, till the time of Iestin ap Gwrgan, the
Last Native Prince who was dispossessed of his territories by a thief called
Robert FitzHamon, (assisted by another Depredator, one William Rufus)
in the year 1089. Surely it is not believed in Heaven, nor even in Hell that
human beings can be so far depraved as to boast of their descent from such
atrocious Villains as the Stealers of Kingdoms, &c States are, who to secure
to themselves such thefts murder the wretched inhabitants of such stolen
territories, quantum sufficit or down to a number sufficiently small to be
unable to resist those that put the yoke of slavery upon their necks. *Ond
pwy na fyddai brenin? a pha frenin nad yw Leidr* _{a llofrudd} *o Dad i Dad?*

Caractacus. The famous Chief or Prince of the Silures, who for nine years
opposed the whole force of Rome and was victorious in upwards of seventy
battles. It was only by treachery that he was at last vanquished. He was
carried Prisoner to Rome and with him his whole Family, or ^{rather} that of
his Father, of which he his wife and children were members, Bran ap Llyr
his father is said to have been the first that on his return into Britain after
seven years residence as a hostage, introduced the Christian Religion into
this Island, he became a convert at Rome. He is called in our ancient MSS,
Bran Fendigaid, Bran Fendigaid ap Llyr, Bendigaidfran, & Bendigaidfran ap
Llyr, i.e. Bran the Blessed, or Blessed Brân. He is by our ancient writers of
the British Triades, memorials of the Saints of Britain, Genealogists &c called
the Patriarch, or the first of the three holy lines or families of Britain,
the second of these families was Cynedda Wledig, and the third Brychan
Brycheiniog. The Roman Catholic clergy & monks struck the name of Bran
ap Llyr out of this Triad and in its room inserted that of their Joseph of
Arimathea of whom they fabricated a most ridiculous legend. When the
reformation took place, the first and most important thing to be done was
to rescue the Scriptures from the corruptions of Popery, no eye was turned
towards the Ecclesiastical history of this Island which had been equally cor-
rupted by it, Humphrey Llwyd, Dr Powel, and other Welsh Historians took

no notice of <u>Bran ap Llyr</u>, or <u>Bendigeidfran</u>, whence the circumstances of his not being mentioned in our ecclesiastical Histories as the <u>British Apostle of Christianity</u>, it is high time that this plain simple and sufficiently probable account should appear in our Church Histories. and the Fable of Joseph of Arimathea be, perhaps it already has been, expunged for ever out of British History, and never appear but in a History of the lies and forgeries of the Church of <u>Rome</u> a work by far too arduous for an[y] <u>one man</u> for any <u>one hundred men</u>, and those of the most gigantic abilities to undertake, even should all of them live to the age of <u>old Methusalem</u>.

<u>Bran ap Llyr</u> lived according to the oldest of our Genealogist[s] at <u>Dindryfan</u> (Anglice Dunraven) in Glamorgan, now the Seat of Thomas Wyndham, Esqr member for the County, this old castelled house built about 1100, stands in the middle of an ancient triangular <u>Roman</u>, or rather <u>British</u> Camp, or fortification, much of it still pretty entire, whence the name of the house, from <u>Din</u> a fortress & <u>Tryfan</u> a triangle, or triangular, i.e. <u>Triangular Fortress</u>.

<u>Caractacus</u> is in Welsh called <u>Caradawc ap Bran</u>, and is also said to have lived at <u>Dindryfan</u>, he was set at Liberty at Rome, and permitted to return to his own Country but his father and his son, Cyllin, were detained there as hostages for seven years – see British Triades, Genealogical Memories of the House of Iestin ap Gwrgan, <u>Memorials of British Saints</u>, &c.

34. Robert Southey, 'St. David's Day [1797]'

This is the Cambrian's day, their high day this,
When glad of heart, and with an honest pride,
They boast their country; mindful of the hour
Of conquest, and that Champion, whose *green crest*
Play'd foremost in the battle; from whose sword   5
The Saxons fled. His fame had Merlin told:
Old Merlin, wisest of the wizard race –
Wisest and best. Before that unborn babe,
The Patron Saint of Erin, in strange trance,
Stood dumb; then suddenly, with lips unloos'd,   10
His upward eye kindled with prophetic fire,
Announc'd the glories of that child, conceiv'd
In sin, and born in *shame; yet doom'd by Heav'n
In youth his Country's Champion, and in age
Her Hermit Saint.
           The lonely vale lay deep   15
Amid encircling mountains, where the cell
Of David, its rude arch with ivy hung,
Pierc'd the dark rock. His hand, that with such force
So firmly grasp'd the sword, was wither'd now;
For abstinence and age had loosen'd all   20
Its strong-strung sinews; and when rais'd in pray'r
It shook with very weakness; and his eye,
So fierce in battle once, fix'd heav'nwardly
So meek a look of patient humbleness,
As truly told all vain and earthly thoughts   25
Had long forsook the soul that spake in it.
Long has the Solitary's soul surviv'd,
And long his fame shall live! A gallant race
Still cheerly hold their Champion's festival,
Proud of their Country; and it is a pride   30
That well becomes the children of that realm
Thro' whose long annals many a patriot name,
Amid the gloom of darker ages, shines
Illustrious. He before whose scythed car
The Roman robber fled – Cassibelan;   35
And that good King, whose undefeated soul
Superior to his fortunes rose, and aw'd

The Con'quor on his throne; and she† whose voice
Rous'd up against the th' invader's tyrant reign
Glorious rebellion; and the theme of song,   40
The minstrel's darling theme, Arthur the good,
The gallant Arthur, round whose festal board
The goodliest company of Knighthood sate
That ever yet did meet in bow'r or hall.
Nor least in fame, Llewellyn, gallant Chief,   45
Who, for his Country's freedom liv'd in arms,
And with his Country's independence died.
Long shall your honours bloom, heroic names!

* The mother of St. David was a Nun.

† Bonduca.

35. Robert Southey, 'Lines, Written Amid the Ruins of Abergavenny Castle'

And is not this a scene that overpays
The toil of our long way? Yon mountain range,
Here rich with woods, and cultur'd where its slope
Sinks gradual to the vale; beyond their side,
Brown with short turf, till with the distant sky   5
Far off their summits blend, while bright below
Along the valley's green fertility,
The Usk streams sparkling on; a scene like this,
My friend, presents no object to disturb
The heart's delight: even these castle walls,   10
Amid whose mould'rings ruins now we stand,
No melancholy feelings wake; no thought
Of mem'ry and regret. The day has been
When Treach'ry spread the feast, and Murder here
Receiv'd the guests; when yonder tott'ring tow'r   15
Re-echoed to her cries, who in the morn
A wise and mother rose in liberty,
Ere night a widow, and the slave of him
Whose sword had made her childless. God be thank'd
That, in our better age, a tale like this   20
With wonder strikes the half-incredulous ear!

36. Robert Southey, 'Ode' ['In vain the trav'ller
seeks Aberffraw's tow'rs']

In vain the trav'ller seeks Aberffraw's tow'rs,
    Beside the running stream,
    There, in th' ocean lost,
In vain his eye the palace site explores.

Still to the ocean flows th' eternal stream,   5
    But now no palace tow'rs
    Shadow its sparkling tide;
Fall'n is the seat of heroes and of kings.

Long, Cambria, has thine ancient throne been broke,
    Long has a stranger sway'd   10
    The sceptre of thy kings,
O land of heroes! but thy fame survives.

But still th' immortalising page proclaims
    His praise, the gallant chief,
    Who on Caer-Caradoc   15
Wag'd his last warfare with the Roman host.

But still those old, delightful strains shall tell
    Of Arthur's peerless deeds;
    But still the high-ton'd harp
Echoes to Owen's and Llewellyn's fame.   20

Nor shall thy spirit in its halls of bliss
    Hear no applauding verse.
    Last of her line of kings,
O martyr of thy country's liberty!

Poor was the triumph of thy Saxon foe,   25
    Thee villain fraud betray'd,
    Thee force subdu'd unarm'd, –
No Muse for Edward wreathes th' unwithring crown.

What tho the shout of rabble praise resounds
    Loud as the thunder peal,   30
    Where vict'ry wings her flight,
The voice that makes immortal is not there!

For virtue was that noble meed design'd,
    And, in the good cause gain'd,
    Alike the Muse respects   35
The Conqu'ror's laurel, and the Martyr's palm.

Thro' London's streets the savage multitude
    Beheld Llewellyn's head
    In barb'rous mock'ry borne,
And with her gallant Prince his country fell.   40

But not inglorious, nor to evil doom'd,
    Fell Cambria and her King.
    The patriot's praise is his, –
A deathless meed his conqu'ror shall not know.

And what tho' of Aberffraw's royal tow'rs   45
    No time-worn trace remains;
    Tho' Cambria's throne be fall'n,
Her antient sceptre in the Saxon's sway;

From her own mountains Freedom hath not fled,
    She never shall forsake   50
    Her old and fav'rite seat,
And with her, erst a stranger, sojourns Peace.

37. David Thomas (Dafydd Ddu Eryri), 'Verses written on the late Victory
gained over the French Squadron by Sir John Borlase Warren'

Inscribed to the loyal Parys Mountain Volunteers – (a hasty production, the
author was obliged to compose the following in about half an hour's time
in order to answer a temporary purpose) –

When <u>Warren</u> on Hibernia's coast
With boldness Hem'd the raging main
Proud Gallia's sons on Ocean tost
Were Shatter'd, Vanquish'd <u>torn</u> and slain
    Rule Britannia & &

Let Britons glory in the day   5
When Warren swept the swelling main
Let all attune the lyric lay
And chaunt the bold triumphant strain
    Rule &

May Britons long in peace remain
From vile oppression even free   10
Their ancient liberties retain
Till blust'ring Wars no more shall be
    Rule &

Ye loyal sons of Mona, thank
Undaunted in the royal cause
While bold Arvonia's towering land   15
Shall yet resound your high applause
    Rule &

Let Peace descend, – and guard our Isle
No longer may the cannons roar
May bounteous heaven with Pity Smile
Protect the rich, defend the poor   20
    Rule &

Health to the Sailor, bold and brave
Who scorns to fear the dart of Death
But cries, O God! my country Save:
Ever with his latest, latest breath
        Rule &

O soon may fierce contention cease   25
May Plenty bless fair Mona's shore
May Uxbridge keep our Isle in peace
While Parys yelds [*sic*] the glittering ore
        Rule &

                    D. Thomas

38. 'A Lady', 'Bangor Ferry'

'Sir,
The following Stanzas are transcribed from the walls of a room of the Inn
at Bangor Ferry. If you think with me, that they convey an interesting
picture of a young mind, just escaped from the horrors and turbulence of
the sister country to the repose and delight which Bangor is so well calculated
to produce, I have no doubt of them finding a place in your entertaining
Magazine.
Viator'

Bangor Ferry.
10th April, 1799.
By a Lady.

1.
From civil feuds and bloody fields,
The rebel pike and trumpet's clangor;
The exil'd fair to fortune yields,
And finds a short relief at Bangor.

2.
Ye verdant rocks! ye peaceful floods!   5
To turbulence unknown, as languor;
Save, then the wild winds bow your woods,
The sole annoyance felt at Bangor!

3.
No refuge these for guilt or shame,
The progeny of pride and anger;   10
But love, or friendship's holy flame,
Might hope ambrosial food at Bangor!

4.
Yet, while she dwells on every charm,
(Tho' critics yawn, and cry out, "hang her"),
The oak crown'd hill, sequester'd farm,   15
And bid a long adieu to Bangor:

5.
Accept these thanks – here care and pain
Subsided first, that wont to pang her;
For Bath, and pleasure're varying train,
Can ne'er efface the spells of Bangor!   20

39. *Richard Llwyd,* Beaumaris Bay, A Poem *(extract)*

. . .

The Green's attracting charms, the Muse shall tell
That all-inviting – ever-varying Mall,
That checks, with pebbly beach, the pressing tides
Where Commerce, in her swelling canvass prides;
And Mona's offspring seek testaceous* wealth,   135
And every Zephyr brings the bloom of health;
Here, Britain's safety, Glory's tempting car,
Inspire the martial mind to dare the war;
The tactic page, with prying eyes explore
To scare the rash invader from the shore –   140
Here school-boys crowd to face the *fancied* foe,
And little breasts with hostile ardour glow;
The war in miniature – the mimic boy –
The bloodless battle – and the hour of joy –
The Muse beholds! and, in the bright presage,   145
The Marlboroughs, Nelsons, of the rising age;
And though no phalanx fall, no heroes die,
Yet Beauty darts around the conquering eye,
Through pleas'd platoons the graceful footsteps bend,
And evening suns on tales of love descend.   150

Here earth is loaded with a mass† of wall,
The proud insulting badge of Cambria's fall,
By haughty Edward rais'd; and every stone
Records a sigh, a murder, or a groan.
The Muse of Britain, suff'ring at its birth,   155
Exulting sees it crumbling to the earth.
Ah! what avails it that the lordly *tower*
Attracts the thoughtless stare and vacant hour!
If ev'ry Bard with indignation burns,
When to the tragic tale* the eye returns;   160
If for his haunted race,† to distant times,
There's still reserv'd a vengeance for his crimes.
. . .

NGLISH-LANGUAGE POETRY FROM WALES

[Line 135] * In this channel, the large oysters called the *Penmon*, are taken by the dredge, a great quantity of which are pickled annually, and sent to different parts of the kingdom, in small neat casks constructed for the purpose.

In an old plan of Beaumaris, there appears a wind-mill on the eminence between the green and the friary, and its removal is a matter for general regret, the neighbourhood, and particularly the poor, being always distressed, in the summer months, by the difficulty and additional expence of having their corn ground at *Aber* and other places.

Near this spot, at the end of *Llangoed* land, was fixed in a wall, a stone, with a head of *St. Francis*, the patron of the adjoining monastery, carved thereon, and to which our ancestors were obliged to make observance as they passed, or pay a fine to the Monks. – *P. G. MSS.*

[Line 151] † This castle is the last of the three great fortresses erected by Edward I; on the conquest of Wales in 1295, he fixed upon this spot with a view of surrounding it with a *fosse*, for the double purpose of defence, and bringing small craft to unload their cargoes under its walls, by a canal; part of which, called *Llyn y Green*, was, till lately, remaining.

Within the castle is an area or square of 190 feet, with obtuse corners; on the right is the chapel, an admirable piece of masonry, and the only intire [*sic*] part of the building; opposite to the south-east entrance is the great hall, 70 feet long and 23 broad, having a range of five elegant windows, and forming a front that (its turreted angles excepted) has a rather modern appearance: and although, upon the whole, a fortress of prodigious magnitude, yet its low situation, and the great diameter of its nearly-circular towers, takes off considerably from its height and appearance.

The stile [*sic*] of architecture in Edward's different erections, is rather Asiatic than Gothic, a taste which he probably acquired in his excursions to the Holy Land; he found the land upon which he built in possession of the posterity of *Gweryd** ap Rhys Goch, Einion ap Meredydd, Gryffydd ap Evan*, and *Einion ap Tegeryn*; these he removed by *excambius:* the first to *Bodelwyddan*, in Flintshire, where their descendants (the Humphreyses) resided till lately; to the other three he gave lands in the townships of *Erianallt*† and *Tre'r ddol*, free from rent and service, and bestowed their possessions on the corporation. In this transaction, the King seems to have been just; but how he came by the lands which he gave in exchange, does not appear. – *P. G. MSS.*

So effectually did English policy operate to the exclusion of the natives from these strong holds, and the towns which gradually grew near them, that in a rental of the borough property, taken so lately as 1608, I find but seven British names, and one burgage, described as some little time before, in the tenure of *Gronwy ap Evan*, Welshman, perhaps the only native resident at the time.

The history of these fortresses is a continued series of oppression and irritation: in a skirmish between the garrison and the country people, on a market day, called the Black Fray (*y ffrau ddu yn y Bewmares*) *Dafydd ap Evan ap Howell*, of *Llwydarth*, Esq. is said to have fallen, and, however gratifying it may be to the reflecting mind to see these enormous masses in a state of dilapidation, and totally useless as to their original design, it is at the same time a matter of some regret, that their structure is such as will always resist every idea of converting them to any useful purpose of rational existence. – *See Appendix.*

* *Gweryd ap Rhys Goch*, Founder of one of the Fifteen Tribes, resided at *Caerdegog*, in *Talebolion*, the tenements adjoining being still called after his sons and grandsons, as *Gwely Howel*, *Gwely Meurig*, &c. I find but one family existing in the male line from *Gweryd* – the Foulkeses, of *Gwerneigron;* the leading branch of the Humphreyses of *Bodelwyddan*, and the Lloyds of *Lligwy* and *Gwaredog*, having of late years become extinct. By heirs female the Wynns of *Bodewryd* are represented by J. T. Stanley, Esq. jun. of Adderley; and the issue of the Rev. E. Hughes of *Cinmel*, T. P. Jones of *Madryn*, and G. LL. Wardle of Hartsheath, Esqrs. representing another branch, ought particularly to quarter, in order to preserve the honorable bearing of *Gweryd*, which according to some authors, is *Argent on a bend sable, three lions' heads caboched of the first;* to others, *three leopards' faces;* but the true coat is, *tri phen Gwyddel ar drawst du, yn y maes gwyr.* The ancestors of *Gweryd* beging among the *Hualogion* (vide Triades) at the defeat of *Sirigi*, the Irish Rover, at *Cerrig Gwyddel*, in Anglesey. The coat of *Ednyfed Fychan*, *Gules a chevron ermine, between three Englishmen's heads couped*, is a similar instance, a distinction bravely acquired in the war against Randolph, Earl of Chester.

† On a farm of this name, and in this neighbourhood, were born three brothers of the name of Morris, men of worth, and of uncommon abilities. The Rev. *Gronwy Owen*, in his monody on Lewis Morris, Esq. (one of the most perfect compositions in this language of modern times) has the following lines:

> "Er eidduned taer ddynien,
> Er gwaedd mil, er gweddi mon,
> Ni adfer ner amser oes."

> Nor Heaven revokes the destin'd hour,
> Though ev'ry prayer ascends to save,
> A thousand sue, and Mona crave.

This gentleman, to much general and useful learning, added a critical knowledge in the antiquities, language, and poetry, of ancient Britain.

[Line 160] * The most effectual of the means resorted to by Edward, for securing the submission of his new subjects, was the extirpation of the Bards. Sensible of the influence which this order of men had on the public mind, they were, by,

> "Edward's cruel sword, consign'd
> To slaughter all."   *D. Ddu Feddyg.*

> "On dreary Arvon's shore they lie,
> Smear'd with gore, and ghastly pale:
> Far, far aloof th' affrighted ravens sail:
> The famish'd eagle screams and passes by,
> Dear lost companions of my tuneful art."
>   *Gray.*

And the system seems to have been acted upon, though, perhaps, with less rigour, after the death of the bardicide; for, in the reign of Henry IV, *Rhys Goch*, speaking of *Gryfydd Llwyd*, says:

> "Y goreu Bardd a waharddwyd."
> The best of Bards is interdicted.

Of late it has become fashionable to doubt this among other historical facts: but what is to become of the testimony of Sir John Wyatt, and the strains of the sufferers?

[line 161] † "With me in dreadful harmony they join,
And weave with bloody hands the tissue of thy line."
                                    Gray.

40. Edward Williams (Iolo Morganwg), 'Carmen Seculare,
or Jubilant Song for the year ~~1800~~ 1900'

1. <u>Philander</u>.

Amid the rude storm what effulgence of light
Springs up, and delightfully streams
Thro' blackest of clouds, widely pours on the night
A ray that celestially beams:
The gloom, tho' reluctant, will soon disappear,   5
Proclaiming the radiance of glory that's near,
The Sun of our jubilant morn.

2. <u>Alexis</u>.

Tho' days of less Evil are seen from afar
Too soon from the tear we refrain;
Still Kings are unconquer'd, the tygers of war   10
Still throng to their murderful plain:
They see with this dawn renovation appear,
The morn of bright Rectitude's age,
And storming indignant, and madden'd in _{with} fear
They howl in th' abundance of rage.   15

3. <u>Philander</u>.

The reign of their pow'r shall be soon at an end,
For <u>Justice</u> replaced on her throne,
Wide over the world shall her banners extend,
And call ev'ry kingdom her own;
She brings out her Legions in <u>Liberty's</u> cause,   20
Her <u>Truths</u> ev'ry Nation shall scan,
She, quelling the Tyrant, shall urge in her laws.
The <u>Rights</u> and the <u>duties</u> of <u>Man</u>.

4. <u>Alexis</u>.

Tho' millions appear from the <u>Vine-cover'd hills</u>,
Tho' to the sure conquest they fly,   25
Tho' the song of their triumph exultingly trills
And the glories of monarchy die;
Th' atchievements of carnage, the deluge of blood,
Give me but a painful relief,
And fierce as destruction rolls on its high flood   30
In my soul are the torrents of grief.

5. <u>Philander</u>.

This havoc shall end, be forever suppress'd,
War's Hero no more be renown'd;
On <u>Infamy</u>'s roll, an <u>infernal</u> confess'd,
His name shall forever be found: 35
All Discord shall perish, Ambition must yield,
Whelm'd in its own horrible jar,
The merciless monarch shall fall in the field,
Of his own <u>diabolical War</u>.

6. <u>Alexis</u>.

See town-burning flames, that yield rapture to Kings,   40
In volumes tremendous arise,
And War's foaming bloodhounds – detestable things,
Meet rankling ^{aching} humanity's eyes:
Of crowns by the murder of millions impearl'd,
Hear monarchs audaciously boast,   45
With <u>infernalized souls</u>, that are seen by the world,
In deepest brutality lost.

7. <u>Philander</u>.

See <u>Wisdom</u> confounding the <u>king-ridden clan</u>,
See <u>Reason</u> promulgate her lore;
That Science of Princes _{Empire} ^{imperial}, the <u>murder of Man</u>,   50
Shall gorge on its millions no more;

In the deeps of disgrace, in abhorrence forlorn,
See <u>Titled Audacity's</u> band,
On Crowns we now trample, the sceptre is torn,
From shameless <u>Regality</u>'s hand.   55

8. <u>Alexis</u>.

O! tell me, <u>Philander</u>, shall <u>Wisdom</u> and <u>Peace</u>?
Shall new Golden ages return?
Say shall this <u>beking'd infernality</u> cease
We ^{so} long have been destined to mourn?
O say, shall this world with new vigour of youth   60
Find <u>Nature</u> and leave her no more?
And <u>Man</u>, shall he study the dictates of <u>Truth</u>?
The lovely <u>Celestial</u> adore?

9. <u>Philander</u>.

Proclaiming her blessings, unfolding her plan,
See <u>Peace</u>, a bright Angel, descend,   65
Singing joy to the mourner, and <u>Wisdom</u> to <u>man</u>
All the <u>virtues</u> her footsteps attend;
O! give the new song to the Regions around!
Her <u>Monarchy Reason</u> regains!
The path, long entangled, of <u>Nature</u> is found,   70
The _{To} ^{Realms} where <u>Felicity</u> reigns.

10. <u>Alexis</u>.

My soul is all joys, kindled up to thy strain,
I tune to new transport my voice
<u>Peace</u> dwelling with Man! O! retune it again!
Till mountains and Valleys rejoice!   75
Till Oaks of the Forest harmoniously sing,
Of <u>Justice</u> now leading the van!
Till Rocks become vocal! till all the worlds ring!
Of <u>Peace in the dwellings of Man</u>!

11. <u>Philander</u>.

This world shall rejoice in a speedy relief,   80
All <u>Rapine</u> shall soon be subdued,
All tears be dried up, and forgotten all grief,
All nature be nobly renew'd:
All Error detected, all pravity flown,
<u>Felicity's</u> ages restored,   85
The <u>Father of All</u> in his <u>Love</u> shall be known,
In his <u>Truth</u> be forever adored.

41. George Davies Harley, 'Sonnet II: Penman-Mawr'

Prodigious PENMAN-MAWR! whose stature fills
    With wild delight the wond'ring mind of man!
Monarch of beetling rocks and rugged hills,
    Vast buttress of the main – thou land Leviathan!
O'er thy bleak brow when IRIS, colour-proud,   5
    Far from the wave hath wrapt her crescent warm,
(The vaulted sky thy roof, thy cap a cloud) –
    The seaman's morning sign, that soon shall raise the storm;
How have I seen thee, when the vengeful wave
    Split its white fury 'gainst thy Druid face,   10
Mock its proud might, til' it hath ceas'd to rave,
    And the spent surge of foam ran rippling round thy base.
So stands stern TRUTH, in batter'd grandeur bold,
Tho' madd'ning Malice roar, and fretful Falshood scold!

42. George Davies Harley, 'Sonnet III: On Seeing a
Poor Welch Girl Pass My Window in a Storm'

Sweet lovely Lass! though of the low degree,
    Thy long black locks, 'all drench'd in this foul storm,'
    With thy blue mantle just to keep thee warm,
And hide thy bare clogg'd foot, thy naked knee –
Thou art of ancient CAMBRIA's hardy race,   5
    Inur'd to toil, and ev'ry gust that blows,
    Or this rude wind would ravish the fresh rose
But now just op'ning on thy fancy face!
Thou art of VIRTUE! for thy unpress'd breast,
    Of rounded beauty, swells upon the sky,   10
    While the bright lustre of thy dark-brown'd eye,
And simple seraph smile, speak PEACE AND REST.
GOD of the good! be these her future dow'r,
And screen with thy big wide wing this else unshelter'd flow'r!

43. George Davies Harley, 'Sonnet IX: The Peasant of Anglesea'

Encircl'd by thy Naiads' arms,
And far from warfare's wild alarms,
    Know that I envy thee
Thy healthful toil, thy humble lot,
Thy little but contented cot –   5
    Peasant of Anglesea!
Thy wall-fenc'd fields, thy wave-wash'd shore,
The scudding sail, the surge's roar,
    These, these I envy thee!
Thy wishes few, thy cravings small,   10
By labour just indulg'd in all –
    Peasant of Anglesea!
And with warm heart thy untam'd temper greet,
Rude as thy rugged rocks – but as their herbage, sweet!

44. Anon., 'The Widow'

Pale grief sits on the widow's cheek,
    Her eyes are dim'd by tears;
Oblig'd her hard-earn'd bread to seek,
    'Midst cares and anxious fears.

Far better days she once had known,   5
    When life was in its prime;
But ev'ry comfort now is flown,
    Lost in the lapse of time.

Time was, the widow could dispense
    With joy, her little store,   10
And shar'd the gifts of Providence,
    And cheerful work'd for more.

Time was, a husband's tender smile
    Her frugal cares repaid,
Whose converse kind, could woes beguile,   15
    With bright religion's aid.

Not for herself her throbbing heart
    Beats in her anxious breast,
Six helpless ORPHANS' wants impart,
    Cares that deny her rest.   20

When sunk upon the bed of death,
    Their hapless parents lay,
Their groans explain'd with dying breath,
    Far more than words can say.

"Ah! cease those piercing groans, she cried,   25
    For heaven your souls prepare:
My bread (by Providence supplied)
    Your children dear shall share.

I'll teach them on Almighty good,
      To fix a steadfast eye,   30
I'll work with them to earn our food,
      And blessings will be nigh."

Now when the early morning shines,
      Their labour is begun,
And when the Sun to West declines,   35
      Their task is still undone.

Hope! deign to shed one glim'ring ray,
      One cheerful smile impart,
And gild the orphan's rising day,
      And cheer the widow's heart.   40

Wrexham, July 27, 1802.

45. Richard Llwyd, 'The Address of the Bard of Snowdon,
to his Countrymen, Written in June, 1803,
During the Threats of Invasion'

To Sir R. Williams, Bart. M.P. for the County of Carnarvon;
As leader of the Men of Snowdon,* and the representative of a race, in
which the Virtues of the Soldier and the Patriot have long been considered
as hereditary,† this address is, with peculiar propriety, inscribed.

The Bard of Snowdon, to his Countrymen.

Ye, (1) whom Britain's *earliest* day,
Saw among her meadows play:
Unconscious yet, that ocean's waves,
Form'd the isle, it loves (2) and laves.

Lords of realms, as yet unknown,   5
A blest creation (3) all your own;
A region yet by blood unstain'd,
Where native Peace unruffled reign'd.

Till Ceasar saw, from heights (4) sublime,
Beyond the deep, a distant clime;   10
His legions led, to guiltless lands,
And forc'd to arms your pastoral bands.

'Twas yours to share the general doom,
To brave, in vain, resistless Rome;
Yet Claudius saw, from Empire's seat,   15
A Briton (5) even in bondage GREAT.

Allur'd by Rapine, Fraud, and Spoil,
Marauding Saxons trod your soil;
And Bards, in strains of sorrow tell,
That Britain's offspring fought and fell.   20

Whene'er the Raven's (6) winds were spread,
From Odin's den, the hordes were led;
And, Britain's then, unguarded coast,
Felt the fell, the savage host.

Lost your own paternal plains,   25
Sylvan shades, and green domains;
Ye follow'd Hope's inviting eye,
To Cambrian vales, and summits high.

Ye, there, (7) with calm indifference saw,
Another crew give *both* the law;   30
Their claims a Norman tyrant spurn,
Oppress th' oppressors in their turn.

Intrepid, (8) amid cliffs of snow,
Ages saw you brave the foe;
Till Concord came, with efforts blest,   35
And sooth'd Contention's roar to rest.

United now, to England's throne,
Your Sires (9) return'd, resum'd their own;
And still, as in her EARLIEST day,
Britannia's wider sceptre sway.   40

O'er Britain's fertile varied face,
One great, one rich, and potent race;
In honour high – and high in fame –
The first of nations – BOASTS YOUR NAME!

BRITONS hear, that NAME's (10) a host,   45
And forms a bulwark round your coast;
And Fame shall tell, in records fair,
You're worthy of the NAME you bear!

The foe that racks a suffering world,
At you, the bolt of war has hurl'd;   50
And dares, in language, loud and high,
Your warriors to the field defy.

Dares and hopes, by threats and wiles,
To ravage, rule, the Queen of Isles;
'Tis your to stem his despot stride,   55
Unhelm, and humble, lawless pride.

By genuine Freedom's holy flame,
By Dragon-crested, (11) Arthur's name;
By Deva's (12) waves, when Saxons fled,
By Mona's (13) sons, when Mervyn led.   60

By Rodri's heir, (14) whose vengeful sword,
Bright gleam'd in Conway's lucid ford;
By Euloe's (15) forests, Berwyn's (16) heath,
Where Owen gain'd th' immortal wreath.

By every patriot-warrior's name,   65
By all that fills the rolls of Fame;
Unfold your banners, rend the air,
And proudly show the shields [17] you bear!

Sons of Snowdon, yours the MEED, [18]
Like Britons live, like Britons bleed;   70
Your Country, Parents, Children, save,
Or fill one great and glorious grave! [19]

* The Snowdon Rangers – Llanciau'r Eryri.

† It appears from the extent of North Wales, taken the 26th of Edward the 3d, that the descendents of the celebrated *Ednyved Vychan*, held that part of his great property, called *Tre'r castell*, in Anglesey, by the tenure of serving the Princes, in their wars with England, at their own charge, within the limits of Wales but beyond the Marches, at that of their country, and with this highly honourable condition annexed, that their leader must be *Toto sanguine ipsius Ednyved*, or, in local language, "O waed côch cyva Ednyved."

Similar to this, was the spirited, and, *to us*, not less honourable tenure, by which *Nigellus*, Baron of Halton, held that Barony and Castle, viz. that in the Earl's wars with Wales, the Barons of Halton were the *first* to enter it, and the *last* to leave it.

(1) Aborigines.

(2) "Anwylyd y moroedd."   Anon.
Beloved of the Ocean.

(3) "Diducta Britannia Mundo." Claudius.
"Toto divisos Orbe Britannos." Virgil.

(4) The Alps.

(5) CARADOC (*Caractacus*) the Silurian and Ordovicean chief, or, as Tacitus says, he described himself "*Plurium gentium Imperator.*" – Having bravely defended his country against the Roman power, for 16 years, was, at length, betrayed by Cartismundus, Queen of the Brigantes, and sent prisoner to Rome.

> "And, borne in chains, from Cambria's summits bleak,
> Rais'd Virtue's generous blush, on Cæsar's cheek."

His manly and dignified deportment in the Roman Senate, procured him his freedom, and the esteem of Claudius. – The well-known speech of this Chief, will be found re-delivered by the Muse, in the Juvenilia of Mr. J. H. L. Hunt.

(6) The Danish standard. – The nations inhabiting the immense region called Scandinavia, under the general name of Danes, at this period, plundered and desolated the shores of a great part of Europe; an ancient Bard, thus quaintly describes the different hordes that invaded Britain in succession –

> "The Romans, next the Picts, the Saxons, then the Dane,
> All landing in this Ile, each like a horrid raine."

(7) The invasion of the Normans – the decisive battle of Hastings – and the immediate and disgraceful submission of the Saxon or English people, was looked upon by the Britons as a war between two *strange nations* – a quarrel with which they had nothing to do.

(8) An ancient historian says, that the hearts and hills of the *Ordovecean* and *Silurian* Britons, kept them free for a long time, both from the Roman and Saxon yoke, opposing themselves to the former, till the reign of Domitian – and to the latter, till that of Edward the First.

(9) The restoration of the British Dynasty, in the house of Tudor. – This revolution was doubtless alluded to by Taliesin, in the sixth century.

> "I Vyrthron DYMBI,
> Gwared gwnedd ovri."

> There will be to the Britons,
> A deliverance of exalted power.

As this event was the first that had any tendency to heal the laceration of ages – to conciliate inveterate foes – and to soften and humanize the nations, it was no wonder, therefore, that Sion Tudor, in the Ode addressed to Queen Elizabeth, thus exultingly exclaims –

> "I Harri lan, hir lawenydd,
> Yr hwn a'n rhoes ninnau'n rhydd,
> I Gymru, da vu hyd vedd;
> Goroni'r gwr o Wynedd."

> Our Henry, happy may he be,
> The chief that set his country free;
> Blest be the day, of blissful date,
> That saw him plac'd on Empire's seat.

And if the battle of Bosworth, which effected this happy change, was the last and the least of the thirteen, which had desolated the Kingdom, and destroyed at least One Hundred Thousand of its Inhabitants, during the contention of the Houses of York and Lancaster, it was the first and the greatest in its consequences; by the marriage of this Prince with the Heiress of York, it united the rival houses: by that of his daughter, with James the 4th, of Scotland, it united the rival nations – it associated the Rose of the South, with the Northern Thistle, in this instance (the *Carduus Benedictus*) and formed a great National *Bouquet*, that promises a perennial verdure; and, finally, it eventually placed, under one head, the British Isles, and in that head, aboriginal rights – the claims of connexion – and the pretensions of conquest, are happily concentred.

(10) Cambria shall rejoice, and Cornwall (Britons also) shall be glad, the Isle shall resume its ancient *Name*, and that of Strangers shall perish: so said Merlin, and Time has verified it.

(11) Our historians agree, that King Arthur bore upon his helm, a Red Dragon, it was also, the cognizance of his father Uther, thence called *Pen-dragon*; Henry the 7th knew this, and sensibly appealing to that union of local attachment – innate honor – and, perhaps prejudice, which constitutes what is called Nationality, displayed a red dragon upon a standard of green and white silk, at Bosworth; this, when Sir William Brandon, his standard-bearer, fell, in a personal rencontre with King Richard, Henry judiciously gave to *Rhys ap Meredydd*, of *Hiraethog*, a man of great personal strength and prowess, whose tomb is still to be seen at *Hosputty Evan*, in Denbighshire; and those of my countrymen who *correctly* bear *Gules, a lion rampart argent*, will find this hero of *Hiraethog*, among their forefathers; of these, the Wynnes of *Voelas*, and the Prices of *Rhiwlas*, are leaders.

The Red Dragon was borne as one of the supporters to the Royal Arms, from the succession of the Tudors, to that of the Stuarts, when it gave place to the Unicorn, as now depicted; it also gave rise to a department in the College of Arms, called, *Rouge Dragon*.

Upon a late re-arrangement of the National quarterings, Taste, Science, and Conciliation, would have pointed out the adoption of this ancient Symbol – would have allotted one compartment in the Regal Escutcheon, to that Charge which originally occupied the whole, and the omission is the more apparent in its inducing a repetition (of what is erroneously called, the Arms of England, the Lions, or Leopards, as an English Bard calls them,

> "Our Leopards, they so long and bravely did advance,
> Above the Flower-delice, even in the heart of France."

in the first quarter, being those of Normandy, Guienne, and Aquitaine) and in the appearance of a paucity which does not exist in an Empire composed of four Nations.

(12) The Saxons in 617, under Ethelred, King of Northumberland, made war upon the Britons, and invited to the assistance from Ireland, where he had committed great ravages, Garmond, a Pagan and Norwegian pirate, being instigated thereto by Augustine the Monk, who persecuted the Christians of Britain, because they would not conform to the Romish regulations; to these *Brockwell*, Prince of Powis, and Earl of Chester (who resided at *Pengwern Powis*, or Shrewsbury, upon the site of the old Church of St. Chad) opposed himself: Brockwell was twice defeated near Chester, and more than a thousand of the Religious of the oldest Monastery in Britain (the neighbouring one of *Bangor is y Coed*, upon the Dee, who had come to pray for his success, barbarously murdered.) After this, to prevent their entering Wales, *Brockwell*

retired over the Dee, and defended the passage, till he was joined by Cadvan, Prince of N. Wales, Meredydd, Prince of S. Wales, and Blaiddrys, of Cornwall, and giving the ferocious enemy battle, routed them with great slaughter.

Those *Powisians*, whose paternal Sheild [*sic*] is *Sable, three Nag's heads, erased argent*, will find the intrepid and patriotic *Brockwell*, among their ancestors – of these, the Lord Blaney (*Blaenau*) of Ireland, is one.

(13) Egbert, the powerful King of the West Saxons, who reduced to his obedience all the Princes of the Saxon Heptarchy, invaded Wales, "even unto Snowdon," and crossing into Anglesey, committed great devastation, but *Mervyn Vrych*, (or the freckled) who had married *Esyllt*, Heiress of N. Wales, defeated him, in the "sore battle" of *Llanvaes*, upon which he evacuated the country.

(14) In 877, the Danes and Saxons united to make war upon Wales, but were met at *Camryd*, near Conway, by Anarawd, Prince of N. Wales, and routed. This battle is sometimes called by historians, that of *Camryd*, and sometimes *Dial Rodri* (or Rodri's revenge) – Anarawd's father, Rodri, having a short time before, fallen in battle in Anglesey, called *Gwaith dydd-sul yn Môn*, the work of Sunday.

(15) and (16) In the forests of Euloe, in Flintshire, and on the mountain of Berwyn, in Merionethshire, the fortunes of Henry the 2d, the Power of England, aided by a diversion from Ireland, upon the coasts of Wales, and a full exertion of the old maxim, *Divide et impera*, gave way to a combination of elemental warfare, an inaccessible country, and the prowess of Owen Gwynedd.

Gray, with his usual spirit and ability, has versified the translation of a British Ode, called *Arvyain*, or triumphs of Owen.

(17) Note omitted to Shields, in last line, page 191.
In the ages of contention and discord, before the incorporation by which we became one great and happy people, the now-neglected language of Shields, of Chivalry, and Arms, was that which symbolically recorded the actions of those to whom their country was indebted for safety in the hour of danger: whose names it is grateful to recollect, and whose exploits it is glorious to emulate. Of these, those of *Gweryd ap Rhys Gôch, Ednyved Vychan, Carwed of Twrcelyn, Meurig,* from *Hêdd Moelwynog, Howel y Vwyall, Davydd Gam* (see History, battle of Agincourt) and that of the family of *Bôd Idris* in *Iâl*, are particularly instructing and interesting.

(18) Note omitted to MEED, first line, page 192.
To incite to Patriotism and to Glory, by reciting the virtues and the exploits of their ancestors –

> "To sing the shades of Chiefs in battle slain,
> And burn to join them on th' ethereal plain;
> For Warrior's souls, they sung, would deathless bloom,
> When their cold limbs lay mould'ring in the tomb."

To raise, in the hour of danger, the "Exclamatur ad arma," and to announce the moment of battle, by singing the *Unbennaeth Brydain*, was the sacred – the inspiring duty of the Bards – and theirs also, the immortal Meed – the wreath of everlasting verdure – the trump of Fame; without this, the heroes of *Marathon, Salomis, Platæa*, might indeed have saved their country, but their exemplary efforts would have been unknown, and their God-like actions unconsecrated by the voice of ages.

(19) Note omitted to *grave*, the last word of the Poem.
Such was the determination of *Grydneu, Henven,* and *Aedenaw*, recorded in the 27th *Triade*.

> "Nad eynt o gâd, namyn ar eu helorau."
> To leave the battle, only on their biers.

Upon the subject of these ancient and curious documents, the *Triades*, which record so many otherwise-unknown events in the infancy of Britain, much light has lately been thrown by the Rev. Peter Roberts, in his intelligent "Sketch of the early History of the Cymry."

———

The Levy *En masse*, so much talked of lately, is not new; for I find a Commission issued the second of Edward the 6th, directed to Sir Rhys ap Gryffydd, of Penrhyn, and the Bishop of Bangor, to train all the Men in Carnarvonshire, above the age of sixteen.

46. *Robert Holland Price,* The Horrors of Invasion; A Poem

'Prepare War, wake up the Mighty Men, let all the Men of War draw near: let them come up. Beat your plough-share into swords, and your pruning hooks into spears: let the weak say I am strong.' Joel c. 3, v. 9, 10.

The favourable reception this little Poem has received, and the encreasing demand for it, induces the Author to present the public with a second edition, and to add a few more applicable notes suitable to the times, and the subject. The Author has not the vanity to suppose that its own merits drew upon The Horrors of Invasion the flattering approbation it has met with from all quarters; but attributes it to that generous encouragement which the British nation is ever ready to bestow on any undertaking, though humble, that accords with the known spirit of loyalty, pervading each rank in this kingdom. Happy concordant quality! though France, and such another neighbour leagued, should pour their myriads on our shores, while unanimity prevails, what have we to fear. What a proud day for Britain; to see a whole nation, rising as one man, and rallying round the throne of a beloved Monarch! the Father of his People! When we behold such as scene as this, how well may we repeat, in the language of our immortal Bard:

> Come the three corners of the world in arms;
> And we shall shock them, --- Nought shall make us rue,
> If Britain to itself to rest but true.

O was I gifted with that heavenly fire!
That once the great *Aneurin** did inspire;
Dwelt in the royal *Llywarch's** hardy breast
And shone conspicuous on brave *Owain's** crest:
My muse would then to martial ardour yield,   5
And spirit up each Briton to the field!
Still, though on humble pinions rais'd on high,
She'll try to wing her passage through the sky;
Till on the top of Snowdon,* perch'd amain,
She sounds her trumpet o'er th' adjacent plain;   10
The hills re-echo with its thund'ring roar,
And spread th' inflaming blast from shore to shore.
And thus she cries, "Brave Cambrians to the field,
For scythe and harrow, sword and buckler wield:

Put off the soft habiliments of peace,   15
And prove yourselves no base degenerate race:
Sound all the lofty instruments of war,
And to the tented field with haste repair;
Let the shrill trump, the ear piercing fife,
Provoke the brave to sacrifice his life   20
To honor's call, and his dear country's cause,
(What other death can merit such applause?)
For Bonaparté threats to cross the waves,
And turn our free born Britons into slaves!
Nay dooms to slaughter those that dare oppose*   25
The hellish fury of these barb'rous foes."
Then, if the ocean wafts the impious band,
And lands the Gallic tyrant on our strand,
O Noble Britons! to your posts repair,
And loosen all the fury of the war!   30
Pour like a deluge on the guilty foe,
Rise to the stroke, and aim the mortal blow.
Shew them the gen'rous stock from whence you spring,
Defend your country, guard your pious king!
Protect your homes, your altars, and your laws,   35
Nor fear to perish in so just a cause!
How did our naked ancestors of old,*
With front undaunted, firm, and bravely bold,
Oppose great Caesar! hasten from afar,
And 'gainst his hardy legions wage an equal war: 40
Tho' cased in steel, school'd to the battles rage,
Yet did the Britons dare their arms engage!
And shall they now, with ev'ry means to boot,
Crouch at a vile usurper's bloody foot,
Forbid it heaven! no, rather let this Isle   45
(On which, in happier days, fate seem'd to smile)
Be shaken to its centre! let the main
Break through its bounds and deluge all the plain!
Ere this fair country be enslav'd by those,
Its bitterest enemy and mortal foes.   50
Think not if once the tyrant's num'rous host,
Shou'd land in safety on our sea-girt coast:
And that a fatal day (avert the while!)
Beholds him lord of Britain's fertile soil;

O think not then his fury at an end,   55
Nor dare upon such wretched hopes depend.
His fury but begins! his blood hounds then,
Will prowl the country with a fearful din:
On our beloved homes, their vengeance pour,
And seek, like Satan, whom they may devour!   60
The reverend head of age does not escape
These savage monsters cloth'd in human shape;
They snatch the infant from the mother's grasp,
In their fell grip he breaths his latest gasp!
Or else they spit him on the pike's keen point,   65
Or tear him limb from limb, and joint from joint:
O God! what horror must the mother feel,
To see her darling writhing on the steel!
Nor she alone, more wretches join her moan,
And answer sigh for sigh, and groan for groan.   70
Some for their husbands, fathers, brothers weep,
These slain in battle, those plung'd in the deep.
The shrieking virgin from the spoiler flies,
And fills the valley with her piercing cries;
He heeds them not, but seizes on his prey,   75
And bears in triumph the poor maid away.
Perhaps her vows were plighted to some swain,
Who watch'd the flock, or till'd the neighb'ring plain;
Whose heart exulted in the honest pride,
Of fetching home his fair and lovely bride!   80
Already thought he had her in his arms,
And fancy'd o'er her many nameless charms!
But when he learns her hapless, dreadful fate,
Forc'd to this loathsome violated state,
With madness stung, he rushes on his doom,   85
And seeks for peace within the silent tomb.
These are the fruits of war? whose foul pestiferous breath,
Blasts all the land, and crams the maw of death.
The young and aged, good and guilty feel,
The sharpen'd edge of the destructive steel.   90
The yellow harvest floating o'er the field,
The fruits the orchard, grass the meadows yield,
Towns, hamlets burn, in one great ruin lie!
Their smoke ascends in columns to the sky.*

O heaven forbid! that e'er our eyes should see   95
The dismal havoc of that dreadful day!
Nor view the Tyrant's bloody banners wave,
O'er British Freedom, and the patriot's grave!
And you, ye warriors of my natal land,
A firm, and brave, and well compacted band;   100
Who first drew breath on wand'ring Deva's* side,
Whose Holy waters† through the valley glide
Of fam'd *Llangollen*,* (where in calm retreat,
The noble Ladies† chose their rural seat;
Honor'd, esteem'd, their sex's boast and pride,   105
In blissful solitude, they wait life's ebbing tide.)
Friends! Neighbours! Kinsmen! O with speed advance,
To check the progress of ambitious France;
To guard each blessing that endears our lives,
Protect our parents, sweethearts, children, wives!   110
Led by the gallant *Biddulph** face the foe,
Attack their legions, lay their chieftains low;
Till panic-struck they scour along the plain,
Each Briton mounts on hillocks of the slain!
With eyes of fury, see where *Horsley*† stands   115
And seals destruction through their fainting bands;
With lightning's speed, behold his sabre flies,
And every stroke it gives, a warrior dies!
There, *Roberts*,* *Youde*,† there *Lloyd*‡ the foe engage,
And in the thickest of the battle rage,   120
With purple faulchion mow their furious way,
Nor cease from slaughter, 'till the close of day!
Wynne,§ *Jones*,|| and *Edwards*,¶ share the glorious toil!
With Frenchmen's richest blood they crimson o'er the soil.
And *Price*,* and *Hughes*,† and *Morris*,‡ well do shew,   125
Their native courage on the flying foe.
So will each man I trust, that form this band
Of warriors, fighting for their native land!
Earn deathless laurels, and increase his fame,
To times unborn, an ever grateful theme;   130
So that in ages hence, in far revolving years,
The song of praise may be, *Chirk Hundred Volunteers*.§
Why lovely health, from out my longing arms,
Ah! why withdraw thy ever blooming charms;

While all the British youth in gallant plight,   135
Eager t' engage, are panting for the fight;
Of fighting for my dear and native soil!
How often has the sun in constant roll,
Pursu'd his annual rout from pole to pole;
How oft the months and years pass'd o'er my head,   140
Since health! sweet health! first disappear'd and fled:
But let me bend submissive and resign'd,
And bear with patience and a contrite mind,
Whate'er the will of God has so design'd,
And O! thou eternal ruler of the skies!   145
Look down in pity on our doleful cries;
Stretch out afar thy great almighty hand!
And save! O save! this war devoted land.
Protect thy servant *George* our gracious King!
Preserve him safe beneath thy shelt'ring wing.   150
Pity this ball of earth, this globe, this world!
And let thy heavenly standard be unfurl'd:
At sight thereof, the furies fly away,
And *Peace* once more shall hail the coming day!

[Line 2] * Aneurin, was stiled [*sic*] Mychdeirn Beirdh, or Monarch of the
Bards: he flourish'd about the year of our Lord 510, and fought personally
against the invaders of those days.

[Line 3] * Llywarch-hên had passed his youthful days in the court of
King Arthur. He was sovereign of part of Cumbria, and also a noted bard
and a warrior. He had four-and-twenty sons, who all died in defence of
their country! Two of them were slain on Bwlch y Rhiw Felen; on which
occasion, the princely bard, their father, deplores their loss in an Elegy, of
which these lines are a fragment;

> Bedd Guell yn y Rhiw Felen,
> Bedd Sawl yn Llan-Gollen.
> "Guell found a grave in Rhiw Felen,
> Sawyl in Llan-Gollen."

The battle in which he lost Cynddelw, the last of his numerous sons, was
fought on Rhiwaedog, or the Bloody Brow: a spot not far off, called Pabell

Llywarch-hên, or the tent of the Monarch, is supposed to have been the place where he rested the night after the battle, and where he finished that pathetic Elegy, in which he laments the loss of all his sons; in it, he this directs the last,

> Cynddelw, cadw deitheu y Rhiw
> Ar y ddêl, yma heddiw
> Cudeb am un mab nyd gwiw.

"Cynddelw, thou defend the brow of yonder hill, let the event of the day be what it may, when there is but one son left, it is vain to be overfond of him."

[Line 4] * Owain Cyfeiliog, was prince of Powys in the twelfth century, and a distinguished bard: his Poem, made on the gaining of a great victory over the Saxons in the Maelor, entitled Hirlas Owain, or the Drinking Horn of Owain, is a noble piece of poetry, and has been finely translated into English verse, by the late Reverend Mr. Williams, of Fron.

[Line 9] * While Wales was governed by its native princes, the territory of Snowdon was divided into five baronies, and was all that the brave but unfortunate Llywelyn ab Gruffudd could stipulate for in the short and ruinous peace of 1277. Five years after he was betrayed into the hands of his vindictive enemies, by the lords of Buellt: discovering their treachery, he endeavoured to escape and join a body of his troops that were posted on a neighbouring mountain, but in making this attempt, he was observed by an English knight named Adam de Francton, who, not knowing his quality, and seeing the prince unarmed, and incapable of resistance, plunged a spear into his body. Thus fell Llywelyn by the arm of an assassin! and with him the only remaining sovereignty of the ancient British Empire. A people like the Welsh, forced into a long and unequal contest in defence of their native rights, with few other resources than their valour, and a fond attachment to their liberties, which they preserved through various fortunes for a length of time, against all the power of imperial Rome, and withstood the utmost efforts of the Saxon and Norman princes to reduce them, for more than eight hundred years! Such a people, I say, claim the esteem, and must excite the admiration of the world, as long as manly sentiment and freedom shall remain. May the Britons of these days emulate the magnanimity of their renowned ancestors, may they put on a resolution to conquer or to die in the defence of their beloved country! and either by their courageous efforts preserve its glorious constitution free and inviolate from the threatened contamination of the Corsican, or seek an honourable grave in its ruins.

[Line 25] * The first Consul, in his instructions to the French Invading Army, orders them on their landing in this island, to put every inhabitant they find bearing arms, to immediate death.

[Line 37] * The Ancient Britons were so anxious for the preservation of their country and its liberties, that they esteemed it a happiness not only to fight, but even to sacrifice their lives for them. They were also so courageous, that they dared engage with men covered with armour, and by their activity and their valour, they often came off conquerors. Henry the Second had frequent engagements with the Welsh, and was as often defeated by them, and his person more than once endangered. In a letter to Emanuel, emperor of Constantinople, he gives the following testimony of their courage; "The Welsh nation is so adventurous that they dare encounter naked, with armed men, ready to spend their blood for the country and pawn their lives for praise."

[Line 94] * The reader must not suppose this description exaggerated, would to God such scenes existed only in the poets imagination! but alas! these and others, if possible more dreadful, have been performed by the present sanguinary despot of France. Witness the cool blood massacres, and the poisonings in Egypt; his bloody acts in Italy and Switzerland. The intolerable oppressions and burdens laid, with the most presumptuous arrogance, on the Spaniards and the Dutch, whom he farcically stiles [*sic*] his friends and allies (though with much more propriety and truth he might have termed them his slaves and servants) and with an insulting contrariety, pretends to acknowledge them as free and independent. Nor can I now pass over his unjustifiable seizure of Hanover, and his arbitrary and cruel treatment of the inhabitants---a people, who, forming part of the Germanic body, were at that very time in profound peace with this perfidious nations.---When such objects as these are placed before our eyes, can Britons hesitate upon what conduct to adopt. No! they have but one alternative, conquest or death! Britain victorious, or Britain annihilated.

[Line 101] * Classical name of the river Dee.

[Line 102] † No river in Great Britain has been so much celebrated for its sanctity as the Dee. It was also particularly venerated in former days for the prophetic quality it was supposed to have of fortelling [*sic*] events by the change of its channel. Giraldus Cambrensis, who was secretary to king Henry the Second, and accompanied archbishop Baldwyn in his progress into Wales, anno 1187, is the first who informs us of it possessing those virtues. This notion was continued for ages after. The eminent English Poets, Spencer,

Drayton, and Milton, make frequent mention of the presaging qualities of the Dee,* and bestow upon it the attributes of Holy and Divine.

* Vide, Spencer, stanza 39, Canto 11, Liber 4.
    Drayton, Song 10, and Milton's Lycidas.

[Line 103] * Llangollen is most romantically situated in a small dale closely environed with mountains; on the point of one of them, just above the town, are the remains of Castle Dinas Brân, a most majestic ruin; once the residence of the Madocian line of the princes of Powis. In the same vale stands what the corroding hand of time has left, of the celebrated abbey of Llanegwast: its ragged sides overhung with ivy, and placed in a situation truly awful and sublime.---For a further description of this delicious spot, I must refer my reader to Miss Seward's elegant Poem of Llangollen Vale.

[Line 104] † The right honourable Lady Eleanor Butler and Miss Ponsonby.

[Line 111] * Robert Myddelton Biddulph, Esquire, Lieutenant Colonel Commandant of the Chirk Hundred Volunteers.

[Line 115] † Heneage Horsley, Esquire, son of the Right Reverend the Lord Bishop of St. Asaph, and Major of the Chirk Hundred Volunteers.

[Line 119] * Edward Roberts, Esquire, Dinbren Hall, ⎫ Captains of the
[Line 119] † Edward Youde, Esquire, Plas Madoc, ⎬ Chirk Hundred
[Line 119] ‡ Godfrey Lloyd, Esquire, Tŷ Issa, ⎭ Volunteers.

[Line 123] § Mr. Edward Wynne, Dolfawr, ⎫ Lieutenants in the
[Line 123] || Mr. John Jones, Bache, ⎬ Chirk Hundred
[Line 123] ¶ Mr. John Edwards, Pen-y-Bryn. ⎭ Volunteers.

[Line 125] * Mr. Robert Price, Tower, ⎫ Ensigns in the
[Line 125] † Mr. Edward Hughes, Pentre Felin, ⎬ Chirk Hundred
[Line 125] ‡ Mr Griffiths Morris, Pengwern Hall, ⎭ Volunteers.

[Line 132] § Since the publication of the first Edition a promotion has taken place among the officers. Lieutenant Wynne has been advanced to the command of an auxiliary company at Llansantffraid, Glyn Ceiriog. Ensign Price succeeded Captain Wynne as Lieutenant, and has also been appointed Paymaster to the corps, and Mr. Richard Jones of Rhysgog succeeds Lieutenant Price as Ensign.

47. *Joseph Reade,* Invasion! A Poem *(extract)*

Dedication.
To the Right Hon. the Earl of MOIRA.

My Lord,
In dedicating the following Poem to your Lordship, I do not harbour an
Idea that it is worthy of your Attention as a well-executed Performance, on
the contrary, the existing Defects strike my Eye with peculiar Force when
I consider that they may also meet yours; but flatter myself the Sentiments
it contains are those which you wish to inculcate in every Briton's Heart,
and the Tendency (if effectual) such as must be conducive to the Welfare
of our Country.
. . .
   I confess, that an interested Motive has also actuated me to dedicate this
Trifle to your Lordship. ADDISON has justly dwelt on the Consequence of
a Person's State of Mind in perusing a Work, upon which its Success greatly
depends, as its Tenor is wholly biased by the accidental Disposition of the
Reader. When therefore those who honour this Poem with a Perusal, observe
the Name of a distinguished Patriot affixed, they will insensibly borrow a
Spirit that will pervade the Whole, and the dull Lines will imbibe a genial
Infusion.

I have the Honor to remain
My Lord,
Your Lordship's
Devoted and obliged Servant,
The Author.

To the PUBLIC.

Though the Author has given his Poem the Garb of Blank Verse, it is
not to be understood that he has adopted that dignified Strain which the
Celebration of Heroic Deeds requires. He has attempted to vary his Stile
[*sic*] with his Subjects; where argumentative, his Muse essays her plainest
Tone, in Exhortations she assumes somewhat of a loftier Note, when locally
descriptive, bold or soft as the Situation described demands, and in Parts
representing a Scene of Agitation, a hurried, breathless Stile seems appropriate,
consisting of short, disjointed Sentences, and a kind of explicable Confusion
(if the Term may be allowed). The chief Part of the Poem is however familiar;

but just steering clear of the Dryness of Prose, the Author seldom launches out far beyond the Borders, fearing he would be hid from the Generality of Readers.

From Canto I

Awake! Arise! and from the slothful Bed
Of fond Security ideal, that
Lulls to Lethargy the nobler Senses
As steeped in Waters of Oblivion.
Oh! Britons start! To me the clatt'ring Sound   5
Of thund'ring Cannon with approaching Din
From common En'my, is less terrific
Than is the distant, comprehensive Threat
Of bold Invasion! Menace of Portent!
When lightest deem'd of heaviest Import   10
Made. But hold; that awful Dread, that barring
To the fated Wretch, Hope's swift-genial Beam
Stagnates each Faculty, be far from thee!
Full strong upon thee glares the Sun of Hope.
For steel'd in Unanimity, thou'lt prove   15
The Enemy Presumptious. Thy Swords,
On Hone of Courage staunch, if keenly whet,
In Gall of Injury infus'd, with Fire
Of Indignation, if thy Muskets flash
And Shots of Anger point their Aim, vainly   20
A Host of Enemies, 'gainst Instruments
Stimulated this, their Ammunition
By indecisive Purport faintly urg'd
Oppose. With Intrepidity if met
A War most fatal to their causeless Ire   25
They wage. Causeless, for to herself untrue
While Peace, its balmy Influence, around
Diffus'd, Gallia beneath a Veil of Smiles,
A hideous Monster hid, to send it forth
At Moment opportune, the World to scare,   30
Each Clime, of its Felicity to cheat,
Herself, 'mid gen'ral Ravage, nothing spared.
Gallia have I nam'd? Statement erroneous!

For Machinations foreign, in Island
Mediterranean, nurtur'd, (thence, on Wings   35
That Subtility and Fortune leagued to form,
Swift wasted) admitted, cherish'd and straight
Adopted, Thousands of Men, of One mere
Tools, in useless War immense; --- Too tamely
When but useless stated; at every Sound   40
Of War's Approach, the truly Brave bewail
With certain Presage the coming Slaughter;
Already to their View, in clotted Mass
Comrades are strewn, nor aught of Crime in them
The Butchery palliating; their Bodies   45
Heedless thrown! for Crows and pecking Ravens
Wantonly reserved! Proud Food! Humbled Man!

    . . . Attention's steady Ear
Awhile inclines; my Lay successful, be
The Fame thine own and mark how Circumstance
With fost'ring Pow'r, to nurture Reason when   115
Time teem'd with Topic (the Muse inviting)
For me the Seat of Solitude selects.
Soft, sweet, around me spreads serene Repose.
Calm, unobtrusive, 'mid ethereal pure
Farthest from Scenes that Sensualists engage,   120
At foot of Cambrian Mountain, in a Place
Where still Reflection liv'd, up-reared a Cot
Of form so rustic and so rural cast
(Contiguous by mould'ring Abbey grac'd
And Lake that doubled Nature's Beauties round)   125
My Muse congenial Temperature hail'd.
Then ye, who rattling in the jumbled Maze
Of arbitrary Cares, a Moment fix
Your wav'ring Eye, digested Warnings judge
And learn what now is due from Man to Man.   130

From Canto II

Dark from yon Southern Hemisphere rolls on
A Thunder-threat'ning Cloud to rouse your fears

This deep, black Aspect that foreboding frowns,
Tow'rds Albion Plains, its Destination points;
It low'ring lingers but t' encrease the Store   135
Of Particles combustible, to show'r
With Fury merc'less and with flaming Rage
Amid your fertile Vales, Destruction dire!
But while in Prospect lies the gath'ring Storm
While yet the mere Horizon it obscures   140
Bright Wisdom's Sun may still Meridian shine
Your Minds t' enlighten and your Hearts to warm;
One genial Fervor cause to glow in all;
Your fires concentrate as a Meteor blaze
Disperse the Cloud and rarify the Air.   145
But stubborn, Wisdom's Ray repelling, should
You 'gainst its Influence salubrious
War, with loud Burst of Storm, the Fiends of Hell
Expect; too late a shapeless Croud, madden'd
You fly to stem the roaring Torrent; or   150
Train'd to Order, if yet unfelt your Wrongs
With Arms unstable, Shots are hurtles aim'd;
Or dream ye, Lenity to find from those
Who issuing from rav'nous Lion's Den,
With View of sharing Plunder stake their Lives,   155
Nerveless your Sword you draw and feebly use.
What burning Energy, thro' your whole Frame
Would spur to Vengeance, when (no longer free)
Your Country's Anguish first assails your Ears,
When lawless Rapine can uncurb'd enact   160
Whate'er it list; nor deem it premature
When I assert, that in the Catalogue
Of human Vice, nor vilest Outrage, nor
Most accur'd Crime exists, at which they would
Demur --- My Witness, Hanover! my Judge   165
Yourself. Demand ye Stimulations still?

Howe'er with Horror harrowing up my Soul
My Thoughts sad Tenor will not I suppress.
To seize my Mind, to agitate my Heart
Dread scaring Scenes intrusively combine.   170
Sorrowing I propose that you should share
Th' Anticipation, at Eve of Battle,

That high your Breasts may heave with honest Rage.
Imagination, now in dread Array
A thousand Terrors forms, and restless wakes 175
To Probabilities too keenly clear.
To Spoilers in dread Perspective black'ning
Our Prospect, deep with sanguinary Hue
Imprinting. --- Expanding now before me
Ruthless Band! Behold what murd'rous Deeds our 180
Land disgrace! Behold that Partner (that twin'd
Around your Heart with Tie endearing) Plain
Amid your Children at your Cottage Door;
Pausing I descry her; at each Whistle
Of the Wind list'ning for your Step in vain; 185
But Fears arise redoubled by the Roar
Of rumbling Cannon from contiguous Camp;
Her youngest babe she snatches to her Breast;
Swift as Lightning (by the Elder follow'd)
Darts onward tow'ards yon Shelter-forming Wood, 190
But quicker still, lo! Frantic she returns;
Her Cot regains; spurning th' opposing Door
Her little Charge within she drives; one look
Now ventures back, then seeks some Instrument
Her frail-formed Cottage-barrier fast to bind. 195
And see, the Cause of her Affright starts out;
A ruffian Herd! Their Swords yet smoaking [sic] with
Your fresh-drawn Blood! Rushing more eager forth
The panting Trembler they pursue. With Strides
Impatient scorn the ling'ring Path and crush 200
The care-rear'd Plants (late Pride of your abode)
Beneath their Feet, indignant of Delay.
Tho' these of Magnitude, alone, you deem
When greater Evils scare, but Trifles prove
And Hark! A Crash strikes harsh upon mine Ear, 205
That Shriek but justifies too well my Dread;
The slender Guardian of the Cottage Wealth
Its splinter'd Strength (Storm-fear'd) in vain it tries.
Alarmed, mine Eye thro' th' Aperture I cast
And view the cow'rdly Conquerors advance 210
(For sure a Spirit dastardly it shews
At pow'less Enemy to stab secure)
Breathless she sees them, with a bursting Heart

Low on her Knee the humble Suppliant craves.
Of human Form partaking, she has Hope   215
That Human Nature dwells within their Breast;
But fierce, with Eye unsoften'd, as they gaze
Their Choler strength'ning, she withdraws her Boon,
And sudden rising, with a manly Strength
Two frighten'd Children clasps within each Arm,   220
"Now let me pass" she cries, and 'twixt them cross'd:
An Instant stand the Men astounded; she
Now forward springs, the Treshold [sic] gains; they start!
A Moment's longer Pause and she were gone;
But hold, the Scene of Horror is to come;   225
The Tumult past but Music, Bliss, will seem
Comparatively shewn, for her the Blow
By yon Ruffian dealt; "Ah! wretched Mother,
See thine Infant fall, thine Arm is numb'd; hark!
Thy Children scream." Her Form (resistless now)   230
The Villains seize; when instant, each other
Echoing, her beauteous Prattlers beg their
Mother's Life, nor beg in vain; a Conflict
Of wilder Passions is she doom'd to feel.
What deep-dyed Fluid's that? What purple Stream?   235
Oh! Height of Mother's Pangs! Her Children's Blood!
The merc'less Monsters, Children's Innocence
And Importunity affectionate
Could ne'er brook; but feel each Pray'r of Infants
A Curse from Nature. --- The Fury darting   240
From those Tyrant's Eye, to what this Moment
I observe in that craz'd Mother, was sure
Meekness mild; boldly now, behold! t' appease
Her Infant's Manes, a Sword she snatches from
The Soldier's Side, and aims a Blow design'd   245
To strike the Murderer's Heart. Poor Suff'rer!
Not to thee is giv'n the Pow'r of Veangeance;
For Heav'n reserv'd! The Climax of her Fate
Draws nigh. Regain'd the Sword, Decision dark
With anger-heated Blood the Men resolve!   250
In their rough Arms (the Weapon weeping warm)
The other screaming Children grasp and forth
Prepare to hurl them to a kindred Fate.
When clatt'ring Clash of heavy Horse's Hoof

Startling, suspends the scaring Steel awhile.   255
Of ruffian Comrades soon a Croud unhorse
With Curses coarse a bleeding Pris'ner thrust
Remorseless in; mean Time the mad Matron
Furious, strong, her tight-held Hands attempts
To disengage. Failing, her Husband's Aid   260
Anguish'd she implores; for her, in this World
The only Hope delay'd, his Life. How short
The Hope delusive stays to sooth her Woes:
To a Corpse she screams! to a Ghost complains!
Too soon the fatal Truth her Senses meets   265
"He fell" the Pris'ner cries, no more she hears,
Her Body sinks; the Ruffian quits his Charge
On the cold stones she falls --- but she's as cold.

With her short Life, close we the fancied Scene,
He fell we heard, the Manner of his Death   270
For your Solution rests; be mine the Task
To urge; 'tis yours not worthless of my Care
To prove. How ample then were my Reward!

Whoe'er among ye, your soft Hours to bless
Such Wife, such Children boast, in Battles' Rage   275
May those soft Hours harden you the more,
Let Wrongs anticipated nerve your Arm,
And Calms precedent, to a Tempest urge!

From Canto III

Resound, rush forth my Lyre with boldest String,
For lofty Souls; a hardy Race I laud.
Cambrians my theme! bids not my Heart aspire   280
In Strains eulogic t' emulate their Zeal.
From their fam'd Bards a Gleam of Life to catch
Their Harp of Spirit and their Touch of Lyre.
Amid the mad Metropolis's Scene
Where Tumult is the Note, where art, the Song.   285
Nor Cambria's Sons, nor Cambrian Deeds were known,
Or, with the Past compar'd, were though inert,

Till the same Wind that wafted Foes from France
Blew Fame of Cambrian Valor's added Store;
For not exclusively is Valor shewn   290
In Firm Deportment at the Wound gangrene,
But acts a strong preparatory Part
While yet Regardless of expected Harm.
Be this their Praise, for lo! they fearless stand
An unexperienced [sic], but a dauntless Throng.   295
Dauntless! far more, they're eager to engage,
And the last Care upon their Minds their Life.
Swiftly the En'my thick'ning on the Shore
With wary Caution and in Silence land.
Quick flies th' Alarm; Invasion stuns the Ear   300
Like Light'ning flashing; Cambrians dart on
Th' encroaching Foe to meet; nor Arms possess
Nor Use of them they know. To Cattles [sic] Care
Solely, the Plough is left; for with the Men
To War the Women speed; the steepest Hills   305
Impatient climb, chiding the seemingly
Retreating Main; at length 'tis spread before
Their gladden'd Sight, and num'rous Foes appear,
And still more Foes arise. To Soldiers train'd
Their Number insignificant; to View   310
Of Country Clowns, a Host! --- With sharpen'd Scythes,
On stoutest Poles uprais'd, gath'ring, they would
Have rush'd the fiercest Fires among; how would
The swol'n Plains have groan'd with *Cambria*'s Sons!
Scarce had they pour'd adown the Mountain's Slope   315
Ere Shots effectual had check'd their Tide;
But now, in Haste, from Southern Coast, a Chief,
Whom Wisdom mark'd for her adopted Son,
Experience seizing, e'er its Tax was paid,
Sudden arrives. Needless, Death's beck'ning Hand   320
He saw them meet; th' impressive Reprimand
He timely gave; shew'd them, if Victory
They meant to purchase, undisciplin'd, they
Dare not tempt the Vale; taught them th' Advantage
Of the Mountain's Height, and that Deception   325
Form'd their only Strength; forthwith, a deep plan'd
Stratagem adopted (solely, willing

Novices at Hand) the Farmers ranging
With their Men, for merest Shew, in Order
Somewhat Martial. Next, on still more distant   330
Hills, o'ertopping those, the Women plac'd. These
With Acquisition of a Handful more
Of war-train'd Men, the Leader's Band compose.
From fancied Penetration blind, the Sons
Of *Gallia* imaginary Thousands   335
(By Height, by Distance delusive, tripled)
Find. "What Legions strong!" exclaim they in wild
Affright. What fancied Myriads croud! Their Arms
Deliv'ring at the earliest Summons,
A bloodless Victory they decide; but mark   340
The Ardour of the *Cambrian* Peasants round,
In Time to gain th' expected Combat's Field.
Each in imagination kills his Man,
Each within his Span already sees him
Grasp'd. Oh! may those Bosoms feel an added   345
Warmth, when Aggravation points the real
Blow; when real Hosts your proud Shores to girt
Advance; your Domain with Chains encircling,
Your Stores their Aim, your Happiness their Ire.
. . .

48. *'Britannus', 'To Bonaparte'*

Scourge of the earth! inhuman Monster! say —
How canst thou hope Britannia to subdue;
Shall Britain ever feel thy iron sway,
Or will an Englishman ere cringe to you?
Curs'd be the thought! perdition catch the sound!   5
Not such the crimson springs their veins supply:
Never was yet a single instance found,
Where Britons doubt to conquer or to die.
Hast thou forgot, or does th' historic page
In vain remind thee of the days of yore;   10
When Albion's sons evinc'd their warlike rage,
And Gallia's plains were deluged with gore.
Hast thou forgot? I'll answer for thee, Not
The siege of Acre in the Holy Land,
Where Bonaparte receiv'd a mortal blow   15
From brave Sir Sidney and his gallant band.
What sad delusion does thy soul impel,
A race renown'd of heroes to annoy?
The sea-girt island soon will make thee feel,
And bring thee into reason yet, my boy!   20
When awful fate has fix'd th' embattled plain,
Where deathless deeds proclaim the hero's fame,
Europe shall know, malgre thy coup-de-main,
That Bonaparte has play'd a foolish game.

Carmarthenshire   BRITANNUS

49. T. Ellis Owen, 'Anglesey Volunteer Song'

Tune – 'The Vicar of Bray'

When conquering Cæsar did draw first,
 The sword of Desolation,
And first, amazed, Britannia saw
 The curse of bold Invasion;
The Druids, fam'd of Mona's Isle,   5
 Did bravely yield their breath, Sir,
And rather than in bondage toil,
 They chose a glorious death, Sir.

Chorus

The Briton's feel a patriot's zeal,
 Attend to Honor's call, Sirs,   10
Resolv'd to see your Country free,
 Or with its freedom fall, Sirs.

When Saxon Hengist rul'd the roast [*sic*],
 Or Norman William reign'd Sir,
Still freedom was the Welshman's boast, 15
 And freedom be maintain'd Sir:
In vain to quell them Edward tried,
 They hurl'd a bold defiance;
But what they to his Arms denied,
 They gave to his Alliance. (a)   20

Chorus

We boast Llewellyn's sacred seat, (b)
 Let's boast his valour too, Sir,
Till low at each true Briton's feet,
 Does crouch the Gallic Foe, Sir.
The sword your Royal Hero bore,   25
 Again shall flame before ye,
And teach his hardy Sons once more,
 To tread the Paths of glory.

Chorus

Hibernia's blood-stain'd rebel dread, (c)
    A Welshman's resolution,   30
Prepar'd Life's last, best blood to shed,
    For King and Constitution.
When France on Pembroke's Plains did flee, (d)
    She met her just reward, Sir,
And Cambrian courage still shall be   35
    A free born Briton's Guard, Sir.

Chorus

On Egypt's plains when Gaul declar'd,
    Invincible her Standard;
But soon by British valour scar'd,
    That boasted flag surrendered;   40
Our Cambrian Heroes still were there,
    Still foremost up the fray, Sir,
A Paget (e) and a Jones (f) to share,
    The lot of that proud Day, Sir.

Chorus

Again, with more that Gothic rage,   45
    She threatens our undoing,
And madly dooms each Sex and Age
    To universal ruin:
But we will meet this daring host,
    With Hands and Hearts united;   50
A wall of steel round Britain's coast,
    We'll see our Country righted.

Chorus

The let old Mona's Sons advance,
    Britannia's rights to shield, Sir,
We'll show these blustering blades of France,   55
    That Britons ne'er will yield, Sir.

So shall our Deeds in every clime,
    Be handed down to fame, Sir,
And on her Rolls to latest time,
    Inscribed a Welshman's name, Sir.   60

(a) Alludes to the Stratagem of Edward the First, respecting the first Prince of Wales of English blood.

(b) Aberffraw in Anglesey, where was found Llewellyn's Sword of State, now in the possession of O. P. Meyrick, Esq. Lieutenant-Col. of the Volunteers.

(c) Sir W. W. Wynne's Welsh Fencibles were the terror of the Irish Rebels last War.

(d) Landing of the French at Fishguard.

(e) The Honorable Colonel Paget, of the 28th Regiment.

(f) Major Jones, of the 23d Regiment.

50. *Richard Llwyd, 'Awdl y Misoedd / Ode of the Months'*

From the British of Gwilim Ddu, of Arvon, Bard to Sir Gryffydd Llwyd, of Tre'r garnedd, in Anglesey, and Dinorwig, in the county of Carnarvon.

Some account of Sir Gryffydd Llwyd, from Rowland's Antiquitatis Parochiales; and Mr. Vaughn of Hengwrt's Notes on Powel's History of Wales.

Sir Gryffydd Llwyd, Knight, ap Rhys ap Gryffydd ap Ednyved Vychan, Seneschal to Llewellyn ap Jorwerth (*Leolinus Magnus*) was a valiant gentleman but unfortunate, "*Magnæ quidem sed calamitosæ virtutis,*" as Lucius Florus says of Sertorius; he was knighted by Edward the first, then holding a Parliament in the castle of Rhuddlan, when he brought him the news of the safe delivery of his Queen, at Carnarvon, of Edward Prince of Wales; but Sir Gryffydd afterwards enraged by the extreme barbarity and tyranny of the English Officers, particularly Sir Roger Mortimer, Lord of Chirk, Justice of North Wales, and unable to procure redress for his Country from the King, excited and led an insurrection, verifying the words of Solomon, that, "Oppression maketh a wise man mad;" he with this view, entered into a treaty with Sir Edward Bruce, brother to Robert then King of Scotland, to make an in-road into the north of England, in order to divide the King's power and attention, while he endeavoured to expel his forces from North Wales, but this treaty, from the exorbitancy of Bruce's terms, not taking effect, Sir Gryffydd, driven to desperation, latinised the Adage, "*Gwell marw vel dyn, na byw vel ci,*" and that it might be intelligible to his enemies, displayed the words *Vincere vel mori* upon his shield and banners, and, in an instant, overran North Wales and the Marches, taking all the strong holds, but was at length defeated, and taken prisoner; what became of him is not with certainty said, but from this, and other poems, it is supposed, that he ended his days a prisoner on the castle of Rhuddlan.

Morvydd, the eldest of his seven daughters and co-heiresses conveyed by her marriage with Madoc of Gloddaeth (the banqueting house) the Mansion of Tre'r garnedd, with its appendages, into that family. The issue of this match was, Gryffydd, whose son Rhys, inheriting the intrepidity of his forefathers, supported Owen Glyndwr, in that last effort to restore the independence of his country and lost his estates, but at the close of that war of nine years, as it was called in 1410, he was restored to a moiety of Creuddyn, the other being sold to Gryffydd ap Gwilim, of Penrhyn: Margaret, sole heiress of his son Gryffydd, carried this property and that of Tre'r garnedd, into the family of Mostyn, by her union with Howel ap Evan Vychan, of that house.

His Coat Armorial – *Gules, a chevron or, and chief ermine*, is paternaly [*sic*] borne *only* by the Davies of Caer Rhûn, of which house was Thomas Davies, Bishop of St. Asaph in 1561, a man who did honor to a Mitre; among other pious actions, the settlement of a scholarship in Queen's College, Cambridge, was one.

Descended from Sir Gryffyd's co-heiresses, the following families do, or may, quarter it – Mostyns of Mostyn, Lloyds of Havodunos; and from his daughter Cecily, the descendents of Sir Henry Sidney, Lord Deputy of Ireland, and Lord President of the Marches of Wales, in the reign of Elizabeth, a name illustrious in both nations, for the virtues and abilities of several of its possessors, the representatives also, if any, of the Griffiths of Llwyn dyrus, Salisburys of Llanrhaidr, Morrises of Treborth uchav, and the Hollands of Hendre vawer, near Abergele. MS. &c.

This poem was the produce of a period of peculiar calamity, when a long and obstinately protracted contest had reached a close, which, it is only surprising, did not happen sooner: when one nation, powerful in its population, and rich in its resources, was contending with the harrassed [*sic*] remnant of another, the proportional ability of which, was but as one to twelve, and which had nothing to oppose to these overwhelming advantages, but a love of Freedom, Fortitude, and Rocks: that the hand of oppression was heavy there are many proofs,* that the colouring is not too high, is confirmed by Gwilim Ddu's contemporary bards; and the reflecting mind will be at no loss to discover the sources of suffering in the insolence of conquest, the reluctance of submission, and the unhumanised ferocity of the age; of this, the revolt of Sir Gryffydd is, in itself, ample testimony, favored [*sic*] and rewarded as he was by Edward, yet the Amor Patriæ glowed too intensely in his bosom for selfish acquiescence; and roused by atrocities to which he might possibly consider himself as having (by inculcating submission, with the laudable hope of a final pacification) in some degree, contributed, he had recourse to arms, the last refuge of the brave, resolving upon a meliorated existence, in which his country might participate, or, on his part, its honourable termination.

---

* See the many pathetic and unavailing petitions to King Edward for redress, in Powel's History of Wales; in which the sufferings of his new subjects are emphatically called *Greefs* [*sic*]. – see also Notes to *Beaumaris Bay*.
To Sir. T. Mostyn, Bart. M.P.
For the County of Flint.

This attempt to renovate, in the language of Modern Britain, the plaintive and grateful notes of Gwilim Ddu, the subject of which, is the magnanimity, patriotism, and beneficence of that Wallace of his Country, Sir Gryffydd Llwyd, his patron, and your illustrious ancestor.
Is respectfully inscribed
By R. Ll.

"Neud cyn nechreu Mai mau anrhydedd."

My days were bright, my hours were gay,
Ere Cambria saw the sun of May;
That erst dispel'd the winter's gloom,
And bless'd the world with love and bloom.

How heavy on this suffering land,   5
Almighty Father,* falls thy hand;
Inflictive falls, as when of old,
The Saviour of the world was sold:
'Tis ours, in these disastrous times,
To suffer as if curst with crimes;   10
To see the ruin widely rage,
And Havoc seize the locks of age;
While slaughter'd vigour loads the earth,
And Vice, triumphant, treads on Worth:
To Heaven, in vain, even Virtue calls,   15
The foe exults – my Country falls!

O! thou, decreed a world to save,
Where can I rest, but in the grave,
Where can I pass the hours of pain,
Forbid even sorrow's soothing strain;   20
Forbid* by foes, whose breasts are steel,
To pour, to Heaven, the pangs we feel.

Can Bards who fill'd the rolls of fame,
Live but to hold an empty name;
Can I, that long, with grateful tongue,   25
Tregarnedd's† warlike-lord have sung,
Live, and in inglorious rest,
Behold my princely Chief deprest.

Like Dunawd's* Bard, whose plaintive tongue,
The woes of other times has sung;   30
So I, on recent sorrows dwell,
And sad, my Country's troubles tell;
To me how glooms the cheerful day,
That spreads around the sweets of May;†
And June, gay Summer's pride and care,   35
But feeds the horrors of Despair;
Alas! if Gryffydd does not live
What joy can varying seasons give;
What pleasure to the breast of pain,
The World itself – exists in vain!   40

There are – who hear, unmov'd the strain,
By Verse and Virtue rous'd in vain,
Whose breasts resist the patriot glow,
Who crouch beneath the foes controul,
And bear the lash, that tears the soul;   45
Be theirs, Depression's abject life,
But mine, the war's eventful strife!

Where is the Hawk* whose wings were spread,
Whose beak, with Saxon blood was red,
That proudly perch'd on triumph's car,   50
With England's Marches wag'd the war;
Our prowess prov'd, aveng'd our wrongs,
And tun'd to joy, unnumber'd tongues?

Where is the Sword of crimson hue,
That gleam'd upon the warrior's view,   55
A thousand feats record its strength,
And terror long shall tell its length;
And well th' indented edge will show,
To days unborn, its deathful blow?

Where's the red Lance that led the way,   60
When Gryffydd won the doubtful day,
That, torch-like, blazing in his hand,
To conquest lest his Country's band;
When foes, invading, fought and fled,
And England's bravest blood was shed?   65

Heroic band – a people's pride,
That stem'd invasion's threat'ning tide,
That stay'd awhile, your Country's fall,
Illustrious Shades! on you I call;
As bending o'er the soil I weep,   70
Where now your peaceful spirits sleep:
And Cambria's tears bedew the grave;
With flowers,* unfading, decks the sod,
And gives your happier souls to God!

Ye scenes, where still my footsteps tend,   75
Where still unwean'd my wishes bend,
Ye domes, where now, I pensive gaze,
Were bright, when beam'd, the social blaze,
When Gryffydd, from a princely store,
Abundance to the banquet bore: 80
Ye storied walls, where Time shall trace,
High Bryn* Euryn's, trophied race;
That rich in glory's proudest lore,
The deeds of other days restore;
Ye roofs that long responsive rung,   85
When Bards the trying conflict sung,
When Joy's exulting voice was high,
When songs of triumph reach'd the sky,
And horns* from Hybla's sweetest stream,
Were fill'd to Gryffydd's glorious name;   90
Alas, the poor no more repair,
His bounty and his smiles to share;
Heart-rending sighs to Heaven ascend,
They mourn, like me, their common friend:
Chill as the cells that hold the dead,   95
The festive halls where crowds were fed,
Where Gryffydd grac'd the frequent treat,
And led the stranger to his seat:
Like generous Nudd,* in days of yore,
So Gryffydd gave – but gives no more!   100

Dismay and terror seiz'd our foes,
When Arvon's towering eagle rose;
Achilles like, with helmet high,
And fury flashing in his eye,

As Urien† bold, the battle's boast.   105
A nation's hope – his arm, an host;
He rush'd, as torrents roll along,
No flattery stains a Gwillim song;
It flows, like Avon's* dulcet stream,
When brave Cadwallon fill'd the theme.   110

At length the fell, vindictive foe,
Has laid Dinorwig's† lion low;
And now with haughty crest relates,
His happier, and our adverse fates;
While Cambria shrinks, with boding fear,   115
And dreads the tale, she's doom'd to hear,
To hear that Rhuddlan towers restrain,
The man, by Virtue, rear'd to reign;
In chains, my chief, of graceful form,
Smiles at insult, braves their scorn,   120
And bleeding, crown'd with honour's wreath,
Awaits, and courts the dart of death;
While now, on every breeze 'tis borne,
With every pang my breast is torn;
I sink to earth, to hear his name,   125
With all that mans, and warms my frame;
Yet Fame, to other times, shall tell,
How Griffith fought, how Griffith fell;
And ages yet to come, shall hear,
As downward rolls, the pitying tear!   130

Misfortunes throng on every side,
Fallen is Mona's strength and pride,
And lofty Arvon, Gwynedd's* tower,
Falls, and feels, the unequal power;
Her sons by Saxon hosts assail'd,   135
At Rheon's ford† – have fought and fail'd;
In vain the phalanx firmly stood,
Till Rheon roll'd a tide of blood;
They fell, o'erwhelm'd a nation falls,
And Saxon power my Prince enthrals;   140
Oppression's plan, at length succeeds,
At every pore, my Country bleeds;

No ray of hope pervades our woes,
No trait of mercy, marks our foes;
And Britain's sons, in vain, are brave,   145
Immur'd within a living-grave!

Affliction wild, with piercing cry,
And dark Despair, with downcast eye;
The manly Mind, that scorns to speak,
The indignant Heart, that swells to break;   150
All agonise my breast to close,
At once – existence and its woes!

[Line 6] * It was not unusual among the Bards, to invoke the Supreme Being in their Odes, and there are instances among the ancients of other nations, though to inferior deities.

[Line 21] * To repress those who were the *living* records of their country and their forefathers; those to whom their contemporaries looked up for fame and immortality, was not new even then in the annals of Tyranny, even so late as 1480, Davydd Llwyd of Mathavarn, in an Ode to Owen Tudur, of Penmynydd, says –

> Gwyddom dewi a goddev.
> We know to suffer, and to be silent.

[Line 26] † Tre'r garnedd (the tumulus farm) in Anglesey, was in 1220, the property and occasional residence of Ednyved Vychan; from him it descended to his great grandson, Sir Gryffydd Llwyd, who, when he revolted, fortified this house with a foss, 8 yards wide and 4 deep, and, at the same time, formed another strong-hold, at a short distance from it, in the Morass of Malldraeth, intended as a retreat, in the last extremity; this he insulated by drawing round it the deep waters of the river Cevni; and sufficient vestiges of both still remain to ascertain their relative strength and situation.

[Line 29] * Son of Pabo Post Brydain, a Bard of the 6th Century.

[Line 34] † The propriety of the title of the poem, "*Ode of the Months,*" does not clearly appear, two of them only being mentioned.

[Line 48] * This is probably an allusion to Carwed, Lord of Twr Celyn, whose crest it was. – The exploits of that Chieftain in the war with Henry the Second being yet fresh in the public voice.

[Line 73] * "Unfading blooms on the grave of the hero, the garland prepared by his country."

Such also, was the sentiment engraved on the pedestal of a column of Norwegian marble, and placed by the gratitude of the Danish nation, on the grave of her brave sons who fell in the bombardment of Copenhagen, by the British fleet, April 2, 1801; and that breast can have little of liberality that would confine the Virtues to the limits of his Country.

[Line 82] * Bryn Euryn, is in the parish of Llandrillo, near Conwy, and of thirteen residences in the possession of Ednywed Vychan, in North Wales, this is said to be the favorite, and to have been "royaly [sic] adorned with turrets and garrets." – Sir Tudur ap Ednyved was one of the Commissioners for negociating a peace between Edward the first and Llewelyn ap Gryffydd; and his descendants, resident at this place, afterwards assumed and bore the name of Conway; and an English family resident at Bod Rhuddlan, also assumed this name, upon marriage with a Lady of this house; both families are now extinct in the male line.

[Line 89] * These were the mead horns of ancient hospitality, and called the Hirlas; that of Owen Gyfeiliog, Prince of Powis, has been the subject of a beautiful Ode, for the appearance of which, in English, the public are indebted to the pen of an accomplished scholar.

An elegant specimen of the antient Hirlas is still preserved at Lord Penrhyn's seat in Carnarvonshire.

> Fill with *Mead* the *Hirlas* high,
> Nor let a bowl this day be dry;
> The hall resounds – the triumph rings –
> And every bard the conflict sings.
> *Ednufed's* trophied shield displays
> Themes of glory – themes of praise –
> A lion, in the tented field –
> A lamb, when vanquish'd heroes yield.
> *Ednufed!* bravest of the brave!
> His name shall live beyond the grave!

> Vide notes to Beaumaris Bay.

[Line 99] * Nudd Hael (or the generous) one of the three liberal Princes of Britain, mentioned in the triades, and sung by Taliesin.

[Line 105] † A Cumbrian or Cumberland Prince, often mentioned by the Bards of the Sixth Century, the pretended assumption of this name (Fitz-Urien) was one of the *reasons* given by Henry the Eighth, for executing that hopeful and accomplished youth Sir Griffith Rice, at twenty-three; the son of Rhys ap Thomas, of South Wales, who had been so instrumental in placing his father, Henry the Seventh, on the throne of England; and a similar *reason* (quartering the arms of their Ancestor, Thomas de Brotherton, fifth son of Edward the first) was found for the destruction of that Mecænas of his day – the Young Earl of Surrey, the Scholar and the Soldier; but the death of Henry, fortunately saved his father, the Duke of Norfolk.

[Line 109] * Avan Verddig, the bard of Cadwallon ap Cadvan, King of Britain, and, in the Triades, is described as one of the three bloody-speared bards of Britain; his patron, Cadwallon, slew Edwin, King of Mercia, in the battle of Meigin, where the men of Powis behaved so well, that they were distinguished with particular privileges, mentioned by Cynddelw, in an ode called *Breiniau gwyr Powys*. – Bede, in his Ecclesiastical History, describes this Prince by the words *Tyrannum sevientem*.

[Line 112] † Situate on the edge of the Arvonian ridge, in the parish of Llanddeiniolen, and within a few miles of Bangor, was one of the many temporary (and in these tumultuous times, necessarily so) residencies of the Princes of Wales; the situation is most inviting, and though the ruins are nearly removed, the dimensions of the great hall, the hospitality of which, Gwilim Ddu so feelingly sings, and which was twenty-four yards long, are still ascertainable. – One of the many favors bestow'd upon Sir Gryffydd, by the King, was Dinorwig, and the continuation of this, and his other property, in his descendents, shows that Edward, in this instance, did not extend the rapacity of tyranny to its seizure, on the revolt of the proprietor. This division continued in that great and leading branch of his family, residing at Penrhyn and Cochwillan, till William Williams, Esq. transfered [*sic*] it to his third son, Thomas Williams, of Vaenol, ancestor to Sir William Williams, Bart. who, dying without issue, left his estates to King William, who granted them to Mr. Smith, Speaker of the House of Commons, in whose descendant Thomas Ashton Smith, Esq. of Vaenol, they now are.

[Line 133] * North Wales, the Venedotia of the Romans.

[Line 136] † A river in Carnarvonshire, now unknown, having probably changed its name.

*51. Richard Llwyd, 'Owen of Llangoed. Founded on fact.
To Fleetwood Williams, Esq. of Liverpool'*

First Part.

Where is the Muse that loves the good,
The plaintive strain to offer;
But to the bright benignant breast,
That feels for all that suffer.

'Tis this that prompts her now to bring, 5
To thee, a noiseless story;
For Fame confines her brazen trump,
To deeds of martial glory.

She flies on every breeze that blows,
To spread her loud narration, 10
Nor Seas resist, nor Alps repel,
The true, or false, inflation.

To her, the Muse consigns the names,
That court Ambition's bubbles;
And sings the hamlet's humbler cares, 15
A peasant's joys and troubles.

Where Courda* once, in days of yore,
Taught Faith a cell to rear;
A cottage stands, beneath the cliff,
To Owen's feeling's dear. 20

To every heart, how dear is home,
(If worth that heart possesses)
It still renews our earliest joys,
A parent's fond caresses.

A brother's, sister's dear embrace, 25
The love-increasing battle,
The little play-things, still preserved,
The first-engaging prattle.

Six Olive branches gather'd round,
This crowded Cottage table,   30
Till Time declar'd, that Owen, now,
To guard the flocks was able.

The Muse records the sorrowing day
When Owen went, though willing,
To earn his bread, a *little man*,   35
A *new* importance feeling.

The tears ran down his mother's cheeks,
His father saw them – sighing;
His play-mates shook his little hands,
And all the group – were crying!   40

The rushy cap now crown'd his pate,
The mystic crook, his sceptre;
The flocks and fields, his people, realms,
And Nature sole preceptor.

With pastoral pipe,* this infant Pan,   45
Commenc'd his new vocation;
Completed soon, his present views,
A shepherd's education.

The linnets lov'd his dulcet voice,
The larks drew near in numbers,   50
And thought they wak'd the morning sun,
From night's protracted slumbers.

They met at noon his brightest blaze,
They join'd their grateful voices;
Thus Nature, in the sweetest strain,   55
Through all her realms rejoices.

'Twas thus when Day's decending [*sic*] boons,
On western waters rested;
They knew their little nests were safe,
By Owen unmolested.   60

And if he had, the Virtues, Muse,
Even Heaven itself had hated;
The impious hand, that touch'd their hopes,
The future song frustrated.

Second Part.

Thus Owen daily kept his flock,   65
On Marian's* summits seated,
And distant saw, the passing sails,
By every breeze inflated.

Now saw on Llangoed's fertile shores,
The placid waters waving,   70
And now beheld, on rocky steeps,
The billowy rollers raving.

A novel wish, in Owen's thoughts,
Intruded now, was growing;
The place they came from, where they went,   75
The curious itch of knowing.

He'd heard indeed, from Mona's sons.
From regions far returning,
That northern seas were lock'd in ice,
That Afric's sands were burning.   80

He'd also heard, though undeter'd,
From parents still deploring,
Of lads that left them, for the deep,
No tidings yet restoring.

He'd heard of Mersey's* crowded shores,   85
The Dee's triumphant neighbour;
Where Commerce, with a smile beheld,
Success reward her labour.

That there she saw, her useful stores,
From every climate swelling,   90
That all the Virtues, Arts were there,
And pleas'd, had found a dwelling.

And Charity* their Heavenly chief,
Her every view revealing;
That every woe, that Misery wears,   95
Her hallow'd hand was healing!

That there, to gladden sightless woe,
A novel path she'd chosen;
For those that go without and eye,
From her, get near a dozen.*   100

That stretching far her friendly views,
To distant Scotia turns,
And beckons to her fostering arms,
The orphans left by Burns.

Sweet rural songster, born for Heaven,   105
Not earth's ungenial region;
A sparkler even in spangled† skies –
A leader in a legion.

O! Currie,* from the Cambrian bard,
This grateful strain be thine,   110
And Fame shall henceforth, write thy name,
In characters benign.

And he† – may Heaven his efforts bless,
Who guides an Empire's cares;
For his *own heart*, a moment steals –   115
A *thought* for Genius spares.

That even by the Nine, by Virtue led,
(Whose voice they all revere)
Desert, at times, their sweetest shades –
Delight to loiter there.   120

Entice'd by Roscoe's tuneful voice,
They leave their fav'rite fountains;
And cliffs that echo, love the lay,
Now miss them in the mountains.

Delightful warbler, Mersey's own,　　　　　　　　125
Thy lot be lengthen'd years;
To charm with Arno's* classic themes,
Thy Country's list'ning ears.

That Cambria, from adjacent cliffs,
With eye of glee looks down –　　　　　　　　　130
Exulting sees, a valued youth,
Her hopes, maternal, crown.

Beholds him with a parent's care,
Her hapless orphans seek;
And lead, for them, the feeling tear,　　　　　　　135
Down many a manly cheek.

Williams,* while Britain's grateful voice,
Applauds they efforts blest,
She gives her native Muse to waft
Her blessing to thy breast!　　　　　　　　　140

He now left Llangoed's pastoral banks,
And Dwynwen's region, Dona,*
Exchang'd for Mersey's busy shores,
His dear maternal Mona.

He soon beheld the turrets tall,　　　　　　　145
The crowded town* denoting;
And saw, with wonder's widest eye,
A people'd forest floating.

There – though in a constant crowd,
He found his footsteps lonely;　　　　　　　150
For Owen's tongue, as yet, was tun'd,
To antient British only.

To any language, on its want,
At sea there's no demurring;
The men of trade meet every tongue,　　　　　　155
Earth's every voice occurring.

Now Commerce in her active crew,
Our youthful shepherd number'd;
While Owen, on the trackless waves,
Nor novel features ponder'd.   160

Each clime that met th' exploring praw,
With thoughtful eye inspected;
So well had Nature stor'd his mind,
Though Art her aid neglected.

The winds, the waves, the current tides,   165
That ocean's surface varied,
The passing ships from ev'ry shore,
The colours that they carried.

O'er these young Owen saw with pride,
His Country's crosses* leading;   170
With pleasure pass'd his youthful day,
A modern Tyrian – trading.

Till Mars – who now – a little while,
Had brooded o'er his thunder,
Awak'd to waste, the social world,   175
And tear its ties asunder.

Third Part.

And sudden on his comrade crew,
Rush'd bands of ruffian sailors;
What once were Britain's gen'rous tars,
Were now – degraded jailors.   180

O! Britain, sure no parent thou,
If thus thy sons are treated;
Thou, that on ocean's proudest car,
By their brave arms art seated!

Repentant, clasp them to thy heart,   185
With warmth maternal cherish;
Let Power the guilty* *only* grasp,
Let Justice *only* punish!

Thy fires shall then, with filial force,
On all thy foes be hurl'd;   190
They'll bid thee, with intrepid front,
Defy an adverse world.

He soon forgot the ruffian gang,
When Britain's foes drew near,
His bosom caught the patriot blaze,   195
Her every field grew dear.

And when the conflict fierce began,
Her every right defended,
As if, on his brave arm alone,
Her every claim depended.   200

Not Blake, who check'd Batavian pride,
On Britain's seas parading;
Nor Russell, when La Hogue beheld –
Her naval Victors leading.

Nor those that with her Hawkes and Howes,   205
Her sceptred seas contested;
Nor when her welfare and her fame,
On Rodney's efforts rested.

Nor yet, when fell infuriate France,
In seas of blood, though wading;   210
Fled, vanquish'd, when her Nelson fought –
St. Vincent – Duncan – dreading.

Not these, nor Valour's stoutest sons,
In Times's transmitted story,
Enjoy'd their Country's triumph more,   215
Than Owen – Britain's glory.

Now Peace came down, her healing wings,
O'er warring worlds extended,
And Discord, for a while, at least,
To Death's dark caves descended!   220

When Britain's warriors left the waves,
Unnumber'd breasts were burning;
Affection, Love, and Hope, and Joy,
To hail her Youth returning.

Fourth Part.

By distance, absence, Home in view,   225
Its every charm was heighten'd,
Though Winter, with a silver vest,
Its lordly cliffs had whiten'd.

Now Prudence, who, with precepts blest,
Had Owen's days directed;   230
To cheer his friends, and gladden home,
Her little hoards collected.

And Memory, too, was all alive,
Her every cell exploring;
Friends, Parents, Play-mates, even his flock,   235
With magic touch restoring.

They all, on recollection rush'd,
Their temper, form, and feature;
The mental tablet well retains,
Th' impressive lines of Nature.   240

Even little Tegan* liv'd anew,
His various freaks and notions;
The faithful cur, whose voice confin'd,
The fleecy nation's motions.

And Jane, who fill's his waking thoughts   245
Of Jane he dreamt, when sleeping;
With him, *her* heart had left its home,
And she, had *his* in keeping.

He saw, even now, her greeting arms,
The welcome kiss, caresses;   250
He top-knots bought, of every hue,
To tie her auburn tresses.

Young Owen's bosom now beat high,
A world of bliss was forming;
'Tis thus, we sometimes paint at night,   255
The sunshine of the morning.

At length, in sight of home arriv'd,
His eyes on Llangoed feasting;
The bliss which Absence *only* gives,
Her treasur'd joys was tasting!   260

In fatal hour, a Fair he met,
And pilgrim-like, enquir'd
What tale employ'd the public voice –
Of what it last grew tir'd.

"On Monday last, a dreadful day.   265
(May Heaven avert another)
At once, in Llangoed, Death entomb'd
A father and a mother.

Ye orphans poor! ye faithful pair!
So Heaven's high will decided,   270
That they who in their lives were one.
Should, dead, be undivided."

Unnam'd, in Owen's boding breast,
The truth terrific thunder'd;
And he, who brav'd the red broadside,   275
By one dread word – was murdered.

Ne'er yet was Sorrow's pointed dart,
With heavier hand inflicted;
That moment, Hope, in happiest hues,
Had joys in view depicted.   280

Thus fell on Owen's suffering soul,
Woe's dull o'erwhelming measure;
Thus fell, from Joy's exulting lips,
The sparkling cup of Pleasure.

[Line 17] * Llangoed, or more properly, Llan Gourda, from Courda, one of the antient Collidees, or Culdeys (so called from *Colendo Deo*) its patron Saint; a parish situate in the eastern extremity of Anglesey.

[Line 45] * In possession of the *Pib gorn*, or pastoral-pipe – a crook covered with characters intelligible only to themselves – a conick cap, made of rushes – and the Ria ro or cry – acquired – a Shepherd is completely such. In Anglesey and other parts of Wales, this is still the employment of the children of labourers, till they are capable of becoming husbandry servants.

[Line 66] * Rocky eminences in Llangoed, and the adjoining parish of Llan Ddona. – One of these is the site of the British encampment, called Bwrdd Arthur, or the round table – anciently called Din Swywy, or the exploratory fort.

[Line 85] * A river of Lancashire, upon the shore of which, stands the *young*, though large and populous, town of Liverpool; this place so lately as the beginning of the last century, was described in the custom-house patent, as a "*Creek of the Port of Chester*," from which, and the estuary of the Dee, it is divided by that part of Cheshire, called Wirral.

[Line 93] * The Asylum for the blind poor. – The Philanthropist contemplates with true pleasure, and institution so novel in its nature, so beneficent in its design, and so honorable to the place which has given it birth; to relieve the *tedium* of sightless solitude, to render it happy and useful to society, those who had hitherto been unavoidably its incumbrances, had long been a *desideratum* in the breast of Charity; and to this chaplet to her benign brows, was reserved for the inhabitants of the town of Liverpool.

It is impossible for a Cambrian not to wish that it were consistent with the regulations of this Charity, and within the pale of its power, to entertain a Preceptor for the purpose of teaching some of its objects to play on the harp: – beneficence would thus find additional resources and the Mansions of Affluence would be enlivened, as of yore, by the sweet and united tones of Music and Charity.

[Line 100] * So exquisitely nice does the sense of feeling become on the extinction of the visual faculty, that the object may literally be said to have acquired ten eyes, in return for the two lost.

[Line 107] † Education, to a certain degree, is, in Scotland, within the acquisition of Poverty itself; for this blessing, it is indebted to its parliament, in 1646, which made a legal provision for the establishment of schools for instructing the poor in *every parish*, – Illustrious Legislators! immortal teachers of Wisdom and of Virtue, your Country owes to your beneficent endeavours, the high and respectable place she occupies in the moral world; ye have also furnished the *experimental* and *exemplary* argument with which those, who assert that Obedience and Industry, are the Offspring of Ignorance, will contend in vain.

[Line 109] * After the death of Mr. Burns, this gentleman edited, in the spring of 1800, a republication of his poems, life, and correspondence, for the benefit of his widow and children; and in such a manner, as at once to do honor to his head and his heart.

[Line 113] † Mr. Addington is said to have patronised the Bard's eldest son Robert: and that the mind that directs the concerns of his Country at a period of unexampled difficulty and danger, should recollect the orphans of genius, in a remote corner of the Empire is surely no common praise; and may his youthful bosom glow as gratefully as that of his father, who, in his letter to Dr. Moore, speaking of his Patron, that "noblest of men, Lord Glencairn," adds the following emphatic line: –

"Oublie moi, grand Dieu, si jamais je l'oublie!"

[Line 127] * Never has the Ausonian Lyre produced sweeter tones than on the shores of the Mersey.

[Line 137] * On the first of March, 1804, a day annually devoted to conviviality by the natives of Cambria, Mr. Fleetwood Williams, with a feeling not very common in *youthful affluence*, introduced Beneficence to the festive board.

"Then Pleasure fir'd her torch at Virtue's flame,
And Mirth took Charity's celestial name!"

He then proposed to the company, the establishment of a School for the Education of Poor Children, born of parents natives of Wales, and resident in Liverpool; upon such a plan as would enable them to begin life with advantage, and to attain, by their good conduct, respectable situations.

This proposal was immediately adopted, and Mr. Williams liberally led a subscription in which he was most cheerfully seconded by the company present; and, it is to be hoped, that the nobility and gentry in North Wales, particularly, will consider this infant institution, as having (from the proximity of Liverpool, and the consequent number of their compatriot residents) peculiar claims to their favor and fostering protection.

[Line 142] * Llan Ddona (so called from Dona, fourth in descent from the celebrated Brochwell, Prince of Powis, who built a cell there, upon the sea shore, in the ninth century) a parish adjoining Llangoed, on the north west: the fair damsels of this district have, for time immemorial, borne the same addition as those of Lancashire, both having been peculiarly favoured by Dwynwen, the Venus of Antient Britain. The parish dedicated to this Goddess (Llanddwyn) on the western shore of the island, has been, for some ages, overflow'd by the sea, determined, as it would seem, to verify the fable in the Heathen Mythology, "that she should rise out of the waves."

Richard Kyffin, Dean of Bangor, was rector of Llanddwyn, in 1485, from this place he corresponded with Henry the Seventh, then an exile in Britanny [*sic*], and took a very active part in North Wales, in conjunction with Sir Rhys ap Thomas, who led South Wales in bringing about his restoration.

Davydd ap Gwilim, the British Ovid, invokes Dwynwen, in favor of Morfydd, the object of his adoration then on her pilgrimage to the shrine of St. David; and this beautiful production has appeared in English, in the Volumes published by Mr. Edward Williams, the intelligent Bard of South Wales.

[Line 146] * Liverpool (within the recollection of a life) little more than a village. – This Emporium of Western Britain, and of the British Mediterranean, is an ample exemplification of what Industry, Exertion, and Enterprise, are capable of producing; that they are rewarded in the attainment of their object, and that the Virtues and the Arts participate in their prosperity, the lover of his Country delights to contemplate.

[Line 170] * The flag called the Union, is composed of the Cross Saltier, Argent, of St. Andrew, for Scotland, surmounted by the English, or Red Cross of St. George.

[Line 187] * *Nulla pœna sine crimine*, is a maxim in our law, and the just and generous sentiment was not unknown to our remote ancestors.

"A vydd ddieuog, a vydd ddiovn."

[Line 241] * Literally, a toy or play-thing; but here, the name of Owen's little cur, and former companion, when a Shepherd.

Once, when passing a farm-house, in the open champaign district of Iâl, in Denbighshire, five of these little animals ran out to bark at us – a gentleman in company asked a neat well-looking woman, whom this uproar had brought to the door, why she kept so many? she sensibly replied, "they are my fences, Sir."

52. 'Breconiensis', 'The Saxon Invasion'

'To the Editor of the Cambrian

Sir,

If the following lines be deemed worthy of insertion in your paper, they are at your service. They were suggested in reflecting upon our Ancient History and Taliesin's description of the Saxon Invasion, the consequent retreat of the Britons into Wales, and there preserving their liberty and ancient language. Modern history has versified the prediction of the celebrated Bard in the well-known words:

> Eu Nêr a folant
> Eu hiaith a gadwant
> Eu gwlad a gollant
> Ond gwyllt Wallia.

Jan. 29, 1805.   BRECONIENSIS

From German climes the grisly monster comes,
    And Britain fills with bloodshed and with woe;
From shore to shore he fiercely stalks along,
    And lays the strength of valiant Britons low.

What horror spreads thro' lovely Albion's coasts!   5
    Her sons bereav'd of by the tyrant's stroke:
But, worse than death! – shall the surviving few
    Bow down their necks unto the Saxon yoke?

Shall Britons captive in their country live,
    And prostrate fall at the barbarians' feet?   10
No! – let them fly – for liberty is fled,
    And trace her footsteps to her lone retreat,

While servile minds bow down to Saxon lords,
    And in their native soil as slaves survive,
'Midst Cambrian hills that pierce the nether skies,   15
    Freedom and Britons shall together live.

There to adore the Lord of earth and heav'n,
    Tho' tyrants drive them from their lov'd domain;
And there, till Britain is an isle no more,
    Their native tongue from age to age retain.   20

53. 'Philopatria', Untitled ['Arise, my muse, and paint the glorious scene']

To the Editor of the Cambrian
Sir,
The Cader Idris volunteers, after ten days' service, completed their course of permanent duty on the 2d inst. under the command of the worthy member for the county, Sir R. W. Vaughn, Bart. The strict attention paid by the Colonel – the superior discipline which the whole corps displayed in going through their several manœuvres – and above all, the diffusive loyalty visible in every countenance, rendered it a scene truly interesting to every beholder, and drew from my pen the following feeble lines.

Dolgelly, Feb. 11, 1805   PHILOPATRIA

Arise, my muse, and paint the glorious scene –
Relate what heroes crowd the martial green:
Thou didst of old Menai's bard inspire,
Warriors to sing, and stern Pelides' ire.
How nobly paints the bard great Hector's breast!   5
Meridian glory plays upon his crest;
The Trojan bands his matchless skill display,
Whose martial ardour nothing can dismay.
Cambria's bold sons in such exalted strains,
O sing, my muse, whose merit claims thy pains;   10
Union and peace pervade the warlike band,
Whose deathless fame re-echoes thro' the land.
Sing too their brave commander, whose renown
His faithful corps with loud applauses own.
Ample the praise his virtuous deeds afford,   15
And Nannau greets him as her ancient lord:
He stands the first in merit, as in place:
True manly courage sparkles in his face.
A train of gallant warriors next appears,
Whose daring bosoms spurn unmanly fears: 20
Each his respective post with honour fills;
Prepar'd t' oppose of war the pendant ills.
Too great the task each hero's acts to name,
Which bear afar their loud-resounding fame:

Their bright examples animate the corps,   25
Who eagerly imbibe the martial lore.
In stately order straight they take the field,
Their chief to follow, and their arms to weild [*sic*];
There nought but ardour reigns in ev'ry eye,
"God save the King" is heard the gen'ral cry.   30
In military arts they all excel;
'With honest rage their hardy bosoms swell:
Whene'er their Sov'reign and their country call,
Her welfare to protect, her laws, her all;
Their furious way thr' opposing bands they'll mow,   35
With breasts undaunted face the haughty foe:
Flock round the standard of their King supreme,
And bravely pledge their lives to guard the same.
Untaught to bear fell slav'ry's galling yoke,
No foreign sway their gen'rous minds can brook;   40
On heav'n to bless their arms they all reply,
Led on to conquest, or like men to die.

54. 'Mary', 'On the Late Splendid Victory off Trafalgar'

Nelson, thy sun is set! Britannia mourns!
Tow'rds her brave fleet her pensive eye she turns;
There Victory droops her head in deep dismay,
And rues the fortune of a glorious day
From her sad brow the bleeding laurels torn,   5
Wash'd by a nation's tears, shall strew thy honour'd urn!

Mary, Carmarthenshire, Nov 9 1805.

55. 'P. H.', 'On the Victory of Cape Trafalgar, and the Death of the ever-to-be-lamented Admiral Lord Viscount Nelson'

Mourn, widow'd England, mourn; thy hero slain,
    The much-lov'd guardian of thy azure throne!
Who now shall hurl thy thunder o'er the main,
    And guard the empire you so nobly won?
The wat'ry world with wild distraction, saw   5
Albion's dread navies triumph o'er the foe.
    Trafalgar's glorious day: its victor slain!
With laurels, green as mortal's brow could grace,
To see entwin'd the cypress' cold embrace,
    What Briton can from joy and grief at once refrain?   10

Deeds such as these, ne'er deck'd the faithful page
    Of history, nor Time's dark flights unfold,
Amongst the annals of each distant age,
    A nobler seat on Fame's proud list enroll'd.
When first our Chief the hostile fleet descried   15
At distance, drifting with the azure tide,
    'Mid his tall gallies to the van he sped,
And, proudly anxious for the coming fight,
Deals out his thunder with such furious might,
    As surpass'd old Ætna from its lowest bed.   20

Now Heav'n's bright host lean'd downward from the skies,
    At this great combat eagerly to gaze;
Our warriors rais'd their wonder and surprize,
    (If ought these blessed spirits can amaze)
Our navies proud, the foaming deep bestride,   25
At once o'erwhelming in the boiling tide
    The deep laid scheme of vaunting France and Spain
While frequent corpses strew the affrighted waves,
Astonish'd Neptune, from his oozy caves,
    His head uplifting, trembled for his green domain.   30

High on the deck the gallant Nelson stands;
    Each brave compatriot with his voice he hails;
Quick to their task they ply their sturdy hands,
    And tenfold fury thro' the whole prevails.

"Britons," he cried, "'tis yours ev'n now to crown   35
Your trophied country with a just renown:
    Europe in you, her hope's last verge confides;
Prove steady champions to avenge the cause
Of heav'n-born freedom, and her sacred laws,
    And curb a tyrant's lust, that half the world bestrides."   40

While this Britannia's dreadful thunder roars,
    To wreak her vengeance on a haughty foe,
And distant echoes from Iberia's hollow shores,
    Each thrilling strain prolong of melting woe,
Fate whisper'd to the breeze – the gale, in sighs,   45
Some direful presage to our ships conveys,
    The fatal hour is come! and doom'd to bleed
Is orphan'd Albion's dearest son confest!
Nor sacred from the foe his star-gilt breast,
    Whose levell'd tube glanc'd just, commits the horrid deed.   50

Thus falls great Nelson, 'mid triumphant cries,
    While Seraph-pinnion'd, to the blest abode,
His mounting soul to kindred spirits flies,
    His blissful home, the bosom of his God.
Alas! could Fate, to fill her dark decree,   55
Demand no other sacrifice than thee?
    Tho' Gaul is humbled in her mad career;
What tho' her tow'ring navies in a heap
Lie buried in the bosom of the deep,
    Our Nelson is the price! The victory's too dear!   60

Rest, glorious hero, in thy calm repose!
    Thy memory shall mock that waste of time;
Thy worth and value in thy country's cause,
    Mark bright examples to each distant clime;
As round thy laurell'd urn, in sad array,   65
Admiring chiefs the tearful tribute pay;
    Thy race is run! O ever-honour'd name!
Nor cold oblivion waits thee in the grave,
A grateful country still records thee brave;
    Thy tomb their hearts, thy deeds their universal theme.   70

P. H., Merionethshire, Dec. 2.

56. 'J. H.', 'On Winter'

Lo! Winter spreads his hoary mantle round,
All nature grieves! – The purling streams are bound.
The drooping flow'rs their lost enamel mourn
Of various hues. – Distorted earth is torn
By ruthless frost. – Where now the gadding bees?   5
Where now the verdant foliage from the trees?
No lambs are seen to frisk about the meads,
Or shepherds heard to tune their oaten reeds.
No blooming nymphs now traverse o'er the plains,
All things are bound in Winter's icy chains. –   10
Ye happy few, on whom kind heav'n bestows
The pow'r to feed, and sooth, another's woes;
Comfort the sick, and cloath the naked poor.
Nor drive the beggar trembling from your door.
Innum'rous ills the wand'ring tribes sustain;   15
Cold, wet, and hunger, and disease, and pain.

J. H., Carmarthenshire.

57. 'W. R.', 'On the Death of Mr. Pitt'

In these rode [*sic*] times, when mad ambition rears
Her speckl'd crest – the stains of many years;
When *Tyrants* wear their diadems by *fraud*,
Rot'd not by wisdom, nor by reason aw'd:
When kingdoms vaunt another's spoil their own,   5
And point, inglorious! at a British throne –
'Tis then, we ask of some paternal hand
To rule with safety and protect the land.
Here let me pause – Great Pitt! we mourn in thee.
With poignant grief, the friend of Liberty: 10
With thee precision rul'd, and art conjoin'd
A copious eloquence and noble mind!
With thee, lov'd Pitt! these virtues we deplore,
Thy hallow'd accents breathe delight no more!
Firm in debate, thy King and Country's friend,   15
Severe, yet just, without one selfish end:
No title gain'd, to grace thy honour'd name,
Naught but thy virtues, and immortal fame!
     In former times we saw with heartfelt pride,
Thy glowing talents stem ambition's tide.   20
But ah! how vain are human hopes below,
To-day its pleasure brings, to-morrow woe.
So when the morning beams its orient ray,
Out eyes enraptur'd hail returning day:
But lost the transitory rapture flies,   25
A sullen gloom envelopes all the skies.
     Thus Chatham shone, the mirror of the age,
Reflecting virtue on th' historic page:
Thus dawn'd reflected genius from his son,
Whose glory set, ere half his race had run.   30
His precepts aw'd, and him, the senate saw
Its surer basis, and its firmer law.
If immortality can live in verse like mine,
Accept, O Pitt! this tribute at thy shrine.
     Where now, Invective, wilt thou draw thy bow,   35
Where point thy arrow in revenge and woe?
Oft' hast thou aim'd with thy malignant arm,
To wound those virtues which no more can charm.

Now break thy bow, and at conviction's shrine,
Be thine repentance, and forgiveness mine.   40

Llanelly, February 3, 1806.   W. R.

58. David Thomas (Dafydd Ddu Eryri),
'An Address to the Snowdon Rangers'

Versified in the Welsh manner

Llangciau Eryri,
A'r gwyngyll a'i hynill hi
    Hên Brophwydoliaeth

Snowdonian swains with hazel crooks in hands
Will long retain their liberties and lands

To the tune of Morwynion glân Meirionydd

Come forth, ye bold Snowdonian Swains
Who tread the plains of Arvon
Oppose, with warm adventurous hearts
Proud Bonapart's [*sic*] intrusion
The hand that saveth you, may sweep   5
Your foes, in deep confusion.

Hark! hark the animating trill
Yon cloud-capt hill resoundeth
Where Wyddfa rears her ramparts high
No danger nigh surroundeth   10
Our comforts flow from realms above
And social love aboundeth

While brave Sir Robert, valiant man
Leads forth the Van of honour
Undaunted, follow loyal Poole   15
Let nothing cool your ardour
Throw vile Oppression's columns down
And Peace will crown your labour.

Defend your country, serve your King
Despise the blust'ring stranger: 20
Ye loyal souls your foes defy
But never fly from danger

So, tranquil Joy, and peace will rest
On every honest Ranger.

Blow! louder blow the clarion shrill   25
Bold Kidwm's hill will answer.
Shall we obey, if foes advance,
Perfidious France? – no never:
But keep with firm unwearied might
Our ancient right forever!   30

Our race from War's destructive ills
Arvonian hills will shelter
Secure, amid romantic rocks
We'll keep our flocks from plunder
And serve with clean and honest hands   35
Him that commands the thunder!

                              D. Thomas
                              Waunfawr
                                        April 1806.

59. 'Mary', 'Written late in the Evening, December 15, 1806'

How dismal sounds the whistling of the wind,
That mournful, murm'ring tells a gale is near,
The ills it whispers fill my boding mind,
And my heart sinks with many an anxious fear.

The shiv'ring hind forsakes his evening toil,   5
And hails the blessings of a shelt'ring home;
There, while the whistling gusts his roof assail,
Wonders how riches lur'd mankind to roam.

His flocks and herds, safe shelter'd from the storm,
No fears of loss his peaceful wind annoy,   10
Stranger to schemes that restless mortals form,
His is a bliss beyond what Kings enjoy.

Not so, the toll-worn mariner who bears
The keenest fury of the piercing blast;
Hopeless his treach'rous habitation steers,   15
And thinks each moment it will prove his last.

Vainly he wishes for the cheerful blaze,
Round which his distant treasures sportive play;
Driven on the furious wave's expanded maze,
No gleam of hope, of comfort, or of day.   20

O curst ambition, thy gigantic head,
When first it rear'd its horrid form to view,
Innumerable ills around it spread;
Thousands to misery, death, and ruin drew,

Destructive war and slav'ry owe thee birth,   25
Thou worst of ills that wretched mortals know,
Full many a hapless head is bow'd to earth,
Oppress'd by slav'ry, heavy chains, and woe.

How many a wretched being frantic raves,
Upon devoted Afric's distant shore: 30
How many tears are wasted o'er the waves,
That lead to realms bedew'd with Afric's gore.

Say, can the fiends that torture human kind,
E'er hope for pardon at the throne of grace,
Can they expect that mercy e'er to find,   35
Themselves ne'er granted to a helpless race?

Do they suppose that when the Judge of Right
Opens the books which has their actions in,
Their souls will stand before him, spotless, white?
No, they'll be blacker than the Ethiop's skin.   40

Britain! knock off the chains thou hast forg'd,
Wipe out the stain that has our isle disgrac'd,
Give pity, mercy, freedom, to the scourg'd,
Nor let thy character in blood be trac'd.

December, 1806   Mary.

60. 'D.', 'On the Present State of the Belligerent Powers of Europe'

With heaps of blood the plains are strew'd,
Blood gluts th' ensanguin'd field;
And nations once with conquest proud,
To a fell despot yield.

See Britain still unshaken stand!   5
Amid these dire alarms,
And bravely on the sea and land*
Wield her resistless arms.

May victory her armies crown,
Her fleets triumphant ride,   10
While her white cliffs with awful frown,
Repel the swelling tide.

Kind Providence our shores defend
From ev'ry hostile wile,
'Till meek-eyed peace from heav'n descend,   15
To bless our favour'd Isle.

December 29, 1806   D.

* Here the glorious battle of Trafalgar, the greatest naval victory ever
obtained, even by Britons; the defeat of Bonaparte's *Invincibles* in Egypt;
and particularly the memorable victory over the French in Calabria – present
themselves to my mind. Could the inhabitants of the continent but catch
a spark of British fire, and lay aside their jealousies, Europe might yet be
saved.

Notes to the Texts

DAVID SAMWELL
(Dafydd Ddu Feddyg; 1751–98)

Samwell was a naval surgeon, poet and Welsh cultural nationalist from Denbighshire in north Wales, but who spent most of his time in London during periods ashore. He served as a ship's surgeon on Captain Cook's third and last Pacific voyage between 1776 and 1780; his account of the voyage was published in 1786 as *A narrative of the death of Captain James Cook*. A founder member of the Gwyneddigion Society and a supporter of the American and French revolutions, Samwell was an important figure in the late eighteenth-century reinvention of Welsh cultural practices such as Iolo Morganwg's bardic gathering, the Gorsedd. His mock-heroic poem 'The Padouca Hunt', published in 1799, portrays a lively Gwyneddigion Society debate on the Madog myth in 1791 (see Martin Fitzpatrick, Nicholas Thomas and Jennifer Newell, *The Death of Captain Cook and Other Writings by David Samwell* (Cardiff, 2007), pp. 135–49, for the text of the poem). 'Ode for the New Year', published anonymously as a broadsheet, was warmly greeted by the *Monthly Review* for February 1790, but criticized by Mary Wollstonecraft ('a prosaic ode') writing as 'M' in the *Analytical Review* for July 1790. The poem was also copied into the commonplace book (dated 15 May 1792) of John Williams, Llanrwst (see NLW 31B, ff. 13–16).

> 1. 'Ode for the New Year MDCC,XC. As it was intended to have been
> rehearsed this Day at St. JAMES's'

Source:
NLW 13221E, ff. 361–3.

32 *mortal* This word has been corrected, by hand, to 'mental'.

WILLIAM SOTHEBY
(1757–1833)

By the 1790s, Sotheby had retired from a career in the army and embarked on a life as a poet, translator and literary host in London and Sewardstone. *Poems* (1790) was his first publication; his translations of Wieland's *Oberon* (1798) and Virgil's *Georgics* (1800) were well received, though he also wrote several verse tragedies that were, with one exception, never performed. Of particular interest is *The Cambrian Hero, or Llewellyn the Great* (*c.*1800), a play that explores both political and psychological turmoil in ways that suggest Sotheby's enduring sense of Wales as a problematic literary subject in this period.

2. 'A Tour Through Parts of South and North Wales' (extract)

Source:
Poems: Consisting of a Tour through Parts of North and South Wales, Sonnets, Odes, and An Epistle to a Friend on Physiognomy (Bath, 1790), pp. 5–40.

[Book One]
84n *Caerfily Castle* Norman castle at Caerphilly in south-east Wales, built in the second half of the thirteenth century.

222 *Hoel* Hywel ab Einion Llygliw (*fl. c.*1330–1770), Welsh bard known for his love poem addressed to Myfanwy Fychan of Castell Dinas Bran, Llangollen. The poem was published in *The Myvyrian Archaiology of Wales* and translated into English (by 'R.W.', probably Richard Williams of Vron) in Thomas Pennant's *A Tour in Wales* (2 vols., London, 1778–84), I, pp. 281–4. *DWB.*

222 *Taliessin* [Taliesin] Sixth-century Welsh bard whose verse is thought to survive in 'Llyfr Taliesin' (The Book of Taliesin), a fourteenth-century Welsh manuscript. The 'Taliesin tradition' foregrounds his poetic craft and his reputed prophetic gifts, which together made him a key figure for later writers. *DWB*; *CC*, s.n. Taliesin.

230n *Caraigcennin* [Carreg Cennen] Welsh castle set on a crag near Llandeilo, Carmarthenshire, with a chequered history of Welsh and English ownership.

234 *beneath yon tow'r* A network of limestone caves lies beneath Carreg Cennen.

269 *Dinevawr* [Dinefwr] Welsh castle just outside Llandeilo with far-reaching views over the Tywi valley.

270 *Towy* [Tywi] river running through Carmarthenshire.

[Book Two]
50 *rude coast's verge* Unidentified point on the Pembrokeshire coastline.

156 Calpe*'s height* Calpe is the Latin name for Gibraltar: the guide is a veteran of the siege of Gibraltar (1779–83) during the American Revolutionary war.

169 *Cadwallader* [Cadwaladr] Seventh-century Welsh prince, depicted in the Welsh medieval political poetry known as *cywyddau brud* as a figure who will one day return to lead the Welsh in victory over the Saxons. *DWB*.

169 *Roderic* Rhodri Mawr ['the Great'] (d. 877), king of Gwynedd, Powys and Deheubarth whose reign loosely united these Welsh provinces for the first time.

239n *Tacitus* Cornelius Tacitus (*c.* AD 56–*c.* AD 115), Roman historian.

239n *the invasion of* Mona Tacitus describes the invasion and conquest of Anglesey ('Mona') in AD 60 in his biography of the Roman governor of Britain, Agricola. *CC*, s.n. Agricola, Tacitus.

239n *Caractacus* Caractacus, or Caratacus (*fl.* AD 43–51) was a British chieftain famed for his resistance of the Roman invasion of Britain, and then for his patriotism and dignity when captured by the Romans. His currency as a symbol of heroic patriotism in the later eighteenth century owes much to William Mason's 1759 poem *Caractacus*. *ODNB* and *CC*, s.n. Caratācos.

ANONYMOUS

3. 'An Ode to Commerce. Inscribed to John Wilkinson, Esq. the distinguished iron master'

Source:
Chester Chronicle, 24 December 1790.

Title *Wilkinson* An English ironmaster and industrialist (1728–1808) who moved to Bersham, near Wrexham in the mid-1750s. His Bersham ironworks became known for producing high quality cannon; by the time of the Revolutionary war with France Wilkinson was producing around one-eighth of Britain's iron. Wilkinson, whose brother-in-law was Joseph Priestley, was a supporter of the

French Revolution, using French assignats as trade tokens at Bersham until stopped from doing so by parliament in 1793. *ODNB*.

36n *the war of Candia* The Cretan War (1645–69), a conflict between the Ottomans and the Venetians over the island of Crete, strategically important for shipping routes. See Gábor Ágoston and Bruce Alan Masters, *Encyclopedia of the Ottoman Empire* (New York, 2009), p. 157.

47 *Kiang* Yangtze River.

57 *De Ruyter* Michiel Adriaazoon de Ruyter (1607–76), Dutch admiral partly responsible for raising the power of the Dutch navy 'to supreme heights'. *WWMH*, pp. 258–9.

57 *Tromps* Sir Maarten van Tromp (1589–1653), Dutch admiral and naval commander. *WWMH*, p. 296.

62 *Nassau* Maurice of Nassau, Prince of Orange (1567–1625), Dutch soldier, stadt-holder and military innovator who secured the independence of the Netherlands from Spain and reformed the Dutch army. *WWMH*, pp. 190–2.

66 *La Hogue* Battle of 1692 in which the French were heavily defeated by the combined forces of the English and Dutch navies. *WWMH*, p. 294.

89n *elegant and useful coinage* A reference to Wilkinson's trade tokens, which were viewed as radical propaganda in the 1790s.

RICHARD LLWYD
(Bard of Snowdon; 1752–1835)

4. 'An Ode for the New Year [1791], Inscribed to Paul Panton, of Plasgwyn, Esq.'

Richard Llwyd (Bard of Snowdon), was a labouring-class Welsh-speaking poet from Beaumaris, Anglesey. Details of his early life remain sparse, though we know that he spent nine months at the Beaumaris Free School before entering domestic service. Llwyd began to publish his poetry in the *Chester Chronicle* in the 1780s, where he became a kind of poet-in-residence. His long poem *Beaumaris Bay* (1800) made his name as a provincial writer. After living in Beaumaris for many years, he moved to Chester in 1807 where he pursued his interests in Welsh antiquarianism and heraldry into the later part of his life. 'Ode for the New Year', unsigned in the *Chester Chronicle*, was republished in the *Gentleman's Magazine* in April 1792 where it was attributed to Llwyd by 'Meirionydd', a correspondent from Bala:

> The Ode was written by a young man, who, to his other productions, which have been pretty numerous, has signed himself Llwyd. Till lately he lived in the next county: where he is now I do not know; but, wherever he is, he is a strong instance of uneducated genius, and, what is still better, a worthy man.

The poem appears in a reworked form as 'Ode to Freedom' in Llwyd's *Poems, Tales, Odes, Sonnets, Translations* (Chester, 1804).

Source:
Chester Chronicle, 7 January 1791.

Title *Panton* Paul Panton (1727–97) was a barrister, antiquary, industrialist and Welsh literary patron from north-east Wales. He held an important collection of Welsh manuscripts at his Anglesey estate, Plas Gwyn.

20 *callous steel-clad crew* An allusion to the invading army of Edward I.

39n *Henry the Seventh* A reference to the belief that the accession of Henry Tudor as Henry VII (1485) represented the restoration of native British blood to the throne in a way that fulfilled the political prophecies of medieval Welsh verse. See Philip Schwyzer, *Literature, Nationalism and Memory in Early Modern England and Wales* (Cambridge, 2004), pp. 13–48, for a discussion of Henry VII in relation to the myth of the *mab darogan* (son of prophecy).

61n *Roderick the Great* See no. 2, note to line 169.

61n *Y tri thywysog talaethog* The three crowned princes.

62n *Dial os daw* Vengeance if it comes.

62n *Nemo me impune lacessit* No one attacks me with impunity.

65n *Evans* Evan Evans (1731–88) was a scholar, poet and cleric, born in Cardiganshire. Several English writers, among them Thomas Gray and Thomas Percy, encouraged him to publish his translations of early and medieval Welsh poetry, which appeared as *Some Specimens of the Poetry of the Antient Welsh Bards* in 1764

– the 'fine collection' mentioned by Llwyd. He received financial help from Thomas Pennant and Paul Panton as an impoverished alcoholic in his later years.

5. 'Ode, for the Anniversary of St. David [1792]'

Source:
Chester Chronicle, 2 March 1792.

5 *Menevia* St David's in Pembrokeshire.

8 *Hermon* A reference to Psalm 133: 3: 'As the dew of Hermon, and as the dew that descended upon the mountains of Zion: for there the LORD commanded the blessing, even life for evermore'. KJV.

16n *Boadicea* Boudica or Boudicca (d. AD 60/61) was queen of the tribe of Britons known as the Iceni who inhabited what is now East Anglia. See *CC*, s.n. Boudīca.

19n *speech of Caractacus* Tacitus's *Annals*, 12.36–7. See J. C. Yardley and Anthony A. Barrett (ed. and trans.), *The Annals: The Reigns of Tiberius, Claudius, and Nero* (Oxford, 2008), pp. 251–2.

DAVID THOMAS
(Dafydd Ddu Eryri; 1759–1822)

Originally a weaver from Caernarfonshire, Thomas later became a poet and schoolmaster. His literary reputation in Wales is mainly based on his Welsh-language verse; back-to-back successes in the *awdl* (a long strict-metre poem) competitions in the eisteddfodau of 1790 (St Asaph) and 1791 (Llanrwst) made Thomas's name as a Welsh poet in the 1790s. Conservative in his politics, Thomas was a corresponding member of the Gwyneddigion Society and a leading figure in the bardic community of north-west Wales. See Cathryn Charnell-White, *Welsh Poetry of the French Revolution 1789–1805* (Cardiff, 2012), pp. 230–73, for the texts of the prize-winning *awdlau* and other poems by Thomas. 'The Banks of the Menai' also appeared, with minor differences, in the *Gentleman's Magazine* in June 1792 (vol. 62, 548) and the conservative Chester newspaper *Adams's Weekly Courant* on 6 November 1792. See Marion Löffler, *Welsh Responses to the French Revolution: Press and Public Discourse 1789–1802* (Cardiff, 2012), pp. 168–9, for this version of the text. It was later reprinted in the anthology of verse Thomas published in 1810 as *Corph y Gainc, neu Ddifyrwch Teuluaidd*, republished in 1834. See *Corph y Gainc* (Caernarfon,1834), pp. 452–4.

6. 'The Banks of the Menai. An Ode'

Source:
The Monthly Register of Literature (2 vols., London, 1793), II, pp. 17–18.

Subtitle *Druidical Society of Anglesey* A charitable and benevolent society which also promoted agricultural improvement, founded in 1772.

Subtitle *Meeting of the Welch Bards* Second meeting of Iolo Morganwg's Gorsedd or bardic gathering. As Cathryn Charnell-White has explained, the Gorsedd was 'part of a pseudo-antiquarian system devised and used by Iolo Morganwg to validate the identity of Wales' (*Bardic Circles: National, Regional and Personal Identity in the Bardic Vision of Iolo Morganwg* (Cardiff, 2007), p. 118), and to contest contemporary notions of its barbarity (p. 78). See ibid., especially pp. 44–81. See also Geraint and Zonia Bowen, *Hanes Gorsedd y Beirdd* (Abertawe, 1991).

19 *Gwalchmai* Gwalchmai ap Meilyr (*fl*.1130–80), an Anglesey court poet and one of the medieval poets known as the *Gogynfeirdd* (the less early poets). His description of the battle of Tal Moelfre (1157), which pictures the Menai Strait filled with blood, was taken up by Thomas Gray in his poem 'The Triumphs of Owen' (see no. 45, note to line 63n). The opening lines of Thomas's poem also suggest Gwalchmai's vision of the bloodied Menai. *DWB*.

21 *Caradog* [Caractacus] See no. 2, note to line 239n.

31 *Britons, of the Tudor's race* See no. 4, note to line 39n.

DAVID SAMWELL
(Dafydd Ddu Feddyg; 1751–98)

The manuscript source for this text (written in Iolo Morganwg's hand) is in a poor state: the section containing the first part of the poem is torn and lines are clearly missing, though it is difficult to tell how many. As a result, lines in the first part of the poem have not been numbered. Line numbers have been added from the point at which the stanzas are numbered in the original.

7. 'The Resurrection of Rhitta Gawr'

Source:
NLW 21398E, f. 29.

Title *Rhitta Gawr* [Rhita Gawr] In Welsh folklore, a regicidal giant who makes himself a cloak from the beards of the tyrants he has killed. See Charnell-White, *Bardic Circles*, p. 40, for Rhita Gawr in Iolo Morganwg's manuscript writings.

Subtitle *meeting of Welsh Bards* See no. 6, note to the subtitle.

[no line number] <u>*Charles*</u> *is dead* Charles I was executed 30 January 1649.

[no line number] *Barbarian he* A marginal note to this line reads, 'Bubble bubble toil and trouble / Cauldron boil and tyrants bubble'.

[no line number] *bombs at Lisle* A reference to the unsuccessful Austrian siege of Lille in September and October 1792.

25 *Taliesin* See no. 2, note to line 222.

38 *Llywarch* Llywarch Hen, a sixth-century British prince and hero of a cycle of Welsh tales dating from the mid-ninth century. See Introduction, p. 28, for William Owen Pughe's 1792 edition and translation of the poetry of Llywarch Hen.

49 *Aneurin* [Aneirin] Early Welsh-language court poet of post-Roman north Britain thought to have written the sixth-century heroic elegies known as *Y Gododdin*. See also no. 12, note to the title.

52 *Cattraeth* [Catraeth] Catterick, north Yorkshire.

GEORGE RICHARDS
(1767–1837)

In 1792 George Richards, later a Church of England clergyman, was a fellow of Oriel College, Oxford. The previous year, *The Aboriginal Britons* (published 1791) had become a prize-winning Oxford poem, which was performed at the Sheldonian Theatre in July 1791, and generally very well reviewed. Richards's 1792 pamphlet-length collection, *Songs of the Aboriginal Bards of Britain*, was similarly well received: in a review that quoted the first twenty lines of 'The Captivity of Caractacus', the *Analytical Review* for February 1792 judged that Richards was 'unquestionably entitled to a distinguished place among modern poets' (162–5). *Songs* was dedicated (dated 1 November 1792) to the MP and courtier George Simon Harcourt, second Earl Harcourt, sponsor of the Oxford poetry prize won by Richards in 1791.

8. 'The Captivity of Caractacus' (extract)

Source:
Songs of the Aboriginal Bards of Britain (Oxford, 1792), pp. 19–28.

Title *Caractacus* See no. 2, note to line 239n.

8 *Siluria* South Wales.

19 *Penmaenmawr* A mountain adjoining the north Wales coast, often noted by travellers in the period for its sublime appearance and for the dangers involved in crossing it.

64 *buckler* A shield, or means of defence. *OED.*

68 *curtled axe* A short broad cutting sword, such as a cutlass. *OED.*

76 *Sarum's plain* Salisbury Plain.

95 *Trisingis* Unidentified.

95 *faulchion* [falchion] A broad sword. *OED.*

109 *Mona* See no. 2, note to line 239n.

150 *Vaga* River Wye.

158 *Plinlimmon* A mountain in mid Wales, source of the rivers Wye and Severn.

WILLIAM SOTHEBY
(1757–1833)

9. 'Llangollen. Written at the close of the Autumn 1792' (extract)

Source:
A Tour through parts of Wales, Sonnets, Odes, and other Poems. With Engravings from Drawings taken on the Spot, By J. Smith (London, 1794), pp. 105–12.

Subtitle *Robert Fulk Greville* Greville (1754–1821) was a courtier and Tory MP.

49n *Dinas Bran* Castle just outside Llangollen, set high on an old hill fort. In 1277 a native garrison 'burnt the castle rather than see it fall into English hands'. R. R. Davies, *The Age of Conquest: Wales 1063–1415* (2nd edn., Oxford, 2000), p. 333.

49n *Pennant's Tour* Adapted from *A Tour in Wales* (1778), pp. 279–80.

109 *the bank* i.e. of the River Dee, which flows through Llangollen.

119n *Drayton's Poly* Probably a reference to Michael Drayton's depiction of the River Dee in Song X of *Poly-Olbion* (1612), a polemical topographical poem on England and Wales: see *Poly-Olbion by Michael Drayton Esq'* (London, 1612), pp. 161–2. It is worth pointing out that in *Poly-Olbion*, Drayton emphasizes 'the burden of various and conflicting histories' and foregrounds conflicts within the Union (Andrew Hadfield, *Shakespeare, Spenser and the Matter of Britain* (Basingstoke,1994), p. 148). Sotheby's quotation, then, adds a further layer to the subtly political nature of 'Llangollen'.

123 CROMLECHS Standing stones, typically a flat stone resting horizontally on two or more vertical stones. *OED.*

124 CARNEDDS Cairns.

EDWARD WILLIAMS
(Iolo Morganwg; 1747–1826)

Edward Williams, better known by his bardic pseudonym 'Iolo Morganwg', was a self-educated labouring-class poet and cultural nationalist from Glamorgan, south Wales, who wrote in both Welsh and English. A stonemason by trade, he was also variously a manuscript collector, an agricultural surveyor and a brilliant forger of Welsh medieval poetry. The publication in January 1794 of his two-volume poetry collection, *Poems, Lyric and Pastoral*, was the culmination of a lengthy and difficult process marked by poverty, precarious mental health, addiction to laudanum, personal tragedy on the death of his three-year-old daughter in April 1793, and an increasingly disturbed political context. Widely known as radical in his religious and political beliefs, Iolo became a founding figure of Welsh Unitarianism in the later 1790s, a period in which he also began to develop his theories of Welsh Bardism in full, some of which were post-humously published in 1829 as *Cyfrinach Beirdd Ynys Prydain* (The Secret of the Bards of the Island of Britain). See *http://iolomorganwg.wales.ac.uk* for more on Iolo's life and work. Charnell-White, *Welsh Poetry of the French Revolution*, pp. 148–201, gives examples of his Welsh-language poetry.

10. 'Winter Incidents, Written in 1777'

Source:
Poems, Lyric and Pastoral (2 vols., London, 1794), I, pp. 121–8.

Title *1777* See Mary-Ann Constantine, '"This wildernessed business of publi-cation": The Making of *Poems, Lyric and Pastoral* (1794)', in Geraint Jenkins (ed.), *A Rattleskull Genuis: The Many Faces of Iolo Morganwg* (Cardiff, 2005), pp. 123–46, for an account of the evolution of this poem 'Written in 1777' into the published text of 1794.

11. 'Solitude. From the Welsh. Written in 1789'

Source:
Poems, Lyric and Pastoral, I, pp. 142–5.

12. 'Ode; Imitated from the Gododin of Aneurin, an ancient British Bard, who wrote about the Year 550'

This poem was printed in full in the *Monthly Review* for April 1794, where it was perceptively described as 'a war-song, which might as well have been written in 1793 in the fields of Flanders, as so long ago in those of Cattraeth' (405–14). An earlier version of the ode appeared in the *Gentleman's Magazine* in November 1789 (1035–6), a piece that marks Iolo's 'literary debut in English' (Mary-Ann Constantine, 'Ossian in Wales and Brittany', in Howard Gaskill (ed.), *The Reception of Ossian in Europe* (London, 2004), pp. 67–90; here p. 74).

Source:
Poems, Lyric and Pastoral, II, pp. 11–19.

Title *Gododin* [Gododdin] Title of a series of strict-metre elegies, dating from the sixth century and thought to have been written by the bard Aneirin, commemorating the fallen warriors of the Brythonic tribe in north Britain. The verses known as *Y Gododdin* survive in the thirteenth-century manuscript 'Llyfr Aneirin' (The Book of Aneirin). See *CC*, s.v. Gododdin.

Title *Aneurin* [Aneirin] See no. 7, note to line 49.

4 *Eudaf* [Eudaf Hir] Rare reference to a female figure in the original *Y Gododdin*, an otherwise overwhelmingly masculine poem.

9 *BRADWEN* Female warrior probably invented by Iolo.

13. 'ADDRESS TO THE INHABITANTS OF WALES. *Exhorting them to emigrate, with WILLIAM PENN, to Pennsylvania' (extract)*

In April 1794, the *Monthly Review* described this poem urging emigration to America as a work that 'will *at this period* be read by many with kindred feelings. Religious intolerance, the policy of little minds, produces, as often as it is revived, the same deplorable effects' (414 – my emphasis). On Welsh emigration generally in this period, see Hywel M. Davies, '"Very different springs of uneasiness": Emigration from Wales to the United States of America during the 1790s', *WHR*, 15, no. 3 (1991), 368–98.

Source:
Poems, Lyric and Pastoral, II, pp. 49–69.

Title *PENN* William Penn (1644–1718) was a Quaker leader and founder of Pennsylvania. America was generally seen as a place of political, civil and religious liberty for Nonconformists in the late-eighteenth century.

9 *claim to peace* A series of laws, collectively known as the Clarendon Code, were passed in the 1660s that aimed to exclude Nonconformists from political life, municipal administration and the universities, and which tried to prevent them from developing their own educational systems. See Christopher Hill, *The Century of Revolution, 1603–1714* (1961; London, 2002), especially pp. 194, 244.

21 *informer* See also no. 18, line 59.

36 *Proctor* An agent or attorney employed to manage the affairs of someone else. *OED*.

57n *16ᵗʰ Car. II. cap. 4* The Conventicle Act of 1664 forbade more than five people over the age of sixteen to gather together for worship except in a church. See Daniel E. White, *Early Romanticism and Religious Dissent* (Cambridge, 2006), p. 192.

64n CAMBRIA *bled* For a discussion of Iolo and Oliver Cromwell, see Marion Löffler, '"Bordering on the Region of the Marvellous": The Battle of St Fagans (1648) in Nineteenth-Century Welsh History Writing', *WHR*, 26, no. 1 (2012), 2–33.

74n *St.* FAGAN'*s reeking plain* See note to line 64.

74n *Parsoncraft* As 'priestcraft', i.e. 'priestly scheming, guile or deceit'. *OED*.

164n *Madoc* [Madog] The eighteenth-century emigration movement in Wales was framed by the sixteenth-century legend of Madog, the twelfth-century Welsh prince thought to have discovered America before Columbus, and the Welsh tribe, the Madogwys, descended from him and thought to be living in North America. In the 1790s other factors – the repression of Dissent and the civil rights of Dissenters, the 'reactionary backlash against Jacobinism', as well as the rapid spread of industrialization, especially in south-east Wales – intensified the appeal of emigration to those who sought fairer and more egalitarian ways of living. See Caroline Franklin, 'The Welsh American Dream: Iolo Morganwg, Robert Southey and the Madoc Legend', in Gerard Carruthers and Alan Rawes (eds.), *English Romanticism and the Celtic World* (Cambridge, 2003), pp. 69–84. See also note to line 188n; no. 18, lines 97–8; and no. 19, line 7.

164n *Owain Gwynedd* (*c*.1100–70) king of Gwynedd in north Wales.

175 LUNDY'*s Isle* Island in the Bristol Channel, usually cited as the starting point of Madog's second journey. Gwyn A. Williams, *Madoc: The Legend of the Welsh Discovery of America* (1979; Oxford, 1987), p. 52.

188n *Dr. Williams's Enquiry* A new version of the Madog tradition appeared in 1791, John Williams's *An Enquiry into the Truth of the Tradition concerning the Discovery of America by Prince Madog ab Owen Gwynedd about AD 1170*, a work that ignited 'Madoc fever' among Welsh radicals. See Williams, *Madoc*, pp. 89–104, for an account of 'Jacobin Madoc'.

14. 'The Horrors of War, a Pastoral'

Source:
Poems, Lyric and Pastoral, II, pp. 136–44.

Subtitle *ELLIOT's Achievements at Gibraltar* George Augustus Elliot (1717–90) was an army officer and governor of Gibraltar who defended Gibraltar through a long siege (1779–83) by the French and Spanish during the American wars.

15. 'Ode on Converting a Sword into a Pruning Hook'

This is one of Iolo's most widely circulated and hence best-known poems. It was reproduced in full in the *Critical Review* for June 1794 (168–75), in part in the *New Annual Register* for 1794 (162–4), and appeared in the *Chester Chronicle* (without stanza five and without the footnotes) on 24 July 1794 (see Löffler, *Welsh Responses to the French Revolution*, pp. 141–4, for this version of the poem). The ode takes its title from a passage of the Book of Isaiah (2: 4) that prophesies a future of peace for all; more generally it also adopts Isaiah's visionary-cautionary outlook as well as its sense of a nation in crisis, gripped by evil-doings – clearly a commentary on Britain as Iolo saw it in 1793–4.

Source:
Poems, Lyric and Pastoral, II, pp. 160–8.

Subtitle *The four grand solemn Bardic Days* See no. 6, note to the subtitle.

15 *Tyrant* A reference to Catherine the Great. See also no. 19, line 26.

25n *strike a peaceful brother dead* A criticism of fast-days, or days of public prayer invoking God's help to defeat the French, viewed as a moral perversion by radicals such as Iolo and Tomos Glyn Cothi (see Löffler, *Welsh Responses to the French Revolution*, p. 41, for Welsh-language reactions to the fast-days). Gilbert Wakefield quoted the 'Ode' in his intensely anti-war pamphlet of 1794, *The Spirit of Christianity, compared with the Spirit of the Times* (p. 30n). See also no. 16.

51n *Churchill* John Churchill, first duke of Marlborough (1650–1722), soldier, courtier and diplomat.

JANE CAVE
(1754/5–?1813)

Jane Cave (married name Winscom) was born in Talgarth near Brecon. Her father was an exciseman and glover and a Methodist, possibly through the influence of the religious reformer Howell Harris. *Poems on Various Subjects* was published by subscription in 1783, the year in which she married Thomas Winscom, also an exciseman, after which Cave lived in Devon and then Bristol, where the fourth, enlarged edition of her poems appeared in 1794. She died in Newport in or before January 1813, when her obituary appeared in the *Gentleman's Magazine*. ODNB.

16. 'THOUGHTS On the PRESENT TIMES; Written some Time after the PROCLAMATION for the late General FAST'

Source:
Poems on Various Subjects, Entertaining, Elegiac, and Religious, By Miss Cave, Now Mrs. Winscom (Bristol, 1794), pp. 197–202.

1 *another Fast* See no. 15, note to line 25n.

17 *e'en a sparrow cannot die* Matthew 10: 29: 'Are not two sparrows sold for a farthing? and one of them shall not fall on the ground without your Father.' KJV.

26n *Gen. xxxvii. 28* 'Then there passed by Midianites merchantmen; and they drew and lifted up Joseph out of the pit, and sold Joseph to the Ishmeelites for twenty pieces of silver: and they brought Joseph into Egypt.' KJV.

29n *Gen. xxxix. 20* 'And Joseph's master took him, and put him into the prison, a place where the king's prisoners were bound: and he was there in the prison.' KJV.

33n *Exod. ii. 3* 'And when she could not longer hide him, she took for him an ark of bulrushes, and daubed it with slime and with pitch, and put the child therein; and she laid it in the flags by the river's brink.' KJV.

36n *Exod. xiv. 27* 'And Moses stretched forth his hand over the sea, and the sea returned to his strength when the morning appeared; and the Egyptians fled against it; and the LORD overthrew the Egyptians in the midst of the sea.' KJV.

61n *Member for Yorkshire . . . Emancipation of the Slaves* William Wilberforce (1759–1833) MP and leading abolitionist.

HESTER PIOZZI
(1741–1821)

Born Hester Lynch Thrale into a Welsh gentry family on the Llŷn Peninsula, Piozzi received a good education, including instruction in languages, logic and rhetoric, first from her mother and aunt and then from Arthur Collier and William Parker. Reluctantly married to the wealthy London brewer Henry Thrale in 1763, Piozzi gave birth to twelve children over the following fifteen years; only four survived to adulthood. She also became a celebrated literary hostess in these years, counting Edmund Burke, Charles and Frances Burney, David Garrick, Oliver Goldsmith and, most famously, Samuel Johnson among her friends. Long an impressive letter writer and author of a rich and lively journal, *Thraliana*, Piozzi only seriously embarked on a writing career after the death of Thrale in 1781. Between 1786 and 1801 she published, with varying measures of critical success, a memoir of Johnson, an account of her travels to Italy, a ground-breaking book of synonyms, a political pamphlet and a popular world history. Her marriage in 1784 to the Italian musician Gabriel Piozzi, widely considered an unsuitable match for her, alienated Piozzi from many of her friends and from her four daughters. She returned to Wales in 1794, lodging in Denbigh before moving into Brynbella, the house she and Gabriel Piozzi had built in the village of Tremeirchion.

17. Untitled ['Can impious France, though frantic grown']

Source:
British Synonymy; or, An Attempt at Regulating the Choice of Words in Familiar Conversation (2 vols., London, 1794), II, p. 340.

3 *royal blood* Louis XVI was executed on 21 January 1793; the execution of Marie Antoinette followed on 16 October 1793.

EDWARD WILLIAMS
(Iolo Morganwg; 1747–1826)

18. 'Church and King rampant or Satan let loose for a thousand years'

See NLW 21401E, f. 15, for an unpublished six-page preface to this poem defending the rights of man and criticizing the exploitation of religion as a counterrevolutionary force, as in the church-and-king mobs that had rioted in Birmingham and elsewhere in 1791. Rather than institutional religion (or what he calls the 'national mode of Christian Worship', or, more aggressively, 'shameless Priestcraft'), Iolo here has in mind a more abstract and idealized sense of Christianity based on its egalitarianism, benevolence and pacifism. See NLW 21334B, ff. 6–11, for a later copy of the poem, possibly dating from 1803.

Source:
NLW 21401E, f. 6.

Epigraph *Tri Dyn* In NLW 21401E, f. 15, Iolo translates this epigraph as 'Three men extort a living from the properties of others, the King, the Parson, and the Thief'.

Subtitle *This piece was occasioned by* A marginal note in Iolo's hand adds 'Come fill the bumpers let us sing / Old England's glory, Church and King'. Elsewhere in NLW 21401E (f. 29), Iolo has copied out four stanzas of John Morfitt's 'Church and King' (including those on Priestley as 'faction's darling child' and on the French as 'democratic demons'), which is probably the poem to which 'Church and King rampant' is responding. Iolo attacked the 'blasphemy false reasoning and servility' of Morfitt's anti-revolutionary poem (f. 29), which he may have read it in the *Gentleman's Magazine*, where it appeared in August 1791, or in *The Antigallican Songster. Number Two* (London, 1793), pp. 9–10, where it was meant to be sung to the tune of 'Rule Britannia'.

5 *pitt* William Pitt (1759–1806), prime minister 1783–1801 and 1804–6. Iolo's attack on Pitt in this poem arises from his fierce opposition to Pitt's pursuit of political radicals and their publications, which suppressed the British reform movement in the 1790s.

18 *pettifogging* Legal trickery or chicanery; petty quibbling. *OED*.

41 *lawless mobs* Church-and-king loyalism periodically spilled over into mob rioting against British Jacobinism, often in conjunction with protests against

food shortages or parliamentary enclosures. The Birmingham Riots of July 1791, in which Joseph Priestley's house and laboratory were destroyed, became a notorious example of mob violence in the period, especially among radicals (see no. 24, line 6).

46 *reaves* John Reeves (1747–1826), barrister and writer who founded the Association for Preserving Liberty and Property against Republicans and Levellers in November 1792, an anti-radical organization that was very quickly and widely adopted in England and in Wales. See Hywel M. Davies, 'Loyalism in Wales, 1792–1793', *WHR*, 20, no. 4 (2001), 687–716, for the Welsh dimensions of popular loyalism in 1792–3. See also no. 19, line 27, and no. 24, line 10.

55 *rule by spies* See John Barrell, *The Spirit of Despotism: Invasions of Privacy in the 1790s* (Oxford, 2006), especially pp. 1–15, for an account of spies and surveillance in the 1790s.

80 *clubs* Loyalty to Church and king intensified, and became more visible, at moments of crisis during the eighteenth century. Church-and-king clubs affirmed the allegiance of their members to the state during the conservative reaction to the French Revolution in the early 1790s.

19. 'John Bull's Litany'

This satirical poem exists in three manuscript drafts in NLW 21401E. The version reproduced below is the first, and longest due to its accompanying footnotes, which are significantly pruned in the other drafts. The mock cover page of the five-page second version replaces references to Burke with references to Paine and republicanism: 'Liberty Hall. Printed by the assigns of Thomas Paine, and sold by Sawney Mac Muir, at the sign of Algernon Sidney's Head, next door to the Common-Sense-Coffee-house, Reason Row, in the year, one thousand seven hundred and nine o clock.' This second copy also includes the following additional stanzas, numbered as they appear in the poem:

> 6.
> From War-songs of Britain still savage and rude,
> From Kings that with Legions infernal becrew'd,
> In humanity's blood have their tallons [*sic*] imbued
>   Good Lord deliver us.

7.
From Courts Pandemonian whence villany springs,
Where fiends in conventions give slaughter its wings,
From the blood-hound abettors of parsons and Kings,
Good Lord deliver us.

8.
From Pot-house and Brothel that shamefully ring
With sounds of rude blasphemy "God save the King"
From the toad-haunted puddles of honour's vile spring.
Good Lord deliver us.

Source:
NLW 21401E, ff. 1–11.

Title *John Bull* Symbol of British (or English) nationalism, representing Britain or the British people. See Tamara L. Hunt, *Defining John Bull: Political Caricature and National Identity in Late Georgian Britain* (Aldershot, 2003).

Title *Litany* A public prayer.

Subtitle *Berwick upon Tweed* In the Middle Ages the border town of Berwick was repeatedly fought over by the English and the Scottish. In NLW 13094E, Iolo made notes on Edward I's siege and sacking of Berwick in 1296: 'War – murders thousands of innocents, burns Towns, Corn, Rapes, famines, and all because one man will be monarch of an insignificant spot' (f. 186). For Iolo, Berwick was a symbol both of endlessly contested territory and of atrocities carried out on an epic scale.

19n *FOX* Extract from a parliamentary speech made by the Whig politician Charles James Fox on 14 December 1792. Irene Cooper Willis (ed.), *Charles James Fox: Speeches During the French Revolutionary War Period* (London, 1924), p. 26.

19n *PAINE* Iolo is quoting from Part Two of *Rights of Man*. See Mark Philp (ed.), *Rights of Man, Common Sense and Other Political Writings* (1995; Oxford, 2008), p. 264.

21 *Edmund O Paddy* Edmund Burke (1729/30–1797), writer and politician. Quickly alienated by the events of the French Revolution, Burke published his *Reflections on the Revolution in France* in November 1790; his book unleashed a

pamphlet war. Iolo's caricature of Burke in this poem is part of a wave of attacks on him by radical satirists.

23 *Fools . . . shoot rashly the bolt* Shakespeare, *Henry V*: 'A fool's bolt is soon shot' (3.7.118–19).

26 *Russian she Bear* See no. 15, note to line 15.

27 *Reeves* See no. 18, note to line 46.

27 *daggers of Burke* A reference to a debate on the Aliens Bill on 28 December 1792, in which Burke threw a dagger onto the floor of the House of Commons as evidence that weapons of revolution were being manufactured in Britain. *ODNB*.

31n *Corinthian Capital* Slightly misquoted from the *Reflections*, where the passage runs 'the Corinthian capital of polished society'. See J. C. D. Clark (ed.), *Reflections on the Revolution in France: A Critical Edition* (Stanford, 2001), p. 205.

35n *thrones . . . supported by Wars* A quotation from Paine's *Rights of Man. Part the Second*. See Philp, *Rights of Man*, p. 320.

37 *special Juries* A special jury consists of 'persons who (being on the Jurors' book) are of a certain station in society' (*OED*), i.e. potentially hand-picked to ensure a particular outcome.

39n *True Blue* This text may be one of several broadsides of this title published in the early 1790s: see, for example, *True Blue, or, the Press Gang* (n.p., ?1790); *True Blue's Toasts & Sentiments in Prose and Verse* (Salisbury, ?1790); *True Blue: or, Heart of Oak for ever* (London, 1792).

41 *Archy MacBlunder* Sir Archibald Macdonald (1747–1826), judge and politician who, as attorney-general, was the prosecutor in the trial of Thomas Paine for libel in December 1792.

44n *Swinish Multitude* A reference to Burke's characterization of the mob as a 'swinish multitude' in his *Reflections*, which was seized upon by his political opponents and by satirists. See also the subtitle to the poem. Clark (ed.), *Reflections on the Revolution in France*, p. 242.

51n *Journey-men K–s* 'Brenin' is Welsh for king, not knave. 'Rheithwyr-anudon' is, as Iolo claims, Welsh for perjured (or forsworne) jury.

JOSEPH HUCKS
(1772–1800)

Joseph Hucks's 1794 walking tour of north Wales, in the company of Coleridge, was published in 1795 as *A Pedestrian Tour through North Wales in a Series of Letters*. Although 'On the Ruins of Denbigh Castle' was not published until 1798, an earlier version appeared in the *Tour* (pp. 46–7). In its allusions to contemporary affairs the poem is clearly, if distantly, part of the public discourse of 1794. Hucks shows elsewhere in *Poems* that he was prepared to voice revolutionary sympathies in the later 1790s; see, for example, his sonnet 'To Freedom' (p. 159).

20. 'On the Ruins of Denbigh Castle, in North Wales'

Source:
Poems, by J. Hucks, A.M. Fellow of Catherine Hall, Cambridge (Cambridge, 1798), pp. 101–4.

Title *Denbigh Castle* Castle built by the English as part of Edward I's efforts to control Wales after the death of Llywelyn ap Gruffudd in 1282.

38 *impotent alarms* In 1794 alarmism is shorthand for fears that a revolution may take place in Britain, though Hucks is here pointing to the false or inflated nature of these fears. For a discussion of alarmism, see John Barrell, *Imagining the King's Death: Figurative Treason, Fantasies of Regicide* (Oxford, 2000), pp. 15–18.

EDWARD WILLIAMS
(Iolo Morganwg; 1747–1826)

21. 'Song. Bella! horrida Bella! Written in Nov' 1794'

Source:
NLW 21392F, f. 22.

Stanza 1 A marginal note to the whole of this stanza, in Iolo's hand, reads 'Laureate of infernal kings'.

2 *Raven muse* A marginal note by Iolo suggests 'Vultures' as a possible alternative.

Stanzas 2 and 3 A marginal note to these stanzas, in Iolo's hand, reads 'Gory plains of Flanders'. See also line 37.

14 *fereful* A marginal note by Iolo suggests 'wrathful' as an alternative.

40 *Britain's Fred'rick* Frederick, duke of York (1763–1827), commander-in-chief of the British army at Flanders in 1793. *WWMH*, p. 325.

41 *Democratic sweater* In the eighteenth century a 'sweater' was variously a street ruffian or thug, and someone who works hard, a toiler. *OED*.

46 *British scamper* A scamp is both a highway robber and a 'ne'er-do-well', a waster, one who scamps (i.e. avoids) work. *OED*.

DAVID SAMWELL
(Dafydd Ddu Feddyg; 1751–98)

This poem was written after Samwell had resumed his profession as a ship's surgeon in March 1793 following the outbreak of the Revolutionary war. It was published in the *Gentleman's Magazine* in February 1795; Anna Seward praised the poem in a letter to Samwell of 17 March 1795 ('the address to the moon is beautiful', Archibald Constable (ed)., *Letters of Anna Seward: Written Between the Years 1784 and 1807* (6 vols., Edinburgh, 1811), IV, p. 40) that also reflects on the 'relentless winter' of 1794–5 and the 'miseries of a rash and ill-managed war' – also the subjects of Samwell's poem. This manuscript version of the ode includes a previously unpublished stanza (stanza 8).

22. 'Ode, Written on a long and uncommonly tempestuous cruise with a Squadron of Men of War in about 63° North Latitude, Dec' 24 1794'

Source:
NLW 13234A, ff. 5–9.

13 *Scald* In general use, a poet, usually applied to Norwegian and Icelandic poets of the Viking period and down to *c*.1250. *OED*.

17 *Purser* Ship's officer responsible for provisions and for keeping accounts. *OED*.

29 *drafts on Billy Pitt* Draft implies the detachment or selection of a party from a larger body for some particular duty, especially military conscription. *OED*. Samwell is suggesting that Pitt should be conscripted.

36 *Dukes Place* Jewish quarter in the City of London.

55 *Endymion* Figure from Greek mythology; the best-known legend associated with Endymion, a beautiful young shepherd, is that of his relationship with Selene (goddess of the moon), who falls in love with him and seduces him. Granted one wish by Zeus, Endymion chooses an eternal slumber in which he remains young forever. Pierre Grimal, *The Dictionary of Classical Mythology*, trans. A.R. Maxwell-Hyslop (Oxford, 1986), pp. 145–6.

56 *Latmos* In differing versions of the Endymion myth, either the mountain on which Selene first sees and falls in love with Endymion, or in which he sleeps in a cave.

74 *Cynthia* Goddess of the evening; also another name for Selene.

HESTER PIOZZI
(1741–1821)

23. 'See, see the mad Marauders come!'

Source:
John Rylands Library, English MS 647, f. 68.

24 *Te Deum* Hymn of praise (originally in Latin and in the form of a psalm), sung as a thanksgiving on special occasions, as after a victory or deliverance. *OED*.

27 *Brunswic* Karl Wilhelm Ferdinand, duke of Brunswick (1735–1806), Prussian general who commanded the Prussian and Austrian counterrevolutionary forces in 1792. *WWMH*, p. 41.

28 *Howe* Richard, Earl Howe (1726–99), English admiral best known for his defeat of the French off Ushant on 1 June 1794, a battle subsequently known as 'the Glorious First of June'. *WWMH*, p. 139.

EDWARD WILLIAMS
(Iolo Morganwg; 1747–1826)

24. 'Newgate Stanzas'

This witty but not necessarily reliable account of Iolo's visit to the Dissenting preacher William Winterbotham in Newgate prison exists in several copies in Iolo's manuscripts. NLW 21401E includes a version of the prologue and stanzas 1–3 of the poem (f. 33), and possibly an early draft (f. 34), titled 'Imitation of Ode 22. lib v of Horace', which Iolo may have split between later versions of 'Newgate Stanzas' and 'John Bull's Litany':

> 1.
> How void of all fear is bold Liberty's son
> That bears no keen dagger, no murdering Gun.
> Like a lion he looks, like a nightingale sings
> Tho' surrounded by Monsters, called Parsons, and Kings.

> 2.
> Undaunted he goes amongst Ruffians and Thieves,
> Sir Archy Macblunder, and Bear-looking ^{featured} Reeves,
> A jacobin _{Democrate} bold he can scare with a frown
> The scoundrel of Banditties at th' Anchor and Crown.

> 3.
> As late I walk'd out with my Soul in a flame
> Up-kindled by songs to sweet Liberty's name
> A gang of Informers came plump in my way.
> I cried room for Tom Paine! and all scamper'd away.
>   I said to th' informers that pestered my way
>   My name is Tom Paine &c

Another copy, in which Iolo has made minor changes, dated 1803, can be seen in NLW 21334B. The poem remained unpublished in Iolo's lifetime. See also G. H. Jenkins, *'Perish Kings and Emperors, but let the Bard of Liberty live'* (Aberystwyth, 2006).

Source:
NLW 21335B, ff. 12–14.

Title *Newgate* Prison in the City of London dating back to the twelfth century.

Prologue *Winterbotham* William Winterbotham (1763–1829), Baptist minister convicted of sedition in 1793. *ODNB.*

Prologue *Horace* Poem contending that the morally upright need not fear misfortune. See *Horace: The Complete Odes and Epodes*, trans. W. G. Shepherd (London, 1983), p. 89.

6 *Mobs* See no. 18, note to line 41.

10 *Reeves* See no. 18, note to line 46.

19 *Kirby* The jail keeper. In NLW 21334B this line runs, 'The <u>Keeper</u> _{Poor Kirby} stood in trembling ^{trembled, struck with} fear'.

25. *'TRIAL BY JURY, The Grand Palladium of BRITISH LIBERTY'*

Iolo performed this poem celebrating the acquittal of Hardy, Horne Tooke and Thelwall in the treason trials of 1794 at the Crown and Anchor tavern on 4 February 1795. The poem was published as a broadside in 1795 and also appeared in the third volume of Thomas Spence's penny weekly *Pig's Meat; or, Lessons for the People* (London, 1795), 58–9.

Source:
NLW 21401E, f. 32.

Subtitle *ACQUITTALS* Thomas Hardy (1752–1832), John Horne Tooke (1736–1812) and John Thelwall (1764–1834) stood accused of high treason in 1794. Hardy's acquittal on 5 November 1794 was quickly followed by those of Horne Tooke and Thelwall. See Barrell, *Imagining the King's Death*, for a complete account of the trials and their significance.

Subtitle *COUNSEL* Thomas Erskine (1750–1823) and Vicary Gibbs (1751–1820), defence counsel in the treason trials.

ANONYMOUS

26. 'For the Chester Chronicle'

Source:
Chester Chronicle, 21 August 1795.

Epigraph *Dum hæc in animo mea revolvo, effundo Lacrymas* While I reflect on these things, I weep.

6 *northern shore* Denbigh is near the north Wales coast.

THOMAS RYDER

Little is known of the Thomas Ryder who contributed his poetry to *The Cambrian Register*, but he may be the London printmaker (1749–1810) who worked for John Boydell in the 1790s and engraved Angelica Kauffman's 'Vortigern and Rowena' in 1803, a scene depicting events leading up to 'The Treason of the Long Knives'. *ODNB*. See Juliet Feibel, 'Vortigern, Rowena, and the Ancient Britons: Historical Art and the Anglicization of National Origin', *Eighteenth-Century Life*, 24, no. 1 (2000), 1–21. See also no. 49, note to line 13.

27. 'Introductory Ode for the Cambrian Register'

Source:
The Cambrian Register for the Year 1795 (London, 1796), ix–xii.

Subtitle LLYWARCH AB LLEWELYN Court poet of Gwynedd (*fl.*1173–1220), also known as 'Prydydd y Moch'. His poetry was reprinted in *The Myvyrian Archaiology of Wales. DWB.*

Subtitle *Merddin* Merlin.

Subtitle MEIRION Pen name of William Owen Pughe, translator of *The Heroic Elegies and other Pieces of Llywarç Hen* (1792).

6 *Plymlumon* See no. 8, note to line 158.

49 *Arthur* Warrior and British leader (*fl.* in or before the sixth century), chief figure of the legendary Arthurian cycle. Arthur features prominently in Geoffrey of Monmouth's influential *Historia Regum Britanniae* (1136).

61 *Cadwallon* Welsh prince (d. 633).

77 *Coel* Coel Gotebauc, ancestor of Llywarch Hen. *DWB*.

77 *Lywarch* See no, 7, note to line 38.

'ELIZA'

28. 'Sketched on a Party down the River Wye, from Ross to Monmouth'

The following poem on a trip down the Wye is taken from a collection of poems published in 1796 by 'Eliza'. The poems of 'Eliza' have sometimes been attributed to Esther Milnes, wife of the poet and philanthropist Thomas Day, but this is unlikely to be the case since several poems in the collection are dated beyond her death in 1792. Other possible candidates for 'Eliza' include the Anglo-Irish poet Elizabeth Ryves (1750–97) and, perhaps more likely, Eliza Day(e) who published *Poems on Various Subjects* in Liverpool in 1798.

Source:
Poems and Fugitive Pieces, by Eliza (London, 1796), pp. 118–21.

10 *Paraclete* The abbey of the Paraclete, or Holy Spirit, near Troyes, Abelard's retreat in Pope's *Eloisa to Abelard* (1717). See Pat Rogers (ed.), *Alexander Pope: Selected Poetry* (Oxford, 1994), p. 192.

14 *Eloisa* Title character and first-person narrator of Pope's *Eloisa to Abelard*.

26 *Kyrle* John Kyrle (1637–1724), the 'Man of Ross', was a philanthropist and landscape designer eulogized by Pope in *An Epistle to Allen Lord Bathurst* (1733), ll. 250–84. See Rogers, *Alexander Pope*, pp. 84–5.

48 *wounded snake* Pope, *An Essay on Criticism*, l. 357. See Rogers, *Alexander Pope*, p. 10.

56 *plumes her feathers* Milton, *A Masque presented at Ludlow Castle, 1634* [*Comus*], l. 377. See John Carey (ed.), *Milton: The Complete Shorter Poems* (revised 2nd edn., Harlow, 2007), p. 199.

58 *nine Aonian Sisters* The Muses.

69 *Vaga echoes* Pope, *Epistle to Bathurst*, l. 251. See Rogers, *Alexander Pope*, p. 84.

83 *dark oblivion* Adapted from 'Virgil's Tomb. Naples 1741'. See Robert Dodsley's *A Collection of Poems in Four Volumes. By Several Hands* (4 vols., London, 1755), IV, p. 114–19, here p. 115.

ANNA SEWARD
(1742–1809)

The Lichfield-based writer Anna Seward became a major poet in the 1780s on the publication of her *Elegy on Captain Cook* (1780), *Monody on the Unfortunate Major André* (1781) and *Louisa, a Poetical Novel* (1784). Her trip to Wales in 1795, where she stayed in Llangollen with Lady Eleanor Butler and Sarah Ponsonby en route to Barmouth, resulted in the publication of *Llangollen Vale, with Other Poems* the following year, a work that shows Seward seriously engaging with Welsh history and landscape, at times through her reading of Thomas Pennant's *A Tour in Wales* (1778–84). *Llangollen Vale* was a well-received and influential collection (see Introduction, p. 29); by the end of 1796 it had gone into a third edition.

29. 'Llangollen Vale, Inscribed to the Right Honourable
Lady Eleanor Butler, and Miss Ponsonby' (extract)

Source:
Llangollen Vale, with Other Poems (London, 1796), pp. 1–11.

2 GLENDOUR Owain Glyndŵr (*c.*1359–1416), Welsh rebel leader, declared Prince of Wales in September 1400, who led a guerrilla war against the English between 1400 and 1415. By 1405, Glyndŵr controlled the whole of Wales, and was planning the creation of a modern Welsh state with an independent church and its own universities. Since the nineteenth century, Glyndŵr has been a powerful symbol of Welsh nationalism. See R. R. Davies, *The Revolt of Owain Glyn Dŵr* (Oxford, 1995).

9n *Iolo Goch* Court poet (*c.*1320–*c.*1398), native of the Vale of Clwyd who wrote praise poems to Owain Glyndŵr.

9n *Pennant's Tour* See Thomas Pennant, *A Tour in Wales* (1778), p. 321.

15 DEATH Probably a reference to Revelation 6: 8: 'I looked, and behold a pale horse: and his name that sat on him was Death.' KJV.

21 *Circean* 'Of, pertaining to, or resembling the enchantress Circe.' *OED*.

ANONYMOUS

30. 'The False Alarm'

This burlesque on the French invasion, possibly by John Wynne Griffith (1763–1834), is part of a miscellaneous collection of manuscripts relating to a Denbighshire gentry family, the Griffiths of Garn, discovered by Mary Chadwick and discussed in 'National Identity, Literature and Manuscript Culture amongst the North Wales Gentry, *c.*1776–1817' (unpublished Aberystwyth University PhD thesis, 2012). See T. A. Glenn, *The Family of Griffith of Garn and Plasnewydd in the County of Denbigh* (London, 1934).

Source:
NLW, Garn Estate Records, FL1/1/11.

15 *Caractacus* See no. 2, note to line 239n.

25 *Abergella* Abergele.

31 *Jervis* John Jervis, first earl of St Vincent (1735–1823), British admiral who secured an important victory over the Spanish fleet at Cape St Vincent in February 1797 (the battle of Cape St Vincent). See *WWMH*, p. 260.

35 *Mrs Griffith* Possibly Jane Griffith (d. 1814), wife of John Griffith.

CÆSAR MORGAN
(1749/50–1812)

Little is known of Cæsar Morgan, who was vicar of Wisbech and chaplain to the bishop of Ely by 1798, according to *A Sermon on Public Spirit* (Wisbech, 1798). Morgan had earlier published *Poems; by Cæsar Morgan* (Cambridge, 1783): sections from 'The Cave of Merlin' (*Poems*, pp. 33–8) were published as a collection of 'loyal' songs, set to music by Highmore Skeats, in 1800. Skeats also composed the tune to 'The Victory of Fishguard': stanza 1 is copied from the musical setting whereas the remainder were printed as verses.

31. 'The Victory of Fishguard. A favorite Song'

Source:
The Victory of Fishguard. A favorite Song. The Words by the Revd. Dr. Morgan, whose Countrymen were forward to repel the French Invaders, who very lately made a Descent in Wales (London, 1797).

HESTER PIOZZI
(1741–1821)

32. 'Written on the Spur of the Moment, to be Sung at the Crown and Anchor'

The title of this poem may be misleading: Piozzi appears to have been planning a new patriotic ballad for some time before this poem was written. On 21 December 1796 she wrote to her eldest daughter, '*My* Ballad is not begun yet but I have a good Plan in my Head'. *PL*, II, p. 411. Edward and Lillian Bloom note that Piozzi 'had in mind a "Song" to be read at the Crown and Anchor, which would have as part of its incremental refrain the name of the tavern . . . [w]hen the Spithead mutiny erupted on 16 April 1797, she found her subject'. *PL*, p. 413.

Source:
John Rylands Library, Eng. MS 647, f. 37.

2 *Democratic Tree* The tree of liberty was a symbol of the American and French revolutions. See Introduction, p. 20, for Piozzi's response to the republican song 'Plant, Plant the tree'.

EDWARD WILLIAMS
(Iolo Morganwg; 1747–1826)

33. 'Song for the Glamorgan Volunteers'

This poem exists in several manuscript drafts: see NLW 21392F, ff. 35–8, for another four versions, variously dated 1797 (f. 37) and 1798 (ff. 35, 38). All of the copies in NLW 21392F and 13116B are accompanied by endnotes that amplify these verses' ambiguous status as a volunteer poem. In the context of the poem as a whole, the potential French invasion of England becomes metaphorical of the actual, historical invasion of Wales: England becomes the common enemy of the Welsh and the French, and the 'Song' becomes as much an anti-conquest poem as one urging defence of Britain through the volunteer ranks.

Source:
NLW 13116B, ff. 292–9.

Title *Glamorgan Volunteers* The Glamorgan, or Cowbridge, volunteers was raised in March 1797. Bryn Owen, *History of the Welsh Militia and Volunteer Corps 1757–1908: Volume 3 Glamorgan (Part 2), Volunteers & Local Militia, 1796–1816, Yeomanry Cavalry, 1808–31* (Wrexham, 1994), p. 27.

Epigraph *Un ac oll* One and all combined / With power all as one.

Epigraph *Yn undawd* The natives will be united as one.

Epigraph *Cynddelw* Cynddelw Brydydd Mawr (*fl. c.*155–*c.*1195), leading twelfth-century court poet.

Epigraph *Bardd wrth fraint a defawd* Bard, according to the rights and privileges of the Bards of the Island of Britain.

38 *Sabrina* River Severn.

39 *Silurians* See no. 10, note to line 18.

39n *Ond pwy na fyddai brenin? a pha frenin nad yw Leidr* a llofrudd *o Dad i Dad?* Who would not be a king? And what king is not a thief or a murderer from father to father?

40 *Caractacus* See no. 2, note to line 239n.

53 *Gasconade* 'Extravagant boasting or exaggeration; boastful or bombastic language.' *OED*.

Postscript *Syrth y Ffranc* The bad Frenchman will fall, mark you! / if he lands in Siluria, / the war-lords of the Vale of Glamorgan / will scowl at their enemy in his final hour. / Iolo Morganwg sang this.

ROBERT SOUTHEY
(1774–1843)

In the early 1790s Bristol-born Southey was a keen supporter of the French Revolution; by 1793 he had already written the first draft of his republican poem *Joan of Arc* (1796). As a young radical, he seriously considered permanently settling in Wales, a likely location, he thought, for the Pantisocracy, the egalitarian community he was planning with Coleridge in 1794. He was deeply interested in Welsh culture; Iolo Morganwg (who Southey memorably described in 1802 as 'brimfull [*sic*] of genius and jacobinism') provided him with material for his epic project *Madoc* (1805), which he was working on throughout the 1790s. The following three poems are part of a sequence of poems on Welsh subjects contributed by Southey to the *Morning Post* in 1798, some of which may have been inspired by a walking tour he made of south Wales in October 1798. See also 'Inscription. For Cardiff Castle, where Robert of Normandy was confined by his brother Henry the First', 'Lines on visiting Llantony Abbey' and 'Inscription for a Monument in the Vale of Ewias', in Lynda Pratt (ed.), *Robert Southey: Poetical Works 1793–1810* (5 vols., London, 2004), V, pp. 237–8, 258, 262–3.

34. 'St. David's Day [1797]'

Unsigned in the *Morning Post*, 'St. David's Day' was attributed to Southey by Kenneth Curry (ed.), *The Contributions of Robert Southey to the Morning Post* (Alabama, 1984), p. 35.

Source:
Morning Post, 1 March 1798.

9 *Erin* Ireland, i.e. St Patrick.

35 *Cassibelan* [Cassivellaunos/Caswallon] War leader chosen by the British tribes to oppose Caesar during his second expedition to Britain in 54 BC. See *CC*, s.n. Cassivellaunos/Caswallon.

36 *good King* Caractacus; see no. 2, note to line 239n.

38n *Bonduca* Boudica. See no. 5, note to line 16n.

45 *Llewellyn* [Llywelyn] Llywelyn ap Gruffudd (d. 1282) was the last prince of an independent Wales, killed in combat near Builth 'in circumstances that are far from clear'. See *CC*, s.n. Llywelyn ap Gruffudd.

35. 'Lines, Written Amid the Ruins of Abergavenny Castle'

This poem, which appeared anonymously in the *Morning Post*, was attributed to Southey by Lynda Pratt: *Robert Southey*, V, p. 262.

Source:
Morning Post, 18 December 1798.

1 *Abergavenny Castle* Norman castle in south-east Wales, where William de Braose infamously murdered the Welsh chieftain Seisyll ap Dyfnwal, his son, and some of his men in 1175 (see Brock Holden, *Lords of the Central Marches: English Aristocracy and Frontier Society 1087–1265* (Oxford, 2008), p. 143). Lynda Pratt notes William Warrington's *The History of Wales* (London, 1786), pp. 341–2, as a possible source of the story for Southey. See Pratt, *Robert Southey*, V, p. 498.

36. 'Ode' ['In vain the trav'ller seeks Aberffraw's tow'rs']

Unsigned in the *Morning Post*, this poem was attributed to Southey by Curry; see *idem*, *The Contributions of Robert Southey*, p. 130.

Source:
Morning Post, 31 December 1798.

1 *Aberffraw* The palace at Aberffraw was the seat of the Welsh princes of Gwynedd.

14 *gallant chief* Caractacus; see no. 2, note to line 239n.

15 *Caer-Caradoc* Hill in Shropshire, supposed location of Caractacus's final battle with the Romans.

20 *Owen* [Owain Gwynedd] See no. 13, note to line 64.

20 *Llewellyn* [Llywelyn] See no. 34, note to line 45.

DAVID THOMAS
(Dafydd Ddu Eryri; 1759–1822)

37. 'Verses written on the late Victory gained over the French Squadron by Sir John Borlase Warren'

This poem was later published in Thomas's *Corph y Gainc* (1834), pp. 461–2.

Source:
NLW 325E, f. 38.

Title *Sir John Borlase Warren* Warren (1753–1822) was a naval officer and MP best known for his capture of a French squadron off Lough Swilly, northern Ireland, in October 1798. *ODNB.*

Dedication *Parys Mountain Volunteers* The Loyal Paris Mountain Volunteers (1797–1802) were raised by Captain John Price from the labour force employed in the Parys Mountain Copper Mines near Amlwch in Anglesey in or around August 1797. See Bryn Owen, *Welsh Militia and Volunteer Corps 1757–1908, 1: Anglesey & Caernarfonshire* (Caernarfon, 1989), p. 97.

13 *Mona* See no. 2, note to line 239n.

15 *Arvonia* Caernarfonshire.

28 *Parys* See note to the dedication.

'A LADY'

38. 'Bangor Ferry'

Source:
European Magazine, May 1799, 331.

RICHARD LLWYD
(Bard of Snowdon; 1752–1835)

39. Beaumaris Bay, A Poem *(extract)*

Beaumaris Bay, published in March 1800, was well received. The *Anti-Jacobin Review* praised Llwyd's 'strong, nervous, and correct verse' (vol. 6, 82) and several major journals printed long extracts from the poem: see for example, the *British Critic* for June 1800, which reprinted lines 131-50 and commented on Llwyd's 'pleasing' versification (vol. 15, 672), and the *Critical Review* for June 1800, which reprinted the closing section of the poem (vol. 29, 235–6). The extract reproduced in this anthology was also quoted by the novelist James Norris Brewer in his tour of north Wales, published in several instalments in the *Universal Magazine* in 1805 (see vol. 3, 27).

Source:
Beaumaris Bay, A Poem: with Notes, Descriptive and Explanatory (Chester, 1800), pp. 13–15.

135n *P. G. MSS.* Plas Gwyn manuscripts. See no. 4, note to the title.

160n *D. ddu Feddyg* David Samwell. The source of the quotation remains unidentified.

160n *Arvon's shore* Gray, 'The Bard', lines 35–8. See Roger Lonsdale (ed.), *The Poems of Gray, Collins, and Goldsmith* (London, 1969), p. 187.

160n *Gryfydd Llwyd* See no. 51, note to the subtitle.

160n *"With me in dreadful harmony . . ."* Gray, 'The Bard', lines 47–8. See Lonsdale, *The Poems of Gray, Collins, and Goldsmith*, p. 189.

EDWARD WILLIAMS
(Iolo Morganwg; 1747–1826)

40. 'Carmen Seculare, or Jubilant Song for the year ~~1800~~ 1900'

Iolo's poem for the new century exists in several manuscript copies. An incomplete but probably earlier version can be found in NLW 21424E, f. 46, where the poem is titled, '<u>Carmen Seculare</u>, or <u>Jubilant Song</u>, for the year 1800. A <u>Pastoral</u>.' It is referred to as 'Carmen Seculare, or jubilant song for the year 1900' in MS 21335B, f. 32; the shift from '1800' to '1900' brings an unsettling, dystopic quality to the text that may, by 1803 – the date of the copy in NLW 21334B – reflect Iolo's uncertainty about the future in general or the return of war in particular.

Source:
NLW 21334B, ff. 12–15.

GEORGE DAVIES HARLEY
(d. 1811)

George Davies Harley was an actor and writer who worked first in Norwich and then, from 1789 onwards, on the London stage. In the summer of 1796, Harley returned to provincial theatre, performing at Bath, Bristol, Birmingham and Manchester. *ODNB*. His poetry collection, *Holyhead Sonnets* (Bath, 1800) was positively reviewed by the *Monthly Mirror* in November 1800 in a review that reproduced the texts of 'The Parting' and 'The Return'. The latter poem also appeared in the *Salopian Journal*, 1 October 1800.

41. 'Sonnet II: Penman-Mawr'

This poem also appeared in the *Shrewbury Chronicle* (2 March 1800) and the *Monthly Mirror* for March 1800 (171), where it was signed from Holyhead and dated 'Nov. 12, 1799'.

Source:
Holyhead Sonnets, p. 6.

42. 'Sonnet III: On Seeing a Poor Welch Girl
Pass My Window in a Storm'

This poem also appeared in *Adams's Weekly Courant* (1 April 1800) and the *Monthly Mirror* for February 1800 (113), where it was signed from Holyhead and dated 'Nov. 14, 1799'.

Source:
Holyhead Sonnets, p. 7.

43. 'Sonnet IX: The Peasant of Anglesea'

Source:
Holyhead Sonnets, p. 13.

ANONYMOUS

44. 'The Widow'

Source:
Chester Chronicle, 8 August 1802.

RICHARD LLWYD
(Bard of Snowdon; 1752–1835)

45. 'The Address of the Bard of Snowdon, to his Countrymen,
Written in June, 1803, During the Threats of Invasion'

This invasion poem was also published in the *Chester Chronicle* in 1803 (5 August 1803), the *Anti-Gallican* in 1804 (no. 4, 139–41) and, without the footnotes, the *Cambrian* in 1805 (27 April 1805).

Source:
Poems, Tales, Odes, Sonnets, Translations, pp. 184–200.

Dedication *Sir R. Williams, Bart.* Sir Robert Williams (1764–1830), of Nant near Caernarfon, commander of the Snowdon Rangers. See NLW 11557D.

Dedication n. *Snowdon Rangers* The Snowdon Rangers Riflemen Volunteer Infantry, raised in 1803.

Dedication n. *O waed côch cyva Ednyved* Entirely of the red blood of Ednyfed.

6n *Diducta Britannia . . . Orbe Britannos* Llwyd may be referring to Ben Jonson's *The King's Entertainment* (1604), which used both of these quotations. The first is from Claudian's *Panegyricuc Dictus Manlio Theodoro Consuli* (line 51), and the second from Virgil's *Eclogues* (1, line 36): both translate as Britain or Britons 'wholly divided/cut off from the world'. See David Armitage, 'Literature and Empire', in N. Canny (ed.), *The Origins of Empire* (Oxford, 1998), pp. 99–123; here p. 112.

16n *Plurium gentium imperator* Emperor of many countries.

16n *borne in chains* Llwyd is quoting George Richards's depiction of Freedom in *The Aboriginal Britons*, published in 1791 (p. 24).

16n *J. H. L. Hunt* See Leigh Hunt's *Juvenilia; Or, A Collection of Poems* (2nd edn., London, 1801, pp. 11–12.

21n *The Romans* Reference to Song VI of Drayton's *Poly-Olbion* (1612). *Poly-Olbion*, pp. 94–5. In this section of the poem, the muse of the river Wye is listing the invasions that have displaced the ancient British peoples.

33n *Ordovecean* 'ancient British tribe in North Wales'. *OED*.

33n *Silurian* See no. 10, note to line 18.

38n *Taliesin* See no. 2, note to line 222.

38n *Bosworth* Decisive battle of the Wars of the Roses, 22 August 1485.

58n *Our Leopards* Reference to the opening section of Song XI of *Poly-Olbion*. See Drayton, *Poly-Olbion*, p. 172.

59 *Deva* River Dee.

60 *Mona* See no. 2, note to line 239n.

60 *Mervyn* Merfyn Frych (d. 844), king of Gwynedd.

61 *Rodri's heir* Anarawd ap Rhodri (d. 916), son of Rhodri Mawr (see no. 2, note to line 169).

63n *Gray* See Lonsdale, *The Poems of Gray, Collins, and Goldsmith,* pp. 228–33, for the text of 'The Triumphs of Owen. A Fragment'. Gray based his poem (written 1760–1, published 1768) on Evan Evans's literal Latin translation of Gwalchmai ap Meilyr's 'Arwyain Owain Gwynedd', written in the twelfth century.

69n *sing the shades* See Richards, *Aboriginal Britons,* p. 22.

69n *Unbennaeth Brydain* Sovereignty of Britain.

72n *27ᵗʰ Triade* See Rachel Bromwich (ed.), *Trioedd Ynys Prydein: The Triads of the Island of Britain* (3rd edn., Cardiff, 2006), p. 40.

72n *Roberts* See Peter Roberts, *Sketch of the Early History of the Cymry, or Ancient Britons, from the year 700 before Christ, to A.D. 500* (London, 1803).

Postscript *Levy En masse* General Defence Act of July 1803.

ROBERT HOLLAND PRICE
(1780–1808)

46. The Horrors of Invasion; A Poem.

Very little is known of Robert Holland Price, though his celebration of the Chirk volunteers (and detailed knowledge of individuals within the corps) and the Ladies of Llangollen in *The Horrors of Invasion* suggests that he was local to the Chirk-Llangollen area. Meic Stephens suggests that he was a gentleman in *The New Companion to the Literature of Wales* (Cardiff, 1998). *Horrors* is his only known work.

Source:
The Horrors of Invasion; A Poem. Addressed to the People of Great Britain, in general, and to the Chirk Hundred Volunteers, and all Welshmen, in particular. Dedicated by permission, to the Right Honourable Lady Eleanor Butler, and Miss Ponsonby (2nd edn.,Wrexham, 1804).

Title *Chirk Hundred Volunteers* A volunteer regiment founded in 1803.

Prologue *Come the three corners* Shakespeare, *King John* (5.7.116–17).

2 *Aneurin* See no. 7, note to line 49.

3 *Llywarch* See no. 7, note to line 38.

3n *Guell found a grave* See Owen Pughe's *Llywarç Hen*, pp. 240–1.

3n *Cynddelw, cadw* See ibid., p. xiii.

4n *Hirlas Owain* See Pennant, *A Tour in Wales* (1778), pp. 288–93, for the text of the poem.

9n *Corsican* Napoleon Bonaparte.

25n *first Consul* Napoleon became First Consul in 1799.

103n *Llanegwast* Valle Crucis abbey.

JOSEPH READE

47. Invasion! A Poem *(extract)*

Source:
Invasion! A Poem, Familiarly didactic and argumentative. In Three short Cantos (Carmarthen, 1804).

Dedication *Earl of Moira* Francis Rawdon Hastings, second earl of Moira (1754–1826), an army officer and Whig politician. *ODNB.*

152 *hurtles* [hurtle] 'The action or an act of hurtling; dashing together, collision, conflict; clashing sound.' *OED.*

244 *Manes* The spirits of the dead. *OED.*

'BRITANNUS'

48. 'To Bonaparte'

Source:
Cambrian, 31 March 1804.

14 *siege of Acre* French siege of Acre, successfully defended by the Turks, which lasted from March to May in 1799. The failure of the siege forced Napoleon to begin retreating to Egypt in May 1799.

16 *brave Sir Sidney* Sir William Sidney Smith (1764–1840), British admiral best known for his role in defending Acre in 1799 by capturing the vessels supplying the French with artillery. *WWMH*, p. 275.

23 *malgre* 'In spite of.' *OED*.

23 *coup-de-main* 'A sudden and vigorous attack, for the purpose of instantaneously capturing a position.' *OED*.

T. ELLIS OWEN
(1764–1814)

Born in Conwy in north-west Wales, Thomas Ellis Owen was educated at Oxford; in 1794 he became rector of Llandyfrydog in Anglesey. Best known as the author of the anti-Methodist pamphlets *Hints to Heads of Families* (1801) and *Methodism Unmasked* (1802), Owen published an eight-page elegy for William Pitt, 'The Tears of Britannia', in Caernarfon in 1809, which also appeared in the *Anti-Jacobin Review* for August 1809 (vol. 33, 529–32).

49. 'Anglesey Volunteer Song'

Source:
Chester Chronicle, 6 July 1804.

5 *Mona* See no. 2, note to line 239n.

13 *Hengist* Saxon leader whose men massacred their British hosts at a feast in the 'Treachery of the Long Knives' (*Brad y Cyllyll Hirion*) in the fifth century, according to the legendary history of Britain. *CC*, s.n. Gwrtheyrn (Vortigern).

20n *Stratagem of Edward the First* Tradition that, on the birth of his son Edward at Caernarfon in 1284, Edward I presented the baby to the Welsh people as a native prince who spoke no English.

21 *Llewellyn* [Llywelyn] See no. 34, note to line 45.

29n *Welsh Fencibles* Sir Watkin Williams Wynn (1772–1840) raised the cavalry regiment the Ancient British Fencibles in 1794, which took part in the suppression of the Irish Rebellion in 1798. *DWB*. See also Hywel M. Davies, 'Terror, Treason and Tourism: The French in Pembrokeshire 1797', in Mary-Ann Constantine and Dafydd Johnston (eds.), *'Footsteps of Liberty and Revolt': Essays on Wales and the French Revolution* (Cardiff, forthcoming).

33 *Pembroke's Plains* See Introduction, p. 31, for the French invasion of Fishguard in February 1797.

37 *Egypt's plains* A reference to the battle of the Nile in August 1798, when Nelson attacked, and completely destroyed, the French fleet while it was anchored at Aboukir Bay. *WWMH*, p. 41.

43 *Paget* Henry Paget (1768–1854), soldier and MP for Caernarfon, was second in command at Waterloo, after which he was created first marquess of Anglesey as a reward for his part in the battle.

RICHARD LLWYD
(Bard of Snowdon; 1752–1835)

50. *'Awdl y Misoedd / Ode of the Months'*

Source:
Poems, Tales, Odes, Sonnets, Translations, pp. 46–64.

Subtitle *Gwilim Ddu* Gwilym Ddu o Arfon (*fl. c.*1280–1320), court poet, author of a praise poem to his lord Gruffydd Llwyd on Gruffydd's imprisonment in Rhuddlan Castle.

Subtitle *Sir Gryffydd Llwyd* [Gruffydd Llwyd] Supporter of Edward I and traditional hero of a supposed Welsh revolt in 1322 who died in 1335. *DWB*.

Prologue *Magnæ quidem sed calamitosæ virtutis* Great but ruinous virtue.

Prologue *Solomon* Ecclesiastes 7: 7.

Prologue *Gwell marw vel dyn, na byw vel ci* Better to die like a man than live like a dog.

Prologue *Vincere vel mori* To conquer or to die.

Prologue *Rhuddlan* Castle near the north Wales coast built by Edward I in the late thirteenth century.

Dedication *T. Mostyn, Bart.* Sir Thomas Mostyn (1776–1831).

Epigraph *Neud cyn nechreu Mai mau anrhydedd* Evan Evans translates this phrase as 'Before the beginning of May I lived in pomp and grandeur'. See *Some Specimens of the Poetry of the Antient Welsh Bards* (London, 1764), p. 47.

21n *Davydd Llwyd* Dafydd Llwyd ap Llywelyn ap Gruffudd of Mathafarn (*c*.1420–*c*.1500), poet best known as the author of some fifty of the 200 extant prophetic poems (*cywyddau brud*) of his generation. *DWB.*

73n *Unfading blooms* Unidentified.

73n *Copenhagen* Expedition led by Nelson which destroyed the immobilized Danish fleet in Copenhagen harbour on 2 April 1801.

89n *Hirlas* See no. 46, note to line 4n.

89n *notes to Beaumaris Bay* See *Beaumaris Bay*, pp. 11, 40.

99n *triades* Welsh bardic triads group together three cognate terms, usually focusing on important historical events and figures or on proverbial wisdom. They served as mnemonic devices for bards in the oral composition of poetry. See Bromwich, *Trioedd Ynys Prydein.*

99n *Taliesin* See no. 2, note to line 222.

51. 'Owen of Llangoed. Founded on fact. To Fleetwood Williams, Esq.
of Liverpool'

Source:
Poems, Tales, Odes, Sonnets, Translations, pp. 68–92.

Title *Llangoed* Village lying to the east of Beaumaris in Anglesey.

Title *Fleetwood Williams* Roger Hesketh Fleetwood Williams (1777–1826).

45n *Pib gorn* [pibgorn] Traditional Welsh hornpipe.

77 *Mona* See no. 2, note to line 239n.

93n *Asylum* School for the blind, opened in 1791. See Gordon Phillips, *The Blind in British Society: Charity, State, and Community c.1780–1930* (Ashgate, 2004), pp. 19–21.

104 *Burns* Burns had died in 1796.

107n *legal provision* Act of 1646 that aimed to establish a system of universal education. See R. A. Houston, *Scottish Literacy and the Scottish Identity: Illiteracy and Society in Scotland and northern England, 1600–1800* (Cambridge, 1985).

109 *Currie* James Currie (1756–1805) was a Scottish physician and author. His four-volume edition of Burns's poetry, with an accompanying biography, *The Works of Robert Burns*, was published in 1800.

113n *Addington* Henry Addington (1757–1844), later first viscount Sidmouth (attacked by Shelley in *The Mask of Anarchy*), was prime minister between March 1801 and May 1804. *ODNB*.

113n *Oublie moi* Great God forget me if ever I forget [it]. See James Currie (ed.), *The Works of Robert Burns, with an account of his life, and a criticism on his writings* (4 vols., Liverpool, 1800), I, p. 56.

121 *Roscoe* William Roscoe (1753–1831), from Liverpool, was a writer, patron of the arts, abolitionist, anti-war protester and MP. See Arline Wilson, *William Roscoe: Commerce and Culture* (Liverpool, 2008).

127 *Arno* River in central Italy.

137n *Then Pleasure* Adapted from the closing lines of Samuel Johnson's prologue to Hugh Kelly's play *A Word to the Wise* (1770).

142n *Edward Williams* See 'The Fair Pilgrim', *Poems, Lyric and Pastoral*, I, pp. 74–84.

172 *Tyrian* A native or inhabitant of Tyre, ancient Phœnician city on the Mediterranean. *OED.*

187n *Nulla pœna sine crimine* No punishment without crime.

187n *A vydd ddieuog, a vydd ddiovn* He who is guiltless will also be fearless.

201 *Blake* Robert Blake (1598–1657), naval and army officer.

203 *Russell . . . La Hogue* Edward Russell, earl of Orford (1652–1727), naval officer best known for his victory over the French at the battle of La Hogue in 1692 (see also no. 3, note to line 66).

205 *Hawkes* Edward Hawke, first Baron Hawke (1705–81), naval officer.

205 *Howes* See no. 23, note to line 28.

208 *Rodney* George Bridges Rodney, first Baron Rodney (1718–92), naval officer and politician.

212 *St. Vincent* See no. 30, note to line 31.

212 *Duncan* Adam Duncan, Viscount Duncan (1731–1804), naval officer.

'*BRECONIENSIS*'

52. 'The Saxon Invasion'

Source:
Cambrian, 23 February 1805.

Introductory letter *Eu Nêr . . . gwyllt Wallia* They will praise their Lord / they will keep their language / they will lose their land / except wild Wales. A passage of prophetic medieval poetry, traditionally attributed to Taliesin. See

Charnell-White, *Bardic Circles*, p. 73, for seventeenth- and eighteenth-century uses of this stanza.

'PHILOPATRIA'

53. Untitled ['Arise, my muse, and paint the glorious scene']

Source:
Cambrian, 2 March 1805.

Introductory letter *Cader Idris volunteers* Volunteer regiment raised by Sir Robert Williams Vaughn in 1803, based in Dolgellau.

Introductory letter *Sir R. W. Vaughn, Bart.* Sir Robert Williams Vaughn (1768– 1843), member of a powerful Welsh gentry family and MP for Merioneth from 1792 to 1836. *DWB.*

4 *Pelides* Achilles, central character of Homer's *The Iliad*.

5 *Hector* Trojan warrior, killed by Achilles in *The Iliad*.

16 *Nannau* House near Dolgellau, home of Sir Robert Williams Vaughn.

'MARY'

54. 'On the Late Splendid Victory off Trafalgar'

Source:
Cambrian, 23 November 1805.

Title *Trafalgar* The battle of Trafalgar, in which Nelson was killed, took place off the Spanish coast on 21 October 1805.

A second poem, which 'Mary'. has given the same title and date of composition, appeared in the *Cambrian* a week later, on 30 November 1805:

While o'er the British Isle a settled gloom
Bespeaks deep sorrow for a hero's doom,
Kind Heav'n, still watchful for our future good
Repairs the loss in gallant Collingwood;
Long, long may he, his Country's bulwark stand,
And bravely execute what Nelson plann'd.

These verses by 'Mary' belong among a cluster of poems on the subjects of Nelson and Trafalgar published by the *Cambrian* in November and December 1805 and January 1806. For other examples, see: 25 November 1805 for W. Williams, untitled ['Lines in praise of a Briton, who has been the greatest champion the world ever saw'], signed from Tenby; 'J. H.', 'On Nelson's Death and Victory', signed from Laugharne; anon., untitled ['On the Same'], signed from Haverfordwest; Walter Churchey, 'An Elegy on Lord Nelson'; 7 December 1805 for anon., 'For the Cambrian' (first line beginning 'Nelson, Britannia's boast and much-lamented son!'), signed from Laugharne; 'Hoddy Doddy', 'Strachan's New Game at All Fours', signed from Denbigh; 21 December 1805 for 'R. W.', 'On the Death of Lord Nelson', signed from Swansea; and 25 January 1806 for George Richards, 'From the Monody on Lord Nelson'.

'P. H.'

55. 'On the Victory of Cape Trafalgar, and the Death of the ever-to-be-lamented Admiral Lord Viscount Nelson'

Source:
Chester Chronicle, 20 December 1805.

Title *Trafalgar* See no. 54, note to title.

'J. H.'

56. 'On Winter'

Source:
Cambrian, 4 January 1806.

'W. R.'

57. 'On the Death of Mr. Pitt'

A week before the appearance of this poem, the *Cambrian* also printed 'On Mr
Pitt's Death', signed from Swansea. See 1 February 1806.

Source:
Cambrian, 8 February 1806.

Title *Death* Pitt died on 23 January 1806.

27 *Chatham* William Pitt, first earl of Chatham (1708–78), prime minister
1766–8.

DAVID THOMAS
(Dafydd Ddu Eryri; 1759–1822)

58. 'An Address to the Snowdon Rangers'

This poem was later published in Thomas's *Corph y Gainc* (1834), pp. 459–60.

Source:
NLW 325E, f. 51.

Title *Snowdon Rangers* See no. 45, note to the dedication.

Epigraph *Hên Brophwydoliaeth* Ancient prophecy.

Tune *Morwynion glân Meirionydd* The fair maids of Merioneth.

9 *Wyddfa* Snowdon.

13 *Sir Robert* See no. 45, note to the dedication.

15 *Poole* William Poole, lieutenant in the Snowdon Rangers. See Thomas,
Corph y Gainc (1834), p. 459.

20 *stranger* Napoleon. See Thomas, *Corph y Gainc* (1834), p. 460.

26 *Kidwm* Thomas glosses 'Kidwm' with the following passage in *Corph y Gainc*: 'Kidwm's Fort, or Castell Cidwm, a stupendous rock, rising abruptly from the margin of the beautiful Lake Cawellyn, in the little Vale of Bettws, on the south-west side of the majestic Snowdon; the sound of the buglehorn reverberating from the centre of the above-mentioned rock, is exquisitely sublime' (p. 460).

32 *Arvonian* See no. 37, note to line 22.

'MARY'

59. 'Written late in the Evening, December 15, 1806'

Source:
Cambrian, 27 December 1806.

5 *hind* Agricultural labourer. *OED*.

'D.'

60. 'On the Present State of the Belligerent Powers of Europe'

Source:
Cambrian, 3 January 1807.

7n *Calabria* British victory over the French at Calabria, Italy on 4 July 1806, known as the battle of Maida.

Select Bibliography

Aaron, Jane, *Nineteenth-Century Women's Writing in Wales* (2nd edn., Cardiff, 2010).

—— 'Bardic Anti-colonialism', in *idem* and Chris Williams (eds.), *Postcolonial Wales*, pp. 137–58.

—— 'Twentieth-Century and Contemporary Welsh Gothic Fiction', *Literature Compass,* 7, no. 4 (2010), 281–9.

—— and Chris Williams (eds.), *Postcolonial Wales* (Cardiff, 2005).

Ágoston, Gábor, and Bruce Alan Masters, *Encyclopedia of the Ottoman Empire* (New York, 2009).

Anderson, Misty G., *Imagining Methodism in Eighteenth-Century Britain: Enthusiasm, Belief, and the Borders of the Self* (Baltimore, 2012).

Anon., *The Antigallican Songster* (2 parts; London, 1793).

Aronstein, Susan L., 'Wales: Culture and Society', in S. H. Rigby (ed.), *A Companion to Britain in the Later Middle Ages* (Oxford, 2003), pp. 541–57.

Bainbridge, Simon, *British Poetry and the Revolutionary and Napoleonic Wars* (Oxford, 2003).

—— 'Politics and Poetry', in Clemit (ed.), *The Cambridge Companion to British Literature of the French Revolution in the 1790s*, pp. 190–205.

Balderston, Katharine C. (ed.), *Thraliana: The Diary of Mrs. Hester Lynch Thrale (Later Mrs. Piozzi) 1776–1809* (2nd edn., 2 vols., Oxford, 1951).

Barrell, John, *Imagining the King's Death: Figurative Treason, Fantasies of Regicide 1793–1796* (Oxford, 2000).

—— *The Spirit of Despotism: Invasions of Privacy in the 1790s* (Oxford, 2006).

—— 'Radicalism, Visual Culture, and Spectacle in the 1790s', 'Romantic Spectacle', *Romanticism on the Net*, 46, May 2007.

—— (ed.) *Exhibition Extraordinary!! Radical Broadsides of the Mid 1790s* (Nottingham, 2001).

—— and Tim Whelan (eds.), *The Political Pamphlets of William Fox* (Nottingham, 2011).

Bhabha, Homi K., *The Location of Culture* (London, 1994).

Bohata, Kirsti, *Postcolonialism Revisted* (Cardiff, 2004).

Bloom, Edward A., and Lillian D. Bloom (eds.), *The Piozzi Letters* (6 vols., Newark, 1989–2002).

Bowen, E. G., *David Samwell (Dafydd Ddu Feddyg), 1751–1798* (Cardiff, 1974).

Bowen, Geraint, and Zonia Bowen, *Hanes Gorsedd y Beirdd* (Abertawe, 1991).

Brennan, Catherine, *Angers, Fantasies and Ghostly Fears: Nineteenth-Century Women from Wales and English-Language Poetry* (Cardiff, 2003).

Bromwich, Rachel (ed.), *Trioedd Ynys Prydein: The Triads of the Island of Britain* (3rd edn., Cardiff, 2006).

Butler, Marilyn (ed.), *Burke, Paine, Godwin and the Revolution Controversy* (Cambridge, 1984).

Cale, Luisa, *Fuseli's Milton Gallery: 'Turning Readers into Spectators'* (Oxford, 2006).

Carpenter, Andrew (ed.), *Verse in English from Eighteenth-Century Ireland* (Cork, 1998).

Carr, Glenda, 'William Owen Pughe and the London Societies', in Jarvis (ed.), *A Guide to Welsh Literature c.1700–1800*, pp. 168–86.

Carradice, Phil, *The Last Invasion: The Story of the French Landing in Wales* (Pontypool, 1992).

Carruthers, Gerard, and Alan Rawes (eds.), *English Romanticism and the Celtic World* (Cambridge, 2003).

Casid, Jill H., *Sowing Empire: Landscape and Colonization* (Minneapolis, 2005).

Chandler, David, 'Walter Savage Landor and Wales in the 1790s', in Davies and Pratt (eds.), *Wales and the Romantic Imagination*, pp. 141–60.

Charnell-White, Cathryn A., *Bardic Circles: National, Regional and Personal Identity in the Bardic Vision of Iolo Morganwg* (Cardiff, 2007).

—— *Welsh Poetry of the French Revolution* (Cardiff, 2012).

Claeys, Gregory, *The French Revolution Debate in Britain: The Origins of Modern Politics* (Basingstoke, 2007).

Clark, J. C. D. (ed.), *Reflections on the Revolution in France: A Critical Edition* (Stanford, 2001).

Clark, Simone, 'Visions of Community: Elizabeth Baker and late 18th Century Merioneth', in Michael Roberts and *eadem* (eds.), *Women and Gender in Early Modern Wales* (Cardiff, 2000), pp. 334–58.

Clemit, Pamela (ed.), *The Cambridge Companion to British Literature of the French Revolution in the 1790s* (Cambridge, 2011).

Colbert, Benjamin, *Shelley's Eye: Travel Writing and Aesthetic Vision* (Aldershot, 2005).

—— (ed.), *Travel Writing and Tourism in Britain and Ireland* (London, 2012).

Colley, Linda, *Britons: Forging the Nation 1707–1837* (New Haven, 1992).

Constable, Archibald (ed.), *Letters of Anna Seward: Written Between the Years 1784 and 1807* (6 vols., Edinburgh, 1811).

Constantine, Mary-Ann, *The Truth Against the World: Iolo Morganwg and Romantic Forgery* (Cardiff, 2007).

—— 'Beauty Spot, Blind Spot: Romantic Wales', *Literature Compass*, 5, no. 3 (2008), 577–90.

—— 'Ossian in Wales and Brittany', in Howard Gaskill (ed.), *The Reception of Ossian in Europe* (London, 2004), pp. 67–90.

—— '"The French are on the sea!": Welsh and Irish Songs of French Invasion in the 1790s', in Louis Grijp (ed.), *Proceedings of the International Ballad Conference, Terschelling, 2010* (Trier, forthcoming).

—— '"This wildernessed business of publication": The Making of *Poems, Lyric and Pastoral* (1794)', in Jenkins (ed.), *Rattleskull Genius*, pp. 123–46.

—— 'Welsh Literary History and the Making of "The Myvyrian Archaiology of Wales"', in Dirk Van Hulle and Joep Leerssen (eds.), *Editing the Nation's Memory: Textual Scholarship and Nation-Building in Nineteenth-Century Europe* (Amsterdam, 2008), pp. 109–28.

—— and Dafydd Johnston (eds.), *Footsteps of Liberty and Revolt: Essays on Wales and the French Revolution* (Cardiff, forthcoming).

—— and Elizabeth Edwards, 'Bard of Liberty: Iolo Morganwg, Wales and Radical Song', in Kirk, Noble and Brown (eds.), *Political Poetry and Song. Volume 1*, pp. 63–76.

Cookson, J. E., *The Friends of Peace: Anti-War Liberalism in England, 1793–1815* (Cambridge, 1982).

Curry, Kenneth (ed.), *The Contributions of Robert Southey to the Morning Post* (Alabama, 1984).

Davies, Andrew, '"Redirecting the Attention of History": Antiquarian and Historical Fictions of Wales from the Romantic Period', in Davies and Pratt (eds.), *Wales and the Romantic Imagination*, pp. 104–21.

—— '"The reputed nation of inspiration": representations of Wales in fiction from the Romantic period, 1780–1829' (unpublished Cardiff University PhD thesis, 2001).

Davies, Damian Walford, *Presences that Disturb: Models of Romantic Identity in the Literature and Culture of the 1790s* (Cardiff, 2002).

—— '"At Defiance": Iolo, Godwin, Coleridge, Wordsworth', in Jenkins (ed.), *A Rattleskull Genius*, pp. 147–72.

—— '"Sweet Sylvan Routes" and Grave Methodists: Wales in De Quincey's Confessions of an English Opium-Eater', in *idem* and Pratt (eds.), *Wales and the Romantic Imagination*, pp. 199–227.

—— (ed.), *Romanticism, History, Historicism: Essays on an Orthodoxy* (New York, 2009).

—— and Lynda Pratt (eds.), *Wales and the Romantic Imagination* (Cardiff, 2007).

Davies, David, *The Influence of the French Revolution on Welsh Life and Literature* (Carmarthen, 1926).

Davies, Diane, 'Towards Devolution: Poetry and Anglo-Welsh Identity', in Keith Cameron (ed.), *National Identity* (Exeter, 1999), pp. 19–30.

Davies, Hywel M., 'Loyalism in Wales, 1792–1793', *WHR*, 20, no. 4 (2001), 687–716.

—— '"Very different springs of uneasiness": Emigration from Wales to the United States of America during the 1790s', *WHR*, 15, no. 3 (1991), 368–98.

—— 'Wales in English Travel Writing 1791–8: The Welsh Critique of Theophilus Jones', *WHR*, 23, no. 3 (2007), 65–93.

Davies, R. R., and Geraint H. Jenkins (eds.), *From Medieval to Modern Wales: Historical Essays in Honour of Kenneth O. Morgan and Ralph A. Griffiths* (Cardiff, 2004).

Davies, W. Lloyd, 'The Riot at Denbigh, 1795', *BBCS*, IV, part I (1927), 61–73.

Davis, Michael T., '"An Evening of Pleasure Rather Than Business": Songs, Subversion and Radical Sub-Culture in the 1790s', *Journal for the Study of British Cultures*, 12, no. 2 (2005), 115–26.

——, Iain McCalman and Christina Parolin (eds.), *Newgate in Revolution: An Anthology of Radical Prison Literature in the Age of Revolution* (London, 2005).

Dickinson, H. T. (ed.), *A Companion to Eighteenth-Century Britain* (Oxford, 2002).

—— (ed.), *Britain and the French Revolution, 1789–1815* (Basingstoke, 1989).

—— (ed.), *British Radicalism and the French Revolution 1789–1815* (Oxford, 1985).

Duff, David, and Catherine Jones (eds.), *Scotland, Ireland and the Romantic Aesthetic* (Lewisburg, 2007).

Edwards, Elizabeth, 'Iniquity, Terror and Survival': Welsh Gothic, 1789–1804', *Journal for Eighteenth-Century Studies*, 35, no. 1 (2012), 119–33.

Edwards, Gavin, *Narrative Order 1789–1819: Life and Story in an Age of Revolution* (Basingstoke, 2006).

Evans, R. J. W., 'Was there a Welsh Enlightenment?', in Davies and Jenkins (eds.), *From Medieval to Modern Wales*, pp. 142–59.

Evans, R. Paul, 'The Flintshire Loyalist Association and the Loyal Holywell Volunteers', *Flintshire Historical Society Journal*, 33 (1992), 55–68.

Farnie, D. A., and W. O. Henderson (eds.), *Industry and Innovation: Selected Essays / W. H. Chaloner* (London, 1990).

Favret, Mary A., *War at a Distance: Romanticism and the Making of Modern Wartime* (New Jersey, 2009).

Feibel, Juliet, 'Vortigern, Rowena, and the Ancient Britons: Historical Art and the Anglicization of National Origin', *Eighteenth-Century Life*, 24, no. 1 (2000), 1–21.

Fitzpatrick, Martin, 'The "Cultivated Understanding" and Chaotic Genius of David Samwell', in Jenkins (ed.), *A Rattleskull Genius*, pp. 343–402.

——, Nicholas Thomas and Jennifer Newell (eds.), *The Death of Captain Cook and Other Writings by David Samwell* (Cardiff, 2006).

——, Peter Jones, Christa Knellwolf and Iain McCalman (eds.), *The Enlightenment World* (London, 2004).

Forrest, Alan, and Peter H. Wilson (eds.), *The Bee and the Eagle: Napoleonic France and the End of the Holy Roman Empire, 1806* (Basingstoke, 2009).

——, Karen Hagemann and Jane Rendall (eds.), *Soldiers, Citizens and Civilians: Experiences and Perceptions of the Revolutionary and Napoleonic Wars, 1790–1820* (Basingstoke, 2009).

Franklin, Alexandra, and Mark Philp, *Napoleon and the Invasion of Britain* (Oxford, 2003).

Franklin, Caroline, 'The Welsh American dream: Iolo Morganwg, Robert Southey and the Madog Legend', in Carruthers and Rawes (eds), *English Romanticism and the Celtic World*, pp. 69–84.

Gee, Austin, *The British Volunteer Movement, 1794–1814* (Oxford, 2003).

Gilmartin, Kevin, *Writing Against Revolution: Literary Conservatism in Britain, 1790–1832* (Cambridge, 2007).

Glenn, T. A., *The Family of Griffith of Garn and Plasnewydd in the County of Denbigh* (London, 1934).

Goodridge, John, '"That Deathless Wish of Climbing Higher": Robert Bloomfield on the Sugar Loaf', in Davies and Pratt (eds.), *Wales and the Romantic Imagination*, pp. 161–79.

—— (ed.) *Eighteenth-Century English Labouring Class Poets* (London, 2003).

—— (ed.) *Nineteenth-Century English Labouring-Class Poets* (London, 2005).

Gramich, Katie, 'Narrating the Nation: Telling Stories of Wales', *North American Journal of Welsh Studies*, 6, no. 1 (2011), 2–19.

Groom, Nick, *The Union Jack: The Story of the British Flag* (London, 2006).

Guest, Harriet, 'The Consequences of War in the Winter of 1794–95', in Geoff Quilley and John Bonehill (eds.), *William Hodges: The Art of Exploration* (New Haven, 2004), pp. 61–70.

Hadfield, Andrew, *Shakespeare, Spenser and the Matter of Britain* (Basingstoke,1994).

Harris, Bob, *The Scottish People and the French Revolution* (London, 2008).

Hill, Christopher, *The Century of Revolution, 1603–1714* (1961; London, 2002).

Howard, Sharon, 'Riotous Community: Crowds, Politics and Society in Wales, *c.*1700–1840', *WHR*, 20, no. 4 (2001), 656–86.

Howell, David, *The Rural Poor in Eighteenth-Century Wales* (Cardiff, 2000).

Innes, C. L., *The Cambridge Introduction to Postcolonial Literatures in English* (Cambridge, 2007).

Jarman, A. O. H., 'Saga Poetry – The Cycle of Llywarch Hen', in *idem* and Gwilym Rees Hughes (eds.), *A Guide to Welsh Literature, Volume 1* (Cardiff, 1992).

Jarvis, Branwen (ed.), *A Guide to Welsh Literature c.1700–1800* (Cardiff, 2000).

Jenkins, Geraint H., *Bard of Liberty: The Political Radicalism of Iolo Morganwg* (Cardiff, 2012).

—— '"A Rank Republican [and] a Leveller": William Jones, Llangadfan', *WHR*, 17, no. 3 (1995), 365–86.

—— '"A Very Horrid Affair": Sedition and Unitarianism in the Age of Revolutions', in Davies and *idem* (eds.), *From Medieval to Modern Wales*, pp. 175–96.

—— 'Clio and Wales: Welsh Remembrancers and Historical Writing, 1751–2001', *THSC* (2002), 119–36.

—— 'The Bard of Liberty during William Pitt's "Reign of Terror"', in Joseph Falaky Nagy and Leslie Ellen Jones (eds.), *Heroic Poets and Poetic Heroes in Celtic Tradition: A Festschrift for Patrick K. Ford*, CSANA Yearbook 3–4 (Dublin, 2005), pp. 183–206.

—— (ed.), *A Rattleskull Genius: The Many Faces of Iolo Morganwg* (Cardiff, 2005).

—— (ed.), *Language and Community in the Nineteenth Century* (Cardiff, 1998).

——, Ffion Mair Jones and David Ceri Jones (eds.), *The Correspondence of Iolo Morganwg* (3 vols., Cardiff, 2007).

Jenkins, R. T., and Helen M. Ramage, *A History of the Honourable Society of Cymmrodorion and of the Gwyneddigion and Cymreigyddion Societies (1751–1951)* (London, 1951).

Johnston, Arthur, 'Gray's "The Triumphs of Owen"', *The Review of English Studies*, 11, no. 43 (1960), pp. 275–85.

Johnston, Dafydd, *A Pocket Guide: The Literature of Wales* (Cardiff, 1994).

—— '*Barddoniaeth Dafydd ab Gwilym* 1789 a'r Chwyldro Ffrengig', *Llên Cymru*, 35 (2012), 32–53.

Johnston, Kenneth R., 'Whose History? My Place or Yours? Republican Assumptions and Romantic Traditions', in Davies (ed.), *Romanticism, History, Historicism*, pp. 79–102.

Jones, David J. V., *Before Rebecca: Popular Protests in Wales 1793–1835* (London, 1973).

Jones, Ffion Mair, *'The Bard is a Very Singular Charater': Iolo Morganwg, Marginalia and Print Culture* (Cardiff, 2010).

—— *Welsh Ballads of the French Revolution 1793–1815* (Cardiff, 2012).

Jones, Tim, *Rioting in North East Wales, 1536–1918* (Wrexham, 1997).

Keegan, John, and Andrew Wheatcroft, *Who's Who in Military History From 1453 to the Present Day* (2nd rev. edn., London, 1996).

Kerrigan, John, *Archipelagic English: Literature, History and Politics 1603–1707* (Oxford, 2008).

Kidd, Colin, 'Wales, the Enlightenment and the New British History', *WHR*, 25, no. 2 (2010), 209–30.

Kirk, John, Andrew Noble and Michael Brown (eds.), *Political Poetry and Song in the Age of Revolution. Volume 1: United Islands? The Languages of Resistance* (London, 2012).

——, Michael Brown and Andrew Noble (eds.), *Political Poetry and Song in the Age of Revolution. Volume 2: The Culture of Radicalism in Britain and Ireland* (London, 2012).

Koch, John T., *The Gododdin of Aneirin: Texts and Context from Dark-Age North Britain* (Cardiff, 1997).

Lewis, Gwyneth, 'Eighteenth-century literary forgeries with special reference to the work of Iolo Morganwg' (unpublished University of Oxford D. Phil. thesis, 1991).

Lichtenwalner, Shawna, *Claiming Cambria: Invoking the Welsh in the Romantic Era* (Newark, 2008).

Löffler, Marion, *The Literary and Historical Legacy of Iolo Morganwg 1826–1926* (Cardiff, 2007).

—— *Welsh Responses to the French Revolution: Press and Public Discourse 1789–1802* (Cardiff, 2012).

——'Cerddi Newydd "Jac Glan-y-gors"', *Llên Cymru*, 33 (2010), 143–50.

—— 'Serial Literature and Radical Poetry in Wales at the End of the Eighteenth Century', Kirk, Brown and Noble (eds.), *Political Poetry and Song. Volume 2.*

Lonsdale, Roger, *The Poems of Gray, Collins, and Goldsmith* (London, 1969).

McCalman, Iain (ed.), *An Oxford Companion to the Romantic Age: British Culture 1776–1832* (Oxford, 1999).

McCarthy, William, *Hester Thrale Piozzi: Portrait of a Literary Woman* (Chapel Hill, 1985).

McIlvanney, Liam, *Burns the Radical: Poetry and Politics in Late Eighteenth-Century Scotland* (East Linton, 2002).

Mee, Jon, '"Images of Truth New Born": Iolo, William Blake and the Literary Radicalism of the 1790s', in Jenkins (ed.), *A Rattleskull Genius*, pp. 173–93.

—— and David Fallon (eds.), *Romanticism and Revolution: A Reader* (Oxford, 2011).

Morgan, Prys, *The Eighteenth-Century Renaissance* (Llandybïe, 1981).

—— 'From a Death to a View: the Hunt for the Welsh Past in the Romantic Period', in E. J. Hobsbawm and T. Ranger (eds.), *The Invention of Tradition* (Cambridge, 1983), pp. 43–100.

Navickas, Katrina, *Loyalism and Radicalism in Lancashire, 1798–1815* (Oxford, 2009).

O'Gorman, Frank, 'The Paine Burnings of 1792–1793', *Past & Present*, 193 (2006), 111–55.

Owen, Bryn, *The History of the Welsh Militia and Volunteer Corps 1757–1908: 1. Anglesey and Caernarfonshire* (Caernarfon, 1989).

—— *History of the Welsh Militia and Volunteer Corps 1757–1908: Denbighshire & Flintshire (Part 1)* (Wrexham, 1997).

—— *History of the Welsh Militia and Volunteer Corps 1757–1908: Volume 3 Glamorgan (Part 2), Volunteers & Local Militia, 1796–1816, Yeomanry Cavalry, 1803–31* (Wrexham, 1994).

Palmer, Alfred Neobard, 'John Wilkinson and the Old Bersham Iron Works', *THSC* (1899), 23–64.

Pennant, Thomas, *A Tour in Wales* (London, 1778, 1784).

Phillips, Geraint, 'Forgery and Patronage: Iolo Morganwg and Owain Myfyr', in Jenkins (ed.), *A Rattleskull Genius*, pp. 403–23.

Phillips, Gordon, *The Blind in British Society: Charity, State, and Community c.1780–1930* (Ashgate, 2004).

Philp, Mark (ed.), *Resisting Napoleon: The British Response to the Threat of Invasion, 1797–1815* (Aldershot, 2006).

—— (ed.), *Rights of Man, Common Sense and Other Political Writings* (Oxford, 2008).

—— (ed.), *The French Revolution and British Popular Politics* (Cambridge, 1991).

Pittock, Murray, *Celtic Identity and the British Image* (Manchester, 1999).

—— *Scottish and Irish Romanticism* (Oxford, 2008).

—— (ed.) *The Edinburgh Companion to Scottish Romanticism* (Edinburgh, 2011).

Pocock, J. G. A., *Virtue, Commerce, and History: Essays on Political Thought and History, Chiefly in the Eighteenth Century* (Cambridge, 1985).

Pratt, Lynda, 'Southey in Wales: Inscriptions, Monuments and Romantic Posterity', in Davies and *eadem* (eds.), *Wales and the Romantic Imagination*, pp. 86–103.

—— (ed.) *Robert Southey and the Contexts of English Romanticism* (Aldershot, 2006).

—— (ed.), *Robert Southey: Poetical Works 1793–1810* (5 vols., London, 2004).

Prescott, Sarah, *Bards and Britons: Eighteenth-Century Writing from Wales* (Cardiff, 2008).

—— 'Anglophone Welsh Women's Poetry, 1750–84: Jane Cave and Anne Penny', in Jacqueline M. Labbe (ed.), *The History of British Women's Writing, 1750–1830* (Basingstoke, 2010), pp. 102–24.

Quinault, Roland, 'The French Invasion of Pembrokeshire in 1797: A Bicentennial Assessment', *WHR*, 19, no. 4 (1989), 618–41.

Rogers, Pat (ed.), *Alexander Pope: Selected Poetry* (Oxford, 1994).

Schwyzer, Philip, *Literature, Nationalism and Memory in Early Modern England and Wales* (Cambridge, 2004).

—— and Simon Mealor (eds.), *Archipelagic Identities: Literature and Identity in the Atlantic Archipelago, 1550–1800* (Aldershot, 2004).

Scrivener, Michael, *Poetry and Reform: Periodical Verse from the English Democratic Press 1792–1824* (Detroit, 1992).

Semmel, Stuart, *Napoleon and the British* (New Haven, 2004).

Shaw, Philip, *Romantic Wars: Studies in Culture and Conflict, 1789–1823* (Aldershot, 2000).

Simpson, Roger, 'Building Arthurian Castles in Spain: William Sotheby's *Constance de Castile*', *Arthuriana*, 11, no. 4 (2001), 77–86.

Smiles, Sam, *The Image of Antiquity: Ancient Britain and the Romantic Imagination* (London, 1994).

Solkin, David, *Richard Wilson: The Landscape of Reaction* (London, 1982).

Stephens, Meic (ed.), *The New Companion to the Literature of Wales* (1986; Cardiff, 1998).

Thomas, Claudia Kairoff, *Anna Seward and the End of the Eighteenth Century* (Baltimore, 2012).

Thomas, David, *Corph y Gaingc, neu, Ddifyrwch teuluaidd*, ed. Ellis Jones (Caernarfon, 1834).

Thomas, J. E., *Britain's Last Invasion: Fishguard 1797* (Stroud, 2007).

Thomas, M. Wynn, *Welsh Writing in English* (Cardiff, 2003).

—— (ed.), *Corresponding Cultures: The Two Literatures of Wales* (Cardiff, 1999).

Trumpener, Katie, *Bardic Nationalism: The Romantic Novel and the British Empire* (Princeton, 1997).

Watson, J. R., 'Wordsworth, North Wales and the Celtic landscape', in Carruthers and Rawes (eds.), *English Romanticism and the Celtic World*, pp. 85–102.

Weinbrot, Howard D., *Britannia's Issue: The Rise of British Literature from Dryden to Ossian* (Cambridge, 1993).

White, Daniel E., *Early Romanticism and Religious Dissent* (Cambridge, 2006).

White, Simon J., *Robert Bloomfield, Romanticism and the Poetry of Community* (Aldershot, 2007).

Williams, Gwyn A., *Madoc: The Making of a Myth* (Oxford, 1987).

—— *The Search for Beulah Land: The Welsh and the Atlantic Revolution* (New York, 1980).

—— *When Was Wales? A History of the Welsh* (Harmondsworth, 1985).

—— 'Romanticism in Wales', in Roy Porter and Mikuláš Teich (eds.), *Romanticism in National Context* (Cambridge, 1988), pp. 9–36.

Willis, Irene Cooper (ed.), *Charles James Fox: Speeches During the French Revolutionary War Period* (London, 1924).

Wilson, Arline, *William Roscoe: Commerce and Culture* (Liverpool, 2008).

Wright, Julia M., *A Companion to Irish Literature* (Oxford, 2011).

Index